THE REGIONS OF BRITAIN

# The Scottish Border and Northumberland

THE REGIONS OF BRITAIN
Previous and forthcoming titles in the series
include:

*The Pennine Dales* Arthur Raistrick
*The Upper Thames* J. R. L. Anderson
*The Lake District* Roy Millward and Adrian Robinson
*North East England* Arthur Raistrick
*Pembrokeshire* John Barrett
*The Peak District* Roy Millward and Adrian Robinson
*Cornwall* W. G. Hoskins
*The Hebrides* W. H. Murray
*East Anglia* Norman Scarfe
*The Cotswolds* H. P. R. Finberg

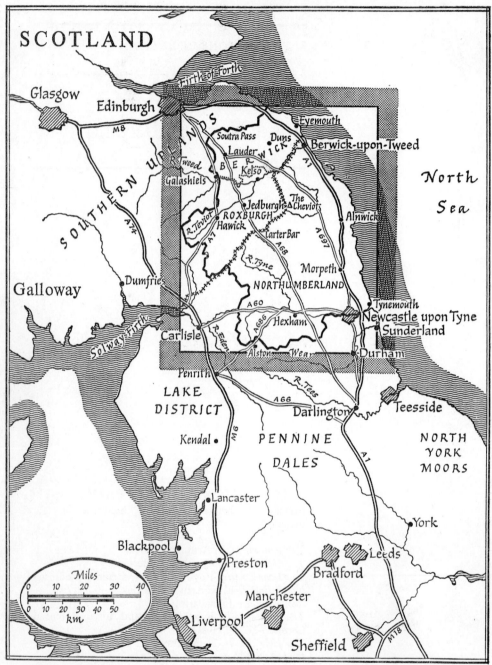

**Map 1** *The Scottish Border and Northumberland in relation to Southern Scotland and Northern England.*

JOHN TALBOT WHITE

# The Scottish Border and Northumberland

Berwickshire, Roxburghshire,
Northumberland

EYRE METHUEN · LONDON

To Dick and Liz Clark
and all my friends on both sides of the Border

*First published 1973*
© *1973 John Talbot White*
*Printed in Great Britain for*
*Eyre Methuen Ltd*
*11 New Fetter Lane, London EC4P 4EE*
*by Cox & Wyman Ltd*
*Fakenham, Norfolk*

SBN 413 28130 2 (hardback)
SBN 413 30270 9 (paperback)

The Scottish Border
and Northumberland

# Contents

|  | Acknowledgements | *page* 13 |
|  | Introduction | 15 |
| 1 | The physical setting | 19 |
| 2 | Flora and fauna | 36 |
| 3 | Briton and Roman | 58 |
| 4 | Church and village and rural scene | 77 |
| 5 | The evolution of the Border | 100 |
| 6 | The landscape of improvement | 122 |
| 7 | Burghs and market towns | 139 |
| 8 | The new age of iron | 159 |
| 9 | The planned environment | 176 |
| 10 | Festivals, fairs and folklore | 189 |
| 11 | Exploring by track and road | 205 |
|  | Select Bibliography | 223 |
|  | Appendices | 231 |
| I | Buildings and structures of special interest | 233 |
| II | National Trust properties | 240 |
| III | Historic houses, castles and gardens open to the public | 241 |
| IV | Museums and galleries | 241 |
| V | Conservation areas and sites | 242 |
|  | Index | 243 |

# Illustrations

*Between pages 32 and 33*  1  The view north-east from Carter Bar
                           2  Looking west over the basin of the Upper Tweed

*64 and 65*  3  St Abb's Head
             4  The Whin Sill and the Roman Wall

*80 and 81*  5  *a* Scrub oak woodland near Rothbury
             5  *b* Remnant alders in Calroust Burn
             5  *c* Grassy ride through Kielder Forest
             6  *a* Seal and calf on the Brownsman, Outer Farnes
             6  *b* Guillemots and kittiwakes on Staple Island
             7  *a* Iron Age hill fort on Blackbrough Hill
             7  *b* Passages and chambers in the drystone wall of
                   Edin's Hall Broch
             7  *c* Iron Age hill fort on Woden Law
             8  *a* Roman camps at Chew Green
             8  *b* Housesteads: three Roman deities
             8  *c* Corbridge: terracotta plaque of the Celtic god,
                   Taranis

*96 and 97*  9  *a* Melrose Abbey
             9  *b* and *c* Anglian carving on St Boisil's tomb,
                   Jedburgh Abbey museum
             9  *d* Norman west door of Lindisfarne Priory

*Between pages 96 and 97*  10  *a* Village green at Ancrum

10  *b* Estate village of Etal

10  *c* Eighteenth-century houses at Stamfordham

*128 and 129*  11  *a* Hermitage Castle

11  *b* Ruins of the castle at Dunstanburgh

12  *a* The White Walls of Berwick-upon-Tweed

12  *b* Corsbie, typical sixteenth-century tower house

12  *c* Queen Mary's house, Jedburgh

*144 and 145*  13  Extract from William Roy's map of 1750

14  *a* Eighteenth-century mansion and parkland at Swinburne

14  *b* Floors Castle

15  *a* Dipping Cheviot sheep at Cocklawfoot

15  *b* Auction of Suffolk sheep at the Hawick Mart

15  *c* Milne Graden, typical 'enclosure' farm group

16  *a* The Royal Burgh of Jedburgh

16  *b* Berwick-upon-Tweed

*160 and 161*  17  *a* The market-place at Alnwick

17  *b* Warkworth on the River Coquet

18  *a* Central Station at Newcastle upon Tyne

18  *b* The bridges of Newcastle upon Tyne

*Between pages 192 and 193*   19   *a* Typical coalfield settlement of Netherton
                                            19   *b* Cumledge, near Duns: nineteenth-century blanket mill
                                            19   *c* The wooden coal staithes at Dunston on Tyne
                                            20   *a* The new Civic Centre of Newcastle upon Tyne
                                            20   *b* Office complex of Swan House

*208 and 209*   21   *a* New pit-head gear at the Lynemouth colliery
                                            21   *b* Health Centre at Kelso
                                            21   *c* Gas Council Research Centre, Killingworth
                                            22   *a* Showing a prize Suffolk ram
                                            22   *b* Bondagers working at Kirknewton
                                            23   *a* The Common Riding at Hawick
                                            23   *b* Salmon fishing on the Tweed
                                            24   *a* Medieval bridge over the Till at Twizel
                                            24   *b* Puffins on the Inner Farnes
                                            24   *c* Bringing sheep down the Kilham Valley

MAPS

1  The Scottish Border and Northumberland
   in relation to Southern Scotland and
   Northern England                    *frontispiece*
2  The Scottish Border and Northumberland    16
3  The physical setting and geological
   structure                                 20
4  Places of special interest                38
5  Roman control of the Northern Border      60
6  Castles and fortified towers in the Frontier
   Zone                                     102
7  Scottish Border Burghs (twelfth–
   seventeenth century)                     140
8  John Gibson's map of the Tyne Collieries,
   1787                                     162
9  Major planning classification areas      177
10 The Border 'Streets'                     206

# DRAWINGS

| | | |
|---|---|---|
| 1 | Sculptured rock variation | 18 |
| 2 | Smailholm Tower | 35 |
| 3 | Thomas Bewick's curlew | 57 |
| 4 | Stone circle near Duddo | 76 |
| 5 | Saxon quoin work | 99 |
| 6 | Gatehouse bastle near Bellingham | 121 |
| 7 | A 'Gin-Gang' horse threshing plant | 138 |
| 8 | The Abbey Tower-house, Kelso | 158 |
| 9 | A Stephenson locomotive | 175 |
| 10 | James Stuart, aged 115 | 204 |
| 11 | Wayside cross, Crosshall Farm, Eccles | 221 |

# Acknowledgements

This book is the result of many years of travel and work in the Borders, years which have been marked by kindness and assistance from many people. To acknowledge everyone who contributed to my appreciation and love of the area would be impossible. I can only hope that they will accept the book itself as a tribute to them.

For specific assistance I would like to thank Mr Gard of the Northumberland County Record Office at Gosforth; Miss Cruft of the Royal Commission for Ancient Monuments in Edinburgh; Mr Crawford of the Berwickshire County Library; Mr Reid of the Eastern Borders Development Association; Mr Hope, National Park Warden; the County Planning Officers of Berwickshire, Roxburghshire and Northumberland; the City Planning Officer of Newcastle upon Tyne; the Rural Community Council at Gosforth; the Department of the Environment at Hannibal House; the National Coal Board at Ashington.

For their hospitality, good cheer and constant encouragement, my special thanks go to Mr and Mrs D. Pallett of Morpeth, Mr and Mrs C. Russell of Killingworth, Mr and Mrs J. Smart of Hexham, Mr and Mrs E. Huntington of Ford Castle, Mr and Mrs G. Robertson of Encampment Farm, Mr and Mrs R. Forman of Alnmouth, Mr and Mrs Hutchinson of Berwick-upon-Tweed, Mr and Mrs A. Anderson of Edinburgh, and Mrs Dunn of The Plough, Yetholm.

To my brother, Percy F. C. White, my grateful thanks for the drawings which appear at the end of the chapters.

Acknowledgements and thanks for permission to reproduce photographs are due to Aerofilms Ltd for plates 3, 11b, 14a, 14b, 15c, 16a, 17b, and 19a; to Hector

Innes for plates 1, 23b, and 24b; to John Dewar Studios for plates 2 and 16b; to J. K. St Joseph and Cambridge University for plates 4, 8a, and 10c; to the Forestry Commission for plate 5c; to Mrs Grace Hickling for plates 6a, 6b, and 24c; to the Ministry of Defence for plate 7c (Crown Copyright); to the Department of the Environment for plates 8b, 8c, 9a, 9b, 9c, and 11a (Crown Copyright); to the British Museum for plate 13; to *Hawick News* for plates 15b and 23a; to the National Monuments Record for plate 17a; to P. J. M. Bailey for plate 18a; to the City Engineer, Newcastle upon Tyne, for plates 18b, 20a, and 20b; to the National Coal Board for plate 21a; to Tweeddale Press for plate 22a; and to the County Archivist, Gosforth, for plate 22b.

Acknowledgement and thanks for permission to reproduce Map 8 and Drawing 9 is due to Christie, Malcolm Ltd, Newcastle upon Tyne, and Robin Gard of the Northumberland Record Office. Drawing 3 is reproduced by courtesy of the Victoria and Albert Museum and Drawing 10 is from William Brockie's *The Gypsies of Yetholm*. The rest of the maps were redrawn from the author's roughs by Neil Hyslop.

# Introduction

In the rolling cornfields by Branxton Church, south of the Tweed at Coldstream, stands a tall stone cross. The single inscription on its base 'To the Brave of Both Nations' commemorates one of the greatest battles to take place on British soil, the bloodiest of all the encounters that scorched the Border between Scotland and England. On a wet September day in 1513, at about four in the afternoon, a Scottish army under the command of the forty-year-old King James IV finally engaged the Earl of Surrey and his armies, mustered hurriedly from the northern counties of England. They fought in the falling dusk, each army facing its own homeland. By the next morning the Scots had left the field to the English victors, leaving the King, the Archbishop of St Andrews and many of their noblemen dead on Branxton Moor.

The monument is not the only physical reminder of the battle known as Flodden Field. Cannon-balls collected in the vicinity can be found by the porch of a local inn. The echoes of the battle still ring in the songs and festivals of the Borders today and the effect of living on a warring frontier is still shown in the physical and social characteristics of the landscape. From the Tyne to the Lammermuirs lies a region united by that peculiar experience. The common history produces similarities in the life style that gives the region its identity – the Eastern Borderland.

At its heart lies the mellow range of the Cheviot Hills and the bright thread of the river Tweed. The region stretches seventy miles from the moorland plateau of Berwickshire to the green pastures of Allendale. To the east, its boundary is the fretted edge of the North Sea coast; to the west, the silent dales of Liddel Water. It encompasses the counties of Berwickshire, Roxburghshire and

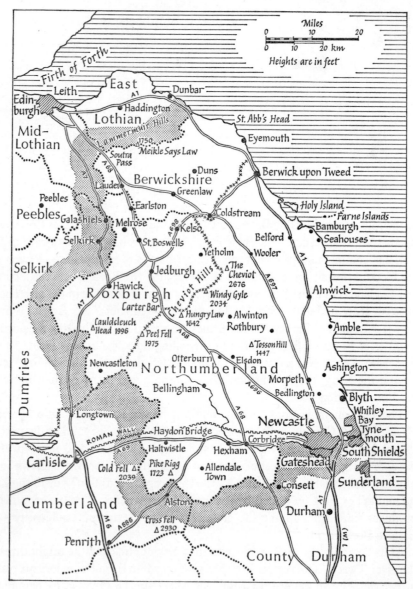

**Map 2** *The Scottish Border and Northumberland.*

Northumberland, an area of great natural beauty, rich wild life, with a wealth of archaeological and historical interest that few regions can match and none surpass.

It was in the period before the evolution of the political frontier that the region had a unity of a different complexion. The territory of the Iron Age Celts, the Ottadini, covered approximately the same part of the north-east before, during and after the Roman occupation. In the same region developed the early Anglo-Saxon kingdom of Bernicia, with its royal vills of Bamburgh and Yeavering. Ultimately it became united with Deira to form the Kingdom of Northumbria, stretching from the Humber to the Forth. It was against the power of Northumbria that the nascent Scottish kingdom steeled itself and achieved the final Tweed–Cheviot frontier.

Today, the region is essentially a rural enclave, left almost as an afterthought in the corner of atlas maps of England and Scotland. But this is no rural backwater, for it contains some of the largest arable farms in Britain and some of the best maintained estates, quite apart from being the most important sheep-breeding area in the country.

Industry lies on the periphery: to the north, the woollen towns of the Tweed, to the south, the heavy industries of Tyneside and the coalfield, the territory of the 'Geordies'. The traditional occupations are under pressure from the economic changes of this century and the whole region suffers from the problems of rural depopulation and an unemployment rate above the national average. Yet this very disadvantage has left the Borders free from some aspects of change that have made so much of Britain less pleasant to inhabit. It is a green and pleasant land still. I have lived, worked and walked in it for many years and found the rich diversity of life, from the fish quays of North Shields to the snow gullies of the Cheviot, a never-failing source of recreation, in the deepest sense of that word. There is no region of Britain where the historic past and the physical present meet with such impact.

In this study, I have followed a broad historical theme from the making of the physical landscape to the final human contribution of new towns and motorways, but, in doing so, I have concentrated on those aspects of the past that are recalled by a physical presence now. The horizon of enjoyment can be enlarged by looking at the total landscape: not just the castles, towers, abbeys and mansions that deservedly occupy so much attention, but also the field systems, the hedgerows, the tracks, the walls and the husbandry that have all played their part in the moulding of the Border story. It is a history, certainly, but a history of the present. The past is still with us, giving a sense of continuity, of belonging.

When trying to organize a wealth of material into a continuous narrative, I came across a comment from an earlier topographer which I can only repeat with feeling. 'Yet it is impossible that any one man, being never so inquisitive and laborious, should attain into the perfect knowledge of all passages, in all places,' wrote William Gray in 1649 in his survey of Newcastle. I have attempted most passages in most places in the region but my bulging notebooks only reveal what a lot I have to learn about the Border and its people. Any such record reflects personal preference and betrays prejudice. I have given most space to the places and people that have given me most pleasure in their recall and I crave the indulgence of all Borderers for the sins of omission.

The general narrative is supported by a series of factual appendices that may help travellers to follow up their own interests and discover new ones. The One-Inch maps of the Ordnance Surveys are essential companions for the Border 'passages' and the following sheets cover the main part of the region:

Sheet 63 – Dunbar
Sheet 64 – Berwick-upon-Tweed
Sheet 70 – Jedburgh
Sheet 71 – Alnwick
Sheet 76 – Carlisle
Sheet 77 – Hexham
Sheet 78 – Newcastle upon Tyne

Some corners overlap on to Sheets 62, 69 and 84.

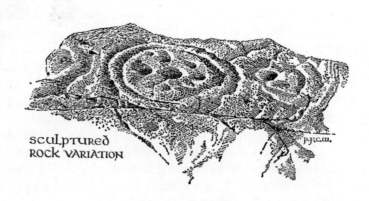

sculptured
rock variation

# I

# The physical setting

He's guided them o'er moss and muir,
O'er hill and houp, and mony ae down;
Till they came to the Foul-bog-shiel,
And there brave Noble he lighted down.

*(The Ballad of Hobie Noble)*

The pleasure of early maps is not just in the ornamental cartouches, the noble ships and fierce marine creatures that fill up the spaces, but in their revelation of a new, refreshing aspect of a familiar area. There is such a map in the National Library of Scotland showing the east coast from Bamburgh in Northumberland to Aberdeen. It was drawn about the year 1584 for Waghenaer's *Spieghel der Zeevaerdt* and shows the Anglo-Scottish eastern Border from the sailor's viewpoint, looking inland from the North Sea. There is the rugged hunchback of Britain bared to the vagaries of the sea. Early topographical writers always stressed the maritime nature of Northumberland and Berwickshire, for the main centres of population were on the coastal plain, especially by the mouths of rivers. The sea itself was the major highway, and the main land route, the Great North Road, ran parallel to the coast. To the south were Newcastle, North Shields and Tynemouth; to the north, Eyemouth and Berwick-upon-Tweed; between them, small harbours in inlets and sheltered coves.

From the seaman's viewpoint, the region is a formidable and dangerous coast, a broad, fertile plain and a distant rim of hills whence the great rivers of Tyne and Tweed flow, gathering tributary waters to create the major estuaries. The sea is still important in the life of the area and the varied coastline from the Tyne to the southern shores of the Forth is one of its greatest assets, but the growth of land transport brings us increasingly to the landsman's view. In spite of the great size of the region, covering three counties, it is possible to gain an overall impression of its physical structure from a vantage-point in the heart of the region, the Cheviot Hills.

Even a comparatively low summit like Coldsmouth Hill at 1300 feet, only a

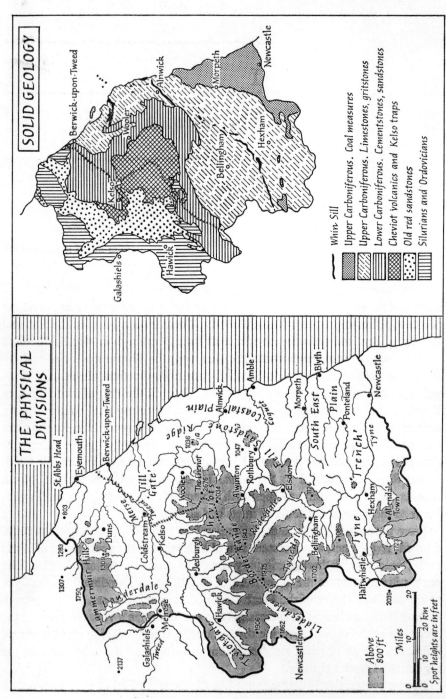

**Map 3** *The physical setting and geological structure.*

short walk from Kilham in the valley of the Bowmont, can give a panorama of the Border's splendours, especially with a brisk wind in the north-west quarter clearing the sky. The Scottish Border lies just to the west of the summit, passing south and east so that the walker here has the additional pleasure of looking *south* from England into Scotland. But the wind is wholly Scottish, blowing from the Highlands and bringing with it the pureness of air that makes the Tweed one of the areas of greatest clarity and loveliest skies in Britain. Visibility of over fifty miles is not unusual.

There at our feet is the great basin of the Tweed, the rich lowland of the Merse of Berwickshire running eastward to the North Sea. Beyond it is the plateau of the Lammermuirs cutting us off from the Lothians and Edinburgh. The hill range continues westward behind Lauderdale across the Soutra Pass to the Moorfoots beyond Galashiels, reaching over 2000 feet in height. The rim swings unbroken to our left past Ettrick Forest to the head of Teviotdale, then merges with the bumpy range of the Border hills somewhere around Peel Fell at 1975 feet, the other side of Carter Bar.

The view along the Border bounces from summit to rounded summit, Windy Gyle, Mazie Law, Rushy Fell, and there, to the south-east, is the great hump of the Cheviot still carrying its cap of snow well into April, with every line of its weathered face etched by the snow-filled gullies, looking near enough to touch. The view swings east now to the sea only twenty miles away across the coastal plain, the great gateway joining the two nations, with the sun sparkling on the sands by Holy Island. Between the Cheviot flanks and the sea the clouds build up in a line marking the ridge of the Fell Sandstone escarpment that begins its long thirty-mile arc, running south and west out of view. All the burns and dykes and waters and rivers in view feed into the clear waters of the Tweed, culminating in the rich salmon fisheries of the estuary at Berwick.

The Tweed basin is one of the major physical constituents of the region and the encircling hills its natural limit, broken by the dales that point long fingers into the interior, especially Tweeddale leading to the inner recesses of the Southern Uplands. The view is also broken by isolated hills like Rubers Law, the Dunion, the Eildon Hills and Dirrington Great Law, volcanic rocks breaking out of the deep layers of ancient sedimentary strata.

We need a change of viewpoint to see the rest of the region or at least its major features. A walk south along the Border to the Cheviot, following the route of the new Pennine Way, brings us to a more constricted view, with the hills carved out of the lava-flows of the old Cheviot volcano dominating the foreground and the burns radiating out from our viewpoint, busily cutting their way down to the Harthope, the Breamish and the Coquet, thence into the broad 'moat' of lowland that encircles the Cheviots. South beyond the moat lies the highest point of the Sandstone Ridge, the easily-recognizable flat top of the Simonsides above Rothbury, beloved of Sunday picnickers and climbers. There in the distance, thirty-five miles away, is the smoky plume from Blyth power station, symbol of the lowlands of the coalfield, the black triangle bounded by the Tyne and the North Sea coast. To the south-west, range on low range of hills greyly cross the view, Redesdale, Tynedale, Wark Forest, the Wall, and at the far limit of vision the Pennines beyond Allendale. On a really good day, I have seen Cross Fell, the highest point of the Pennines at 2930 feet, nearly sixty miles away, the true heart of Britain, near the junction of Northumberland, Durham, Westmorland and Cumberland, beyond the southern limit of our region.

This view encompasses a second great basin, though not so distinctive as that of the Tweed, for most of the water from these hill groups flows into the Tyne, leaving only smaller streams like the Coquet and the Aln to make their way independently to the sea between the basins of the two great rivers.

The limiting rim of hills to the west is more broken than in the Tweed basin. The watershed of the Tyne is less than 500 feet high beyond Greenhead where the main east–west road and railway linking Carlisle to Newcastle follows the trench of the Tyne Gap. The dale of the North Tyne is joined by a deep cut right through the dividing hills with Liddesdale, that isolated extremity of Roxburghshire that faces west and feeds its waters into the Solway Firth.

Eighty miles from the northern watershed of the Lammermuirs to the head of Allendale in the far south; sixty miles from the bleak head of Teviotdale to the rocky shores of Bamburgh; across the heart of this great north-eastern region runs the great watershed of the Cheviot Hills, dividing river systems, dividing nations, and the Cheviot itself, centre of this magic circle.

Berwickshire is traditionally divided into three regions: Lammermuirs, Merse and Lauderdale; Roxburghshire is dominated by Teviotdale, with parts of Liddesdale and Tweeddale. Northumberland is more complex but is basically a series of regions ranging in sequence round the central feature of the Cheviots, the thin lowland belt of the 'moat', then the Fell Sandstone Escarpment, followed by the south-east plain, which is itself broken on closer view by a series of low escarpments also facing the Cheviot. Then the pattern is severed by the Tyne trench with the Pennine foothills south of that line.

There is no simple relationship between land surface and the geological structure as this region has been nearly 400 million years in the making and possibly a land-surface for nearly half that time, during which the rocks have been worn down and weathered to the roots of their original forms. All the major geological systems of the region are from the Palaeozoic (literally 'old life') or Primary Era. This entire 'platform' of ancient rocks, folded, faulted, subject to earthquake and vulcanicity by the great upheavals of earth history, has been modified by the Ice Age, the glacial features of erosion and deposition being amongst the most interesting (and, from the point of view of human occupation, most significant) aspects of the landscape.

It is tempting to start the geological story with the Cheviot itself, that central mass of granite and andesitic lava flows that marks the eroded roots of the volcano, active 300 million years ago on the southern shores of the Devonian land mass, the great hump of peat-laden mountain upon which Daniel Defoe ventured with such fears, wondering if there would be room for himself and his guides on the summit. The 'summit' is so broad that armies could muster there but the brave walkers of today can only claim the summit by aiming at the Ordnance Survey trigonometrical point across a morass of sticky mud. But the geological sequence really begins in the far north where the earliest deposits are found, and unfolds southwards, each rock outcrop supplying to a large extent the materials for later deposition to the south, in a perpetual rhythm of erosion and deposition.

A journey from Newcastle northwards to Coldstream along the A1 and the A697, thence to Soutra *en route* for Edinburgh, is in effect a geological journey in reverse, a journey backwards through geological time which is reflected visually not only in the general landscape but in the materials of the buildings and walls that are passed in succession, from the Coal Measure sandstones of Tyneside to the flaggy Silurians of the Lammermuirs. For this is 'stone country'. The buildings in the rural districts whether castle, church or cottage are of stone (with the exception of comparatively recent brick intrusions), and especially of 'freestone', the masons' term for the sandstones that cut relatively easily into the required shapes. The sandstones are in use for corner work and doors and windows, and between them are the tell-tale patterns of limestones, glacial boulders, and angular volcanic stones that reflect the geological outcrops in the vicinity. Even the sandstones vary enormously in colour and textures, from the honey-colour of Belsay to the bright red of Berwickshire.

It is along that broken coast where the sea has matched its power against the ancient land mass that the secrets of the geology are most readily revealed and it is in the far north, at Siccar Point, one of the wildest parts of this dramatic north-eastern shoreline, that the story begins. It was here that one of the great original thinkers in geological science first gazed in wonder at the chaos of rocks and wrestled with the implications of their fantastic structure. Here, James Hutton developed the ideas that bore fruit in his *History of the Earth,* published in 1785. It is a fairly inaccessible place, away from main roads and needing a long scramble down steep grassy slopes to get down to the sea's edge, where the Silurian sedimentary rocks have been up-ended into an almost vertical position. There, improbably, as if resting loosely upon the broken teeth of the Silurian platform, are horizontal slabs of Old Red Sandstone, a classic example of 'un-conformity'; two sedimentary deposits of different ages and between them a complete break. The Silurian shales, greywackes, grits and flagstones, bearing an abundance of fossils of the earliest forms of life, bear witness to forty million years of deposition, to the earth movements that consolidated them into hard rock and contorted them into deep folds, to the long erosion that stripped them down to a rough level on which new deposition took place. A similar pattern could be seen near Jedburgh, at the base of the red cliffs of the river Jed, another place visited by Hutton, who was a Berwickshire man. Recent slumping has spoilt the exposure, hiding the Silurians at the base, but the Old Red Sandstone strata are still clear. The Silurian rocks, seen both here and at Siccar Point, underlie the great rim of hills (referred to at the beginning of this chapter) that encompass the basin of the Tweed to the north and the west and are one of the main constituents of the range of the Southern Uplands that run south-south-west from the North Sea down to the Solway Firth and Galloway.

The rivers running from these 'Silurian Hills' when they were first formed deposited their material into what Sir A. Geikie, writing in the nineteenth century, has called the 'Cheviot Lake'. These deposits of coarse sandstones and conglomerates are called the Lower Old Red Sandstone and are associated with early volcanic activity, lava flows of up to 1200 feet in thicknesses being found with them. They are best seen on the Berwickshire coast, at Eyemouth, Colding-ham and St Abb's Head. They are comparatively limited in occurrence due to subsequent erosion, from which was derived the next stage of the Devonian deposition, the Upper Old Red Sandstone which gives the characteristic colora-tion to the fields of so much of Berwickshire, especially in that area of undulating country running from Greenlaw to Jedburgh with 'tongues' running north along Lauderdale and east to Mordington near Berwick-upon-Tweed. These coarse red sandstones and conglomerates have been protected from subsequent erosion by their position in the Tweed trough. Within them, sun-cracks and rain-pitted surfaces, a memory of climatic conditions more than 300 million years ago, reflect the conditions of their deposition.

Throughout the period of the deposition of the Devonian System of rocks, volcanoes were extremely active and within what had been the Cheviot Lake erupted the Cheviot volcano, with enormous thicknesses of andesitic lava flows, giving a purply tinge to so much of the Cheviot stone. The andesites often show their origin by the small pits on the surface which were formed by the gases on the surface of cooling lava. Often these pits or vesicles were filled by later minerals of volcanic origin and supply the hunter for semi-precious stones with agates and other varieties of 'Scotch pebbles', now so popular in jewellery and decoration.

Associated with the lava flows were outbursts of volcanic ash which form the agglomerates found on Gaisty Law and in Raven's Cleugh. New intrusions from the weak sides of the old volcano formed dykes of mica felsites and porphyrites which can often be identified not only by their change of colour from the prevalent andesite but also by occasional crags that stand out from surrounding ground. Another feature of the volcanic activity was the upwelling of masses of magma, mostly of granite, that never reached the surface but cooled at depth and therefore are known as plutonic rocks. The fact that they now appear on the surface in so many places is due to the erosion of all the rocks that once covered them. The pink Cheviot granites that now can be found at the head of Langleeford and around Hedgehope, lay deep in the heart of the once-majestic volcano. Other such plutonic masses that now make their mark on the landscape are the elongated dome of Duns Law and the unusually red outcrop of Harden redstone that occurs on the southern flank of the Cheviot lavas at Biddlestone near Alwinton. You can always tell when a road has been surfaced by redstone from the Biddlestone quarry – the roads are redder and brighter than any other. Heavy rains and rivers eroding the lava flows accumulated areas of conglomerates in hollows, the best known exposures being those in Roddam Dene, up the Ingram Valley of north Northumberland.

The Border country, especially north of Kelso, has been described by Sir A. Geikie in his *Scenery of Scotland* as the best possible locality for tracing the influence of igneous rocks on landscape (Map 3). It was during a comparatively late stage in the volcanic story that the flows of olivine-basalt known as the Kelso Traps broke out. They form many of the isolated hills, sometimes up to 1000 feet in height, that stand out from the general lowland of the Tweed Basin and make a focus for the eye looking northwards from the Cheviot Hills. Perhaps of the same period are the three peaks of the Eildon Hills, famous because of their special place in the heart of Sir Walter Scott, dominating his favourite view from the Tweed at Bermersyde. The three peaks are the remnants of a much larger laccolith of plutonic rock that formed at the end of the Devonian system.

Just to the north of the Eildons is a small knoll composed entirely of volcanic ashes and agglomerates that were extensively quarried for the Abbey at Melrose and perhaps for the earlier Roman buildings at Trimontium. The stone used in the Abbey is now almost crumbling into its original constituents (in contrast to the Red Sandstone) but the exposure in Quarry Hill is a fine place to study this rock type.

The olivine-basalt of the Kelso Traps may rival the Eildon Hills in the number of times it has appeared in photographs for it forms the rugged moorland base for one of the most famous Border towers, that of Smailholm.

Even more dominating visually are the isolated outcrops of volcanics, creating a crop of conical hills at and above 1000 feet in height to the south-west of Jedburgh, notably Dunion Hill, Black Law, Rubers Law and Bonchester Hill.

Contemporary with the formation of these trap rocks was the next great period of deposition, the Carboniferous System of rocks that reached their climax in the great coal forests after eighty million years and some 6000 feet of deposition in a subsiding basin to the south of the Devonian volcanics and sandstones. The southern boundary may be taken for convenience as the line of the Stublick Fault that cuts across the southern part of Northumberland to the south of and parallel with the Tyne valley. That fault marks, too, the effective northern limit of plateau-landscapes associated with the Pennines and represents a visual break as well as a geological divide from the land to the south, which has been studied in an earlier volume in this series.[1]

The onset of the Carboniferous deposition was marked by muds, sands, algae and lime-secreting organisms. Up to 3000 feet were deposited in the Tweed area but the strata thin out towards the south. Fossils suggest a lagoonal environment at this time. These so-called Cementstones rarely appear on the surface and have little positive effect on the topography. Although alternating bands make such a fine feature in the Coquet Gorge, just west of Alwinton, deep and steep enough to tempt the army to train men in dangerous pursuits at the end of ropes, the Cementstones provide an easily eroded rock that created the great arc of lowland round the Cheviot Hills, the Cheviot Moat, as I called it earlier.

The loveliest and most effective of the Lower Carboniferous rocks in terms of landscape is the Fell Sandstone. Many people would take the Coal Measures of the south-east to symbolize Northumberland; for me, it is the Fell Sandstone.

[1] A. Raistrick, *The Pennine Dales.*

Durable, lovely in texture, admirable building stone found even in Edinburgh and in Coventry Cathedral, yet uniquely Northumbrian. Weathering into fantastic patterns along its joint lines and along the original bedding planes of the deltaic sands that first formed it, it gives the climber some of the best cracks, chimneys and traverses for his skill, albeit on a small scale. This massive, uniform sandstone is up to 1000 feet in total depth in places. The last quarry using it closed at Doddington in 1969.

Beautiful in itself, the Fell Sandstone also has a dramatic effect on the landscape. So great have been the past convulsions of the earth that this great thickness of solid sandstone has been folded and faulted into a series of blocks forming a general pattern of two broad, broken arcs of high ground swinging across the centre of Northumberland, separated by the basin near Hetton. The complexity of the pattern shows up most strikingly in the earliest edition of the One-Inch Ordnance Survey, mapped in the 1860s.[1] The poor, thin soils and the considerable height of the escarpment, reaching over 1000 feet in several places and a maximum of 1400 feet south of Rothbury, produce a distinctive and varied moorland landscape that stretches from Etal in the north to Elsdon in the west and, incidentally, supplies some fine ridge walks.

The landscape south and east of the Fell Sandstone escarpment is much quieter. Rhythmic variations in the subsidence of the land during the long periods of deposition enabled vegetation to form and the subsequent Scremerston Coal Group contains many seams of up to two feet in thickness, some of the earliest coal formations in the British Isles. This estuarine period was followed by deposition of 3000 feet of rocks, featured especially by limestones in clear, warm, shallow waters where sea-creatures flourished and coral reefs grew. Rich with fossil remains, these Carboniferous Limestones can be studied in detail along the Northumbrian coast, from Alnmouth to Berwick-upon-Tweed, a coastline of such scientific interest and visual attraction that much of it has been protected as an Area of Outstanding Natural Beauty; its possible spoliation has been avoided, temporarily at least. Many lime quarries and old kilns can be found from Beadnell Bay across country to the valley of Deadwater in the North Tyne. Even within the Limestone Group of sediments, many coal seams are found, some still actively worked to the south of Alnwick, at the Shilbottle Pit.

Within the main Limestone Group are many outcrops of sandstone, due to periods of shallower conditions in the limestone seas. These sandstones frequently outcrop in the form of crags and produce small areas of moorland that

---

[1] Reprinted by David & Charles in 1971.

break the generally well-farmed, sweet pastures associated with the limestones. These miniature escarpments are like small copies of the Fell Sandstone Escarpment and are seen to perfection around Rothley and Shafto in mid-Northumberland.

Following the limestones came further sandy conditions forming what is called, most inappropriately, the Millstone Grit. I say 'inappropriately' because the words conjure up the savage landscape of the Kinder Scout and other such hill landscapes of the Pennines. But in Northumberland the gritstones are friable and easily eroded and in most places produce a trough of low ground that runs south-west from the mouth of the Coquet to the Tyne down-stream from Corbridge.

The Millstone Grits are only a brief interlude before the long period of shallow swampy conditions that made the name Tyneside associated nationally with coal, to become one of the cradles of the first Industrial Revolution. The six-hundred-yard depth of the Coal Measures in some places contain seams of coal six feet thick, supporting one of the most important coalfields in the British Isles, partly because of its proximity to the coast and easy transportation to the south and overseas. It is now an area of declining output and closing pits; most of the 'long-life' pits are near the coast and the thick, horizontal seams can be seen in the cliffs, especially north of St Mary's Island. The most impressive exposure is at Lynemouth, near the modern pit-head gear on the cliffs. Here complete fossilized trees of the ancient Carboniferous forest can still be seen standing upright in a matrix of later deposits. The deposition that effectively 'drowned' the trees must have been very gradual at this point, for such upright fossils are rare; they are normally found crushed in a horizontal position. A south-easterly gale often causes the sea to breach submarine coal seams and the small coal is thrown up on to the beaches, giving rise to a thriving local industry in 'culling' such coal for private use.

Finally, desert conditions again replaced the swamps of the Coal Measures and the Permian System of rocks were deposited, which appear in the cliff line in the extreme south-east of Northumberland, at Tynemouth and Cullercoats. It is possible that later systems of rocks may have covered the region, the rocks associated with Southern England south of the coalfields. If they did, there is no evidence of them now and they have been completely stripped from the Carboniferous platform by later erosion. Odd things, such as flints and chalk rubble, are found along the coast, as at Seaton Sluice, but these deposits owe their origin to the ballast of colliers coming back from southern ports, especially Thames-side.

The conclusion of the Permian deposition was accompanied by another major period of earth-disturbance and mountain building known as the Variscan orogenesis. This had the effect of uplifting the entire region and subjecting the rocks to intense pressures. Some folding of the Carboniferous rocks took place, which can be seen along much of the coast, especially in the Limestones, but the comparative rigidity of the rocks led to fracturing and faulting rather than folding. Many of the bays and inlets of the coast owe their existence to such faulting and the whole of the Fell Sandstone escarpment was faulted, leading to the development of a series of isolated blocks and, in one area near Kyloe, to the development of a double scarp.

The weaknesses in the crust caused by these later earth movements again enabled volcanic intrusions from the depths to find a way to the surface. One such intrusion of quartz-dolerite has given rise to one of the most famous geological features in Northumberland, the Great Whin Sill, which is the collective name given to a series of sills that occur right across the county, producing the Farne Islands at the north-eastern extremity, on the angular columns of which one of the most famous bird sanctuaries exists. Many of the greatest castle sites, such as Bamburgh and Dunstanburgh, stand on the same outcrop which has forced its way through the limestone strata, causing a baking effect at the junction of the two rock types. Throughout the county it creates small escarpments but none more dramatic than that on which the Romans built their defensive wall, especially beyond Housesteads, where its steep north-facing slope supplements the defences created by the occupying army.

More volcanic dykes came to the surface during the Alpine orogenesis which created the Alps of Central Europe and buckled up the young rocks of south-eastern England. The Acklington Dyke, composed of fine-grained dolerite, runs right across Roxburghshire, through the Border hills to Rothbury and thence eastward to the village which bears its name. The occurrence of dykes does not have a dramatic effect on the landscape but 'where their outcrops are free from Drift [they] usually form green rather ridgy ground, or else slacks when running across sandstone scars'.[1]

## The Glacial Interlude

The glaciation of the Border region may best be introduced by the existence of certain rock types far away from their source of origin. I have picked up a small boulder of Cheviot granite on the Fell Sandstone ridge above Weetwood and a

[1] C. T. Clough, *Memoirs of the Geological Survey, Plashetts and Kielder* (1889).

hunk of Criffel Granite (from Galloway) in gravels on the north bank of the Tyne. These 'erratic' boulders could not have been transported by normal water activity and, by their presence, not only show the work of ice but indicate the direction in which the ice sheets flowed. Mapping all the known occurrences of 'erratics' gives an overall pattern which indicates three major ice movements, one main glacier coming down the Tweed, being diverted south by another major sheet from Scandinavia (Scandinavian erratics are found on the Northumberland and Durham coasts). Small valley glaciers flowed independently from the Cheviot Massif. The full story of the actual sequence of glacial events is still debated and even such basic facts as to whether the Cheviot itself was ice-covered are disputed. The general traveller is perhaps more concerned with the surface features which resulted from this 'arctic' period, for not only are they interesting in themselves but they have had a decisive effect on man's colonization of the area, his settlement sites and his farming pattern.

The major effect of the periodic onset of the cold conditions that led to the development of ice sheets, which may have completely covered much of the region with the possible exception of the highest hills, was the deep weathering of the rock surfaces by severe frost and then the removal of that weathered layer. But many of the upland features associated with classic areas of glaciation are not well developed and the mountain silhouette is rounded and mature, quite unlike the fretted outline of the peaks of, for example, the Lake District. This may be due to the lower precipitation on the eastern section of the great ice sheets or to less active freeze-and-melt processes. Whatever the reason, the peaks and sharp-ridged *arêtes* do not occur and the corries, the gouged-out 'armchairs' hollowed from mountainsides that are such a feature of highland glaciation, are not readily found. The nearest approximation are the hollows gouged out of the east and north face of the Cheviot – the Bizzle and the Hen Hole, wild places both. The Bizzle has a marked basin shape and a pile-up of morainic material at its lip, but the Hen Hole is a series of rock steps and rugged gorges. There is little doubt that both features are related to the glacial structures known as corries.[1]

Generally speaking, the glaciers occupied existing river valleys, flowed down them, deepened them and widened them to form straight troughs, though the straightness of many of the valleys is due partly to faulting in the Cheviot block. Most of the valleys radiating out from the Cheviot have this form, such as College Valley, Harthope Burn, Kale Water and the Bowmont. The broad valley

[1] C. M. Clapperton, 'The Evidence for a Cheviot Ice-Cap', *Transactions of the Institute of British Geographers*.

that cuts right through the Border range at Deadwater, joining the North Tyne with Liddesdale, also suggests by its shape that it was occupied by a valley glacier. A unique pass, it is used by the road from Kielder to Hawick and the now-disused North Tyne Railway.

Striae, deep scratches on rock faces cut by moving ice, which are useful indicators of ice-flow direction, are not prolific in the region though they can be found on the surface of hard, compact rock faces such as the Fell Sandstone. The best example I have found was on the surface of the Whin Sill above Howden Quarry just after the overburden of soil had been removed in order to start quarrying. The striations or striae were indicating a north–south flow at this point which agrees with the direction shown by erratics. The same direction is followed by deep grooves cut in the same rock on the Farne Islands.

The ability of ice to gouge out and deepen rock-basins even on low ground created deep hollows in which melt waters remained as lakes. Most of the basins became filled with subsequent debris and with peat. Borings through them often bring up lake clay. The greatest of these and one of the biggest hollows in England is now known as the Milfield Plain. Borings have shown a depth of more than 180 feet of fine clay and there is evidence of a shoreline around what was once the 'Milfield Lake' at about 140 feet.

Another such rock-basin, although on a smaller scale, is that of Ford Moss, developed by a fault in the Sandstone Ridge. This is now filled by at least twenty-five feet of peat and mosses, and water. Such hollows are quite abundant and usually recognized by their vegetation, which thrives on wet conditions· Some of the small loughs on the north-west side of the Cheviots may have been formed in this way, such as Pawston Loch and Yetholm Loch, both near Yetholm. Morebattle, near by, is situated on the edge of an old lake or mere (which may account for the town's name). Another group of loughs is north of the Roman Wall where ice scoured against the outcrop of the Whin Sill. Some lakes have been formed by the damming-up process caused by later deposits and each site needs close inspection before one can be sure.

Throughout the region there are hundreds of deep channels, often at high level, cutting across hill spurs, frequently 'dry', with an unusual profile up and down, which cannot possibly have been cut by normal river processes. One of the most spectacular, and historically interesting, is Monday Cleugh above Humbleton, the site of one of the many battles between the Douglas and Percy factions. Another important channel cuts a route for the A697 south of Powburn through the Sandstone ridge. At one time it was held that these channels were cut by water spilling out from the margins of lakes formed by meltwater at the edge of ice sheets. Some may be attributed to this but many must have been cut by meltwater under pressure, probably sub-glacial. The most interesting group of such channels is in the north-east Cheviots, where the ice direction was south and east. The Powburn channel may represent meltwaters escaping under pressure to the south.

Another important group of meltwater channels follows the alignment of the Berwickshire coast near St Abbs, one particularly deep trough now being occupied by the river Eye, the Great North Road and the railway to Edinburgh.

The severity of the climate and the deep frosts that occurred, perhaps most effectively in the inter-glacial periods, that is, when ice was not protecting the ground, is reflected in the existence on the Cheviot summit at 2600 feet of granite that has been so rotted that it can be scooped out with the hands. Inside the twenty feet or so of soft red earth can be found small core stones, the hard little eggs of solid rock that alone have resisted disintegration.

## Glacial Deposition

The great amounts of material weathered from the parent rocks and dragged away by moving ice were then deposited when the ice lost its momentum or by meltwaters running under the ice, at ice margins and even through crevasses in the ice sheet. It has been estimated that in some parts of the Tweed Basin the solid rock surface is masked by 300–400 feet of glacial debris, and the old mouth of the river Tyne (the pre-glacial Tyne) has been filled in with 180 feet of material through which the present Tyne is cutting its course. The general name for this material is glacial till and it supplies some of the best farming land in the region, the clays and sands breaking down to more amenable soils for cultivation than many of the parent rocks, such as the sandstones. Quite frequently, the edge of glacial material can be marked by the edge of cultivated land, with moorland vegetation forming on the uncovered parent rocks.

In parts of the region, especially in the Tweed Valley, the till or boulder clay is formed into long, elongated smooth ridges called drumlins, extremely difficult to photograph from the ground but most distinctive from the air and quite well shown by the contour pattern.

Detailed studies of the boulder clays have shown several different layers, especially on the coast, the one overlaying the other suggesting that ice sheets from different directions overrode previous deposits of other ice.

Another depositional feature that is well-represented in the region is that associated with dead ice, stagnant ice sheets trapped by the relief of the land

1. The view north-east from Carter Bar showing the outlying hills of volcanic rock outcropping through the sedimentary deposits; the granite massif of the Cheviot lies in the background.

2. *Looking west from above Bernersyde Hill over the basin of the Upper Tweed: the Eildon Hills to the left; Melrose and Galashiels in the valley to the right; the distant backcloth of the Southern Uplands. Sir Walter Scott's favourite view was from the road in the foreground above the site of Old Melrose.*

rotting *in situ* to build hummocky ground composed of sands and gravels and distinguished on the maps of the Geological Survey by a quite different colour from that of the boulder clay. This ground is called kettle moraine, after the 'kettle' holes that occur in it, often with standing water, the depth of which varies according to rainfall, for the water seeps readily through the sandy deposits. Large areas of this type occur at both ends of the old Milfield Lake Basin, around Hedgeley and Ilderton and again between Crookham and Cornhill. The old road used to bounce like a switchback through this type of landscape and recent road-straightening has given some good exposures of these deposits.

The frequent association of these sand and gravel deposits with meltwater channels may suggest that some of them were deposited by meltwaters under the ice. The shape of some of the deposits in isolated hillocks and in long winding snakes indicates formation in caves and tunnels under the glacier snouts. These kaims and eskers, respectively, are both referred to locally as kaims, the most famous being the Bradford Kaim which follows a two-mile course south of Spindlestone Heugh. Even more remarkable are the 'kaims' north of Greenlaw, a long snake of sands and gravels winding across the wet moors for nearly four kilometres near the Weststruther Road, a good walk for a day's exploration.

The kettle moraine is found in patches in a zone running south-west from Alnmouth via Morpeth to Harlow Hill, roughly the line of the Millstone Grit trough. This was the zone in which Tweed, Tyne and Cheviot ice sheets met. The road builders making the new Morpeth by-pass have had some difficult encounters with the instability of this material.

The effect of the deposition of this great blanket of glacial materials all over the lowland area of the region, even up on the flanks of the hills in some places at 1000 feet, had the effect of modifying the normal drainage pattern. The return to normal pluvial conditions led to a redevelopment of river systems which were sometimes unable to follow their previous course due to the blocking of channels by drift. This may account for some of the more unusual courses taken by rivers such as the great swing of the Bowmont as it approaches within three miles of the Tweed at Coldstream then proceeds to swing away through a deep trough through the hills, finally finding its way to the Tweed after a diversion of about twenty-two miles. Just to the south-west of this spot, the Kale Water turns abruptly to the west at Morebattle when it seems more natural that it should flow through a deep channel to the east and join the Bowmont. Of course, such complex drainage patterns have a much longer pedigree than that of the Ice period alone.

B

33

Another good example of such diversion is two miles to the south of Jedburgh, where the Jed Water forsakes the channel flowing north-east from Mossburnford and cuts a steep-sided gorge to the Tweed at Nisbet.

Some of the Northumbrian rivers flowing east to the coast may have been similarly affected, the lower courses of many rivers now divorced from what, on the map at least, look like their natural upper courses. But this pattern has another explanation, that of river capture, by which a fast-flowing stream cuts back to 'capture' the headwaters of another river. Hence the Wansbeck is aligned with the Upper Rede, and this 'capture' activity, producing a 'trellis' pattern in contrast to the dendritic pattern (like the veins of a leaf) seen in the Tweed, is much earlier than the glacial period.

The rivers found themselves with enormous amounts of easily-eroded material to re-sort and much of the glacial material has been carried out. In the process, the rivers have formed terraces marking their older, higher courses.

The terraces do not show up well on maps but in the field they are easily recognized by their old river banks, now far from the river course, and they frequently supply sites for villages and farms, being well-drained and away from the greatest dangers of flooding, the low-lying 'haughs' of alluvial land which are still often under water after snow-melt or heavy autumnal rains.

These river terraces may be associated with changes in sea-level after the Ice Age. As the land recovered from the enormous weight of ice, it would rise gently; this is called 'isostatic recovery'. At the same time, enormous quantities of meltwater would cause the sea-level to rise. The two effects are probably still proceeding, and our coastal areas especially reflect this constant readjustment of the land. Just north of Berwick-upon-Tweed is Brotherston's Hole, a good example of an arch cut in the sandstones by present wave action. As sea erosion carries on, this arch may be breached to form a stack, of which there are many examples on this coast. But what is remarkable in this instance is that there is one such stack standing on top of the rocks in which the arch is formed. This stack must have been formed at a time when either the land surface was lower or the sea-level higher. Fragments of 'raised beaches' are also mapped by the Geological Survey, especially in the Bamburgh area, another indication of sea-level changes.

The structure of the coast is disguised by the most recent of geological events, the occurrence of blown sands which have formed dune areas backing the bays of Northumberland, especially between Alnmouth and Warkworth and again north from the north shore of Holy Island to Scremerston. The dunes are constantly reforming before the onslaught of easterly gales. The southerly turn of many river mouths is partly due to long-shore drifting of loose materials, forming sand-spits. A stormy night in 1805 caused the river Aln to cut right across its sand-spit and dunes, cutting the church from its village. A map showing the area before the storm still hangs in the saloon bar of one of the pubs in the main street. The general southerly drift of the sea can even bring timbers and tree branches down from flood waters on the Tweed.

SMAILHOLM TOWER.                    P.J.C.W.

# 2

# Flora and fauna

The hounds ran swiftly through the woods
  The nimble deere to take,
That with their cryes the hills and dales
  An eccho shrill did make.

*(The Ballad of Chevy Chase)*

It was midnight on Midsummer's night and I was sitting in Prior Castell's fifteenth-century tower, gazing out over the scoured, doloritic slab of the Inner Farne, with the light still good enough to see the outer group of rocky islands clearly – Staple, Brownsman, Wamses, Harcar, Longstone. The sky was still busy with Arctic Terns, the sea swallows with their forked tails and aggressive spirit like winged demons. Many were hovering above their nesting places in shallow hollows in the rare patch of sand near the landing inlet. Others were swooping vigorously above the multi-coloured little rabbits[1] that were sporting around like rugby players and venturing too close to the terns' territory. As I went out with my companions into the cold night, the wind was howling from the north-east, unbroken in its fierce fetch from the Norwegian coast. The sea was racing into Churn Gut at the north-west corner of the island, surging beneath the rocks along the eroded joint lines and roaring up through the blow-hole to a height of about thirty feet. A really fierce gale can create a spout of more than ninety feet. It was good to think that the midsummer weather was wild enough to keep us on the island and other visitors off. Three of the sixteen acres of the island are covered with soil and this area was honeycombed by the rabbit burrows and, in many of them, the young puffin chicks were protected. On the steep eighty-foot cliffs, the kittiwakes were nesting, holding their eggs on narrow ledges in the columns of quartz-dolerite, screaming and spitting as we climbed gently down the rock face. There, too, were shags, cormorants, razor bills, guillemots and the cacophony of the sea's edge that still lingers in the ear's memory. Back along the path by the thin glacial soils that once sup-

---

[1] The rabbits are no longer on the island and the vegetation has changed dramatically.

36

ported St Cuthbert's meagre crop of barley and onions, we found the quiet, matronly eider ducks, waiting to escort their young from puddle to puddle down to the sea for the first time. And there looking west to the shadowy presence of the mainland, we could just see the vague silhouettes of three castles – Lindisfarne, Bamburgh, and Dunstanburgh. All round the edge of this island kingdom of wild-life were the bright clumps of campion and thrift removing any sense of desolation. Here was a sanctuary of the earth's original richness and I had three more days in which to discover that sixteen acres can saturate the senses and revive a sense of wonder in the natural scene. As we worked on the shoreline, seals would bob over from Brownsman to have a look at us, honking quietly to each other. They seemed to be as interested in our activities as we were in theirs.

Unfortunately, the Farnes are vulnerable to oil pollution from the North Sea which will, presumably, increase with the exploitation of the mineral wealth out there. The sight and sound of a water-skier towed behind a roaring speedboat circling the island, cutting just beneath the cliffs and causing consternation amongst the bird-life, is even more disturbing, reminding us that the mainland is only a mile away. The small coastal towns from Seahouses to Beadnell are developing as rather bright and brittle seaside resorts, a new crop of entertainment places being grafted on the old fishing harbour and the favoured retreats of retired people and weekenders. During the season, fishermen tout for trips to the Farnes. The area illustrates the whole problem of development and protection, an area needing new economic activities yet in danger of killing the goose that laid the golden egg, the beauty and wild-life of this superb coastline. But at least things are better than they were in the eighteenth century when sporting parties chartered boats to indulge in mass shooting and local fishermen took a regular harvest of eggs.

It was as early as 1923 that a meeting of the Natural History Society of Northumberland, Durham and Newcastle upon Tyne sponsored a public appeal for funds that enabled the islands to be purchased and formally handed over to the National Trust. At least two bird-watchers are maintained on the Inner Farne and on the Brownsman during the breeding season as partial protection for the birds, and a local committee of the Trust administers the islands. The lighthouse on the Inner Farne is now automatic so no keeper is in residence. The extraordinary rabbits are believed to have developed from animals kept by the early keepers. The first official lighthouse was established in 1673, a warning beacon on Prior Castell's tower kept alight by coal and timber brought from the mainland. Another tower on the Brownsman was used in the same way.

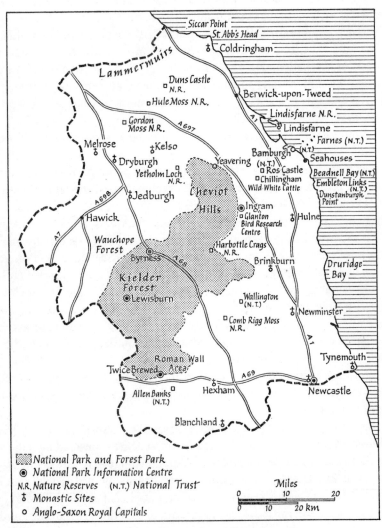

Siccar Point
St. Abb's Head
Coldringham

Lammermuirs

Duns Castle
N.R.
Hule Moss N.R.

Berwick-upon-Tweed

Gordon
Moss N.R.     A 697
Lindisfarne N.R.
Lindisfarne

Melrose                                    Farnes (N.T.)
Kelso                        Bamburgh (N.T.)
Dryburgh          Yeavering (N.T.)    Seahouses
Yetholm Loch                Ros Castle      Beadnell Bay (N.T.)
N.R.            Chillingham     Embleton Links
Cheviot         Wild White Cattle    (N.T.)
Jedburgh         Hills                   Dunstanburgh
Point

Hawick                    Ingram
A 698                     Glanton        Hulne
Bird Research
Wauchope        A 7      Centre
Forest                  Harbottle Crags
Byrness    A 68  N.R.           Druridge
Brinkburn      Bay
Kielder
Forest
Lewisburn        Wallington
(N.T.)           Newminster
Comb Rigg Moss
N.R.                A 1

Roman Wall
Area                            Tynemouth
Twice Brewed
Allen Banks      Hexham         Newcastle
(N.T.)        A 69

Blanchland

National Park and Forest Park
● National Park Information Centre
N.R. Nature Reserves   (N.T.) National Trust
⚑ Monastic Sites
○ Anglo-Saxon Royal Capitals

Miles
0        10        20
0    10    20 km

**Map 4** *Places of special interest.*

The small stunted elder bushes also owe their origin to the lighthouse keepers but at least seventy-eight flowering plants have been identified on the boulder clay soils, which reach a thickness of nine feet in some patches. The sea campion is the most distinctive plant.

The islands vary from fifteen to twenty-eight in number according to the state of the tides, many being rocky islets just near sea-level, very hazardous to shipping. The eroded platform of the Whin Sill dips to the north-east, creating cliffs on the south side with fine stack formations, especially in the Pinnacles of Staple Island. Many of the names are identifiable with those used in ninth-century manuscripts – Crumstone, Longstone, Wamses, Megstone, Oxscar, Scarcar, Harcar – hard names suited to hard places. Sandy areas are rare, the one small bay on the Inner Farne being the main landing place. The whole area was scoured by ice, and deep grooves were scored from north to south across the bare rock. The limited variety of the habitats – rock shelf, rock cliff, sand, boulder clay – suit different birds but cause severe competition for space. The massing of guillemots on the Pinnacles is an object lesson in overcrowding. More than two hundred migrants are visitors to the area but the most common birds seen are the eider duck, the oystercatcher, gulls such as the kittiwake, herring gull and lesser black-backed gull, guillemot, puffin, razorbill, cormorant, shag, a variety of terns (common, sandwich, roseate and arctic) and the more uncommon fulmar petrel and ringed plover. Some of the terns ringed on the islands have been picked up all the way down the west coast of Africa to the Cape of Good Hope, a journey of something like six thousand miles!

Nearly all the birds and mammals are under protection orders and from their sanctuary seek other favourable sites along the whole extent of the north-east coast and enliven the scene wherever fairly inaccessible rock outcrops and cliffs offer them undisturbed territories. Eider duck can often be seen in Amble Harbour, and from there northwards by Alnmouth, Craster, Beadnell Bay to Budle Bay, along to Holy Island, along the Goswick Sands to Berwick-upon-Tweed, by the rugged coast of Berwickshire to the rocky havens of St Abb's Head and Siccar Point a wealth of bird-life can be seen. The southern shores of the Firth of Forth offer a particularly varied type of habitat – rock shores, steep cliffs (comparatively free from human interference), sandy bays, extensive remnants of the once fearsome Coldingham Moor, inland lochs and the deep-cut valleys of the Eye and Ale Waters. In Berwickshire alone more than two hundred and fifty species of birds have been recorded, one hundred and fifty of them breeding in the county, including the first instances in Scotland of the turtle dove, the green woodpecker and the little owl. It was the first Scottish county to support the five breeding species of owl – the Barn, the Tawny, the Long-eared, the Short-eared and the Little Owl. Red grouse, golden plovers, merlin and curlew are all found on the Lammermuirs and the northern rim of hills generally.

The depredations of the larger birds and of the seals have always made the salmon fishing interests of the coast less enthusiastic about wild-life protection than the general public. In March 1971, a fisherman told me that every salmon in a large catch had been rendered unsaleable by the ravages of the seals. Such complaints are not new and a conference of interested parties at Berwick-upon-Tweed in 1956 led on the one hand to a detailed study of the seal colony and on the other to an agreed 'culling' to reduce the numbers. Ironically, some of the complaints coincided with record catches of salmon on the Tweed. But there is little doubt that the seals do frighten the fish away from the nets and their piracy of the fish from the nets is almost comic in its impudence. But it is not so comic for the fishermen and there is also a possibility that the seal is host to a parasitic worm which infests cod.

There is a high mortality rate amongst the young calves resting on the rocky shelves, vulnerable, in spite of their hundred pounds weight achieved in less than a month, to high tides and easterly gales during the breeding season. Yet more than two thousand seals have been recorded in a single month (September) and more than seven hundred have entirely covered the top of the Crumstone. 'Big seals and little seals: grey old bulls, mottled cows and fawnish-brown youngsters; seals asleep and seals awake; seals by the dozen often huddled so closely together that it is impossible to see the rock on which they are lying.'[1] So tight-packed are they on occasions that calves may be smothered by bulls and cows lying on top of them. Mrs Hickling has given a recent (1971) estimate of a total colony of seven thousand seals. Such numbers, together with the puffins and gulls, are destroying the vegetation cover on some of the outer islands, causing erosion of the peaty soil that caps the boulder clay. Some form of management will be needed but this unique breeding colony of grey and common seals deserves protection even at the cost of some fish. The Natural Environment Research Council recommended a cull of about two thousand seals in a report in 1971, a smaller cull actually occurring in 1972. Some of the fishermen profit from their presence by taking visitors out to see them (more than twenty-five thousand people landed on the Inner Farne in 1970) and they have had cause to be grateful during thick sea-fog, hearing the song of the seals (and they do sing) warning them that reefs were near. The very months when seal

[1] Grace Hickling, *Grey Seals and the Farne Islands*.

observation is most rewarding are precisely those when weather and rough seas make landing most difficult and visitors must rely on the experience of the fishermen.

Only five miles to the north-west of the sanctuary of the Farne Islands is that other gem of the Northumbrian coastline, the Holy Island of Lindisfarne. This is in essence a square mile of rock with a long sandy snout, called the Snook, pointing to the sand-dunes of Goswick and Cheswick on the mainland. It is separated from the mainland by a broad area of mud flats and salt marsh crossed now at the narrowest point by a metalled causeway which is covered by high tide. The ebb and flow of the tides through the narrows of Goswick and by Guile Point, the north point of Ross Links, makes the mud flats a graveyard of cars whose owners neglected the tide tables or ignored local advice, and every season brings its crop of salt-ruined wrecks. Some of the safety towers, small wooden structures, still exist, as do the poles which once guided pilgrims across the wet sands to the Priory and St Cuthbert's small islet. The comparatively recent opening-up of the island by the causeway has stimulated the tourist traffic, especially of short-stay coaches, yet the essential atmosphere of the island does not seem to have suffered though the inns pay more attention to licensing hours than they used to when they were effectively isolated. The busy mile from the main village near the priory ruin and the Norman parish church along by the Ouse, the main haven, to the Castle on its volcanic crag contains much that is worth going miles to see, but the wild-life of the island is seen to best advantage on the less frequented east and north shores. Beyond Emmanuel Head is the bird-watchers' paradise, where the three limestone headlands stick their teeth out into the sea and between them lie sheltered sandy bays and beyond them the long sandy bar fronting the Snook, identified always by the surf line racing across towards Goswick. It is the variety of habitats in such small compass that makes the island so rich; mud flat, salt marsh, sand dune, limestone cliffs and skerries, volcanic intrusions and, inland, the marshy 'lough' and farming land on boulder-clay soils. Waders, wildfowl, passerine birds wintering for a while, birds from the moorlands only five miles inland, all meet here. Seals are often seen off-shore. Since 1964, a National Nature Reserve has been developed on 7718 acres of the inter-tidal zone and the sand dunes of the north shore. The eel-grass that flourishes here is one of the main sources of food for overwintering fowl. Wigeon and mallard, the Atlantic race of Brent geese, pink-footed geese, greylag geese, teal, knot, dunlin, bar-tailed godwit, redshank, eider, shelduck, mute swan, whooper swan and even the rarer Bewick swan are all reported here at one time or another during the year. Shooting is still permitted in certain areas and a special panel has been set up to study the management of wildfowl. At certain times of the year bird-watchers are nearly as thick on the ground as the birds, for access is relatively easy. Yet even this favoured place, with one of the lowest rainfall figures in the British Isles and a low incidence of snow cover, can be difficult. I remember trying to free gulls frozen into the sand on which they were resting during the very severe 1962–3 winter. Sea frets can black out many a hot summer's day causing a rapid drop of temperature and, of course, easterly gales can cause bird and seal alike to suffer from exhaustion. But the four-mile walk around the perimeter of the main part of the island is one of the most rewarding in the whole kingdom. The sand dunes of the north shore are fairly active with many blow-outs and, as they move, reveal old mineral railway lines, for limestone and coal have been worked here. Early air photographs confirm the evidence of old maps that some of the land under the dunes was once cultivated. The stabilization of the dunes is a problem, for the sort of afforestation that holds the Culbin Sands in check on the Moray Firth would alter the appearance of the island fundamentally.

The microcosmic world of the sand dunes, which is found also on the mainland from Cheswick and Goswick in the north to Bamburgh, Beadnell and Alnmouth and Warkworth in the south, produces a very special flora. Variations occur from the strand-line, across the active dunes, to the flats and slacks and stabilized dunes to the landward. The active areas of sand-deposition and movement are dominated by sea couch grass, sea lyme grass and the tall spikes of the marram grass with its deep-rooting system. A little stability allows the development of a carpet of fine-leaved fescue grass, speckled with bird's foot trefoil, kidney-vetch, daisies, mouse-ear hawkweed and lady's bedstraw. In the damp hollows where the water-table creates a comparatively stable base-level to the dune formations is the grass of Parnassus and the rarer delights of the close view with the delicate white flowers of the knotted pearlwort, the azure early-forget-me-not and the pink flowers of bog-pimpernel, all less than three centimetres high.

Dune ridges are still actively forming at Goswick around such unnatural obstacles as barbed wire, and a sand-bar is building up between Goswick and the Snook end of Holy Island. Sand extraction south of Bamburgh (surprisingly on National Trust land) and local authority bulldozers creating new car parks south of Blyth have caused local instability and many a recent winter gale from the east has flung sand even as high as the promenade at Whitley Bay.

Much has been written about Lindisfarne but nothing more scholarly and delightful than Richard Perry's *A Naturalist on Lindisfarne*, first published in

1946. His detailed journal illustrates the abundance of bird-life even in mid-winter.

The Farne group is the main concentration of fauna in the coastal region and the concentration of bird-life has its effect all along the coast, especially where sea-cliffs, rocky islands and isolated sandbanks and mudflats offer suitable undisturbed habitats. Since the Second World War, for example, an important site has developed around the whinstone cliffs at Dunstanburgh Castle Point, adding an abundance of birds to the existing pleasures of a dramatic landscape capped by the weather-beaten enclosure of the castle ruins.

It was the pleasures of Dunstanburgh that drew Sir Edward Grey away from the tribulations of foreign affairs and cares of state back to his estate at Falloden. He had so much interest in his 'Green Book' of Northumbrian wild-life that he half hoped to lose each election so as to forsake the human for the natural scene.[1] A monument to him has been erected on a sandstone summit on Ros Castle above Chillingham, another of his favourite spots.

Away from the coast, the most interesting areas are those where semi-natural conditions still exist, beyond the limits of the most intensive arable and pastoral farming. There are few areas where the 'natural' landscape still survives but least modification has taken place on the thin soils and exposed slopes of the moorlands of the interior, especially along the highland rim of the Tweed Basin, and along the Fell Sandstone escarpment.

The verse from *Chevy Chase* that heads this chapter depicts earlier days when hunting took place in the Cheviot forests and summons up a natural scene of woodland and wild-life, yet, even at the time it was written, the woodland cover had already been largely cleared for sheep-walks, by felling for building and fuel and by clearances for settlement and farming. The Tudor landscape was so barren of trees that the Scots raiders included timber amongst the worth-while objectives of their plundering expeditions. The Cheviot area is referred to as early as 1182 as 'the free forest of Chyviot' belonging to Thomas Muschamp of the Barony of Wooler. By the thirteenth century it had been divided into two *moieties*, carefully delineated, though the physical features mentioned in early charters are now very difficult to recognize. They were, on the English side, basically, a northern section, known as Strangeways and a southern section known as Conyers. In the seventeenth century the two sections became known as Selby's Forest and Grey's Forest, names which still appear as names of districts in the Cheviot Hills. A description of 1630 referred to the 'forest, waste

[1] G. H. Trevelyan, *Grey of Falloden* (Longman, 1937).

or chase of Cheviot' and shows the nature of the landscape of the time. 'Forest' was a word used to indicate the land outside the cultivated area in which woodland was only one component. In Leland's much-quoted description, 'in Northumberland, as I hear say, be no forests except Chivet Hills, where is much brush wood and some oak, ground overgrown with ling and some with moss. I have heard say that Chivet hills stretcheth xx miles. There is great plenty of red deer and roe bucks,' and further, 'In Glendale here and there wood, and Chivet serveth them well; but the great wood of Chivet is spoiled now and crooked trees and scrubs remain.' In the words of the County History, 'a forest in the modern sense it never was; it was probably a hunting ground but never, so far as we know, included in the King's forests'.

We know more about the nature of the 'crooked trees' from a report made for the Crown in 1541 which, after a general description of the rivers and mosses, continued: 'there groweth many alders and other ramell wood, which serveth much for the building of such small houses as be used and inhabited by husband-men in those parts'.[1] Oak and alder are the two definite references we have and such 'crooked' woodlands can still be found below Yeavering Bell along the sides of the College Valley, in Langleeford, especially along Calroustburn on the Scots side where there is a clump of the best alders in the hill area. Isolated hawthorns, oaks, birches and alders have survived only where grazing is difficult for sheep, in steep-sided burns and on river cliffs. The Cheviot 'forest' is now an open grassy moorland 'waste' with bracken, heather, moor mat grass and purple moor grass dominant according to local conditions of soil and drainage. Yet birch fragments can still be found trapped beneath the peat hags of the summit as they can be on the treeless plateau of Allendale Common in the south of the county. Research in the peat deposits of Falstone Moss (at 850 feet) have confirmed, by pollen analysis, the once much wider spread of woodland over the hills. The twenty-five-foot deposit of peat (such depths are found in many rock-basins in the region) began forming after the waning of the ice sheets and valley glaciers about eight thousand years ago, and soon birch and pine began colonizing the open tundra. With the so-called 'Atlantic' period of weather reaching the post glacial 'climatic optimum', pine, hazel, elm and oak covered extensive areas. Subsequent wetter conditions about 500 B.C. led to an increase of birch, hazel and alder and of sphagnum moss. Following this phase, a notice-able 'deforestation' took place, probably linked with the pastoral activities of the Iron Age herdsmen whose hill-camps and enclosures are so widespread in the

[1] Calender of Border Papers.

whole region. Another deforestation phase followed between about A.D. 400 and A.D. 950, this time associated with the Anglo–Saxon colonization which started from the east coast and spread by stages into the foothills and up the dales. Following the Norman 'harrowing of the North' came the monastic settlement and their penetration of the hill lands for cattle ranching, their 'vaccaries' and sheep flocks. The monks of Melrose and Dryburgh, for example, obtained many grants of land for grazing purposes in the ancient 'forests' in Tweeddale and Lauderdale, such as Threepwood, Edgarhope and Spottiswoode. Ettrick Forest bounded the Tweed region to the west and here James V of Scotland had a herd of ten thousand sheep in 1530. The existence of many place names with elements indicating woodlands is an indication of previous forest cover. Such woodland names are prevalent, for example, in the Lammermuirs, which were reported as early as the sixteenth century by John Leland as having 'little or no woode', a report confirmed in 1542 that 'there is no store of timber wood in these parties'. Yet in the Lammermuirs, 'morishe evill grounds of little valore', as with the Cheviots and the Allendale Moors, large tree trunks have been dug up.

Part of the great forest that once stretched across the Tweed lowlands and the Merse into Northumberland was enclosed or 'emparked' at Chillingham in the thirteenth century and in it was preserved a number of wild white cattle, the 'Bos primigenius' of ancient times. The descendants of these wild creatures are still preserved in the park, a unique herd of about thirty-six cattle which have survived border raids, sportsmen with itching fingers (including the Prince of Wales in the nineteenth century), severe winters and recent foot-and-mouth outbreaks. The herd is on the estate of the Earl of Tankerville (who is a fellow of the Zoological Society) and is now protected and maintained by the Chillingham Wild Cattle Association, formed in 1939. The largest herd was recorded in 1838, when it was eighty strong, and it declined to thirteen in 1947 after a particularly severe winter when local people told me that they could walk in snowdrifts about the tops of the telegraph poles. The survival of the herd depends on a healthy stock of bulls and especially the King bull, for this is a case where the male animals fight for supremacy, though the contests seldom end in the death of the loser. The skeleton of one such loser, however, is preserved in the Hancock Museum in Newcastle. The cattle are available for public view but it requires patience and a readiness to undertake a good tramp over steep rough slopes through the parkland in the company of the keeper to enjoy a view of these unique animals, for they are dangerous to approach and never seek shelter in other than the lee-side of a wood. A similar herd of cattle is found at Cadzow Park near Hamilton. A splendid view of Chillingham Park can be gained from the summit of Ros Castle on the sandstone ridge to the east of the park, and the cattle can be seen on occasions with good field glasses.

The clearance of the forests led to the decline of wild-life, and a sixteenth-century report by the warden responsible for the safety of Redesdale against robbers and wolves commented 'and there be no wolves'. There were robbers in plenty. Now there are no red deer, either, though roe are abundant, especially in the newly afforested areas. The last wild-cat was reported in Berwickshire in 1849. But the fox, the badger, the otter, the weasel, the stoat, all survive in spite of the attentions of gamekeepers and sportsmen. For the Border region is one in which the large estate is still common and field sports are an important part of the annual rhythm of rural life.

On one December day on the moors above Ryal in the south of Northumberland I came down off the moors and saw in one symbolic vista the hunt silhouetted against the sunset sky returning from the day's work and below them a group of men out from Tyneside for the day with their dufflecoats, Wellingtons and whimpering whippets digging out a badger, one of the men holding a snubnosed pistol ready to dispatch the wild creature. The huntsmen's pink and the thunder of horses, the excitement of hounds and the following caravan of cars and horse-boxes are an essential part of the winter scene.

The season of the hunt, following the harvest, is also that of the shoot, especially for pheasant and partridge. Much of the wild-life of the Borders is not really wild in that it is bred in captivity and fattened up for the ritual slaughter. Shooting game-birds is more than a pastime; it is also business where shooting rights on the moors are rented out to syndicates. The preservation of game is all-important on many estates and the gamekeeper is one of the key men in the social hierarchy of the rural communities, feared to some extent for his power. Birds of prey, otters, badgers, even domestic animals such as cats that might interfere with the raising of the favoured game-birds are unpopular with gamekeepers and liable to meet a sudden end. It is still not unusual for a gamekeeper or a tenant farmer to show that he is ridding his land of 'pests' by stringing crows, rooks and moles along the fences. Recently, I counted 204 moles on a wire fence at Deadwater, blind snouts turned to the sky, strong yellow hands widespread, skins wasting. Moleskins were once one of the perks of the trade but are seldom utilized now because of the effort involved.

Ironically, many of the great pioneer naturalists gained much of their knowledge and their affection for wild creatures at the safe end of the gun and many of the landowners who participate in the winter field sports are amongst the most active members of conservation councils and naturalists' clubs. Several cooperate with the Nature Conservancy in establishing sites of special scientific interest on their land, which does not, of course, indicate public access.

It is fascinating to read the words of one of the great northern naturalists and see the attitudes implicit in his description of the Cheviots:

> that mountain land which remains as created, unaltered by the hand of man – the land 'in God's own holding' – bounded by the line where the shepherd's crook supplants the plough: where heather and bracken, whinstone and black-faced sheep repel corn, cattle and cultivation; where grouse and blackcock yet retain their ancient domain, excluding partridge and pheasant; and where the ring-ousel dispossesses the blackbird.[1]

We know that 'that mountain land' which he loved and recorded so faithfully had altered a great deal in its long evolution from the post-glacial tundra; that the shepherd and his black-faced flock are no more indigenous than the corn that still grows on the foothills. But it is pleasant to think of him in his garden near Wark in the sheltered valley of the North Tyne recording the arrival of the birds. February: the peewit, golden plover, skylark, curlew and pied wagtail. March: titlark, black-headed gull, stock dove, redshank, wheatear, ring-ouzel. April: sand martin, chiff chaff, dunlin, sandpiper, willow wren, redstart, swallow, whinchat, house martin, pied fly-catcher, cuckoo. May: landrail and nightjar.

Many sea birds make their appearance on the uplands in summer. But the curlew is the symbol of the hills, its haunting cry mingling with that of the peewits being one of the most characteristic sounds of all the moorland areas in the region, the most musical accompaniment to the lone walker invading their territory beyond the stone dykes. I associate it especially with those un-enclosed peaty moors in the Allendale district where it seems most prolific. The sign of the curlew appears on all the stone indicators that ring the Northumberland National Park from the Roman Wall in the south to Kirk Newton in the north. Many birds of prey are still found in the hill zones, such as the peregrine falcon, the buzzard, the kestrel, the merlin and the short-eared owl, and sightings have been reported of the golden eagle. Increased numbers of these birds are recorded after plagues of voles, two of which were known in the last quarter of the nineteenth century. The extensive use of pesticides, however, is making the future of these birds here, as elsewhere, more hazardous.

[1] Abel Chapman, *Birdlife of the Borders* (1907).

Adders, common lizards and slow worms are found on the hills. The adders can be a problem. They curl up in the warm sun by stone dykes, on screes and amongst the bracken and are not easily seen. I have often nearly trodden on one. Lambs can be killed by them, though a full-grown ewe usually survives their bite. Human beings need medical attention quickly if bitten, though strong boots or Wellingtons are some safeguard as the bite is usually above ankle level. One of the natural enemies of the snakes is the goat, and a number of wild goats are known to roam the Cheviots, though I cannot be sure I have ever seen them. Henry Tegner, a prolific writer on the wild-life of the Borders, favours the hills on the west side of the College Burn, up on Newton and Easter Tors. The herd there once numbered twenty-three but was reduced to seven by shooting. They might have become extinct but for the introduction of a healthy wild male from the Scottish side of the Cheviots by Sir Alfred Goodson, a local landowner, which assisted a recovery of numbers. The goats are either grey-blue in colour or a 'skewbald pattern of brown and dirty-white'.[1]

Other herds on the fringes of the Kielder Forest and at Wark have been kept down by shooting in recent years, presumably for the damage they would do to grazing lands and to new afforestation.

The vegetation of the hill areas is now predominantly grassland of various types, depending on the soils, drainage and long history of settlement and grazing. Visitors to the Borders are always surprised at the greenness of the hills. Apart from isolated areas near the summit of the Cheviot, the hills throughout the region are gently-rounded, devoid of the ruggedness of the Lake District or the Scottish Highlands. They are an 'oldland' in which rock outcrops are comparatively rare: they are suited to the walker rather than the climber. Arctic-alpine flora is rare and found on parts of the Cheviot summit where rocks have been shattered and up-ended by frost action and in the steep ravines and glaciated corries of the Bizzle and the Hen Hole. Here the flora includes alpine scurvy grass, chickweed willow herb, alpine willow herb, hairy stone-crop, mossy saxifrage, dwarf cornel, bog whortleberry, alpine club moss, bryophytes and lichens. But most of the level summits are covered by wasting blanket bogs of peat now eroding rapidly. On the peat hags, which can be very dry and powdery in summer, heather and cloudberry grow. On wetter areas, cotton sedge, deer sedge, crowberry and bilberry are found.

The steeper, well-drained slopes support the swards of bents and fescues which are important for grazing livestock. Here the sheep's fescue and bent

[1] H. Tegner, *Beasts of the North Country* (H. Hill, 1961).

grasses are joined by sweet vernal grass, tormentil, heath bedstraw, bilberry and the woodrush. Wherever soil depths are greater than about nine inches bracken invades and flourishes. Farmers have a saying that 'under bracken is gold' and there is plenty of evidence that some of the gentler slopes, even at 1000 feet, have been ploughed in the past. Bracken is prolific throughout the hill country and makes walking after a wet summer's day something of a trial, giving more of a wetting than the rain falling from above. It also hides the sheep and the adders. Its luxuriance may be due partly to the replacements of cattle grazing by sheep which do not destroy the young bracken by treading in the way that cattle do. Cutting it is a long and arduous process but many efforts have been made to improve hill grazing by eradicating bracken by crushing and cutting regularly. The bracken is very thick on the lower slopes of the hills where glacial drift gives a deep, clayey soil as distinct from the thinner, stoney upper slopes. Overgrazing of the bent-fescue grassland encourages the growth of *Nardus stricta*, the moor mat grass, especially between 1000 and 2000 feet, where a higher precipitation causes greater leaching of the soil. A grass of low nutritional value, it is joined by rushes, bilberry, heath bedstraw and tormentil and the wood anemone. The purple moor-grass, *Molinia caerulea*, is found in the wetter pockets, often in association with bog myrtle, bog moss and deer sedge.

The relic woodlands of alder, birch, oak, hazel and ash which are usually found on the lower slopes of steep valley sides have their characteristic plant communities, amongst which are found wood sorrel, primrose, foxglove, bluebell, golden saxifrage, meadow sweet, yellow flag, dog mercury, water mint, tufted hair grass, angelica and many ferns.

The broad, stone-strewn valley floors, with small burns winding across glaciated valleys, have patches of soil, though subject to occasional inundation after snow-melt or a rainy autumn, but one of the great sights is the flowering gorse which thrives on these ridges and bars of river boulders. In June it can set a whole valley ablaze with its yellow blossom. In this region, the *ulex europaeus*, the common gorse, is known as the 'whin', a word of Scandinavian origin. At one time it covered vast areas of the lowlands now farmed. Clearing the whin was one of the greatest problems for the eighteenth-century agricultural improvers. Many an earlier ambush took place under the cover of the shrub and gave the main road by the west side of the Milfield Plain the reputation amongst the Scots as the 'ill road' during the raiding days. It is usually thought of as a plant of the wasteland yet it was once cultivated, used for hedgerows, for thatching, for yellow dye and even for cattle fodder. A 'whin stone' (not to be confused with

49

the volcanic rock bearing the same name) was used to bruise the gorse and make it more palatable. It is still grazed by sheep when other grazing is poor, producing a low, close-cropped bush.

The pattern of hill vegetation is again undergoing comparatively rapid and dramatic change. Throughout the region, the tell-tale furrows of deep-drainage ploughs are scoring the landscape; in nearly every valley, the dark regiments of young conifers are beginning to change what has been regarded as the traditional open landscape. Tree planting is nothing new and the scrubby remnants of an eighteenth-century sycamore clump or an eighteenth-century group of pines break the bleakness of many a moorland vista. Many fine plantations of long standing clothe the lower hills above Duns and along the banks of the White-adder Water where it cuts down through the slopes of the Lammermuirs. But the scale of operations has suddenly increased and new forests are replacing sheep-walks on large private estates. Dramatic changes have occurred above Alwinton since 1970 and recently I walked over the wet brim of the moors from the Ingram Valley into the bleak basin of Threestone Burn and was surprised to see the entire upper basin scored with the preparations for new afforestation. New roads were cutting fresh scars through the drift soils and new fencing was being erected to protect the young trees. The bulldozers and drag-ploughs were thundering across the wet moors and what had been a very isolated shepherd's holding had suddenly become the centre of a new industry. This was a new venture by the Forestry Commission from its base at Chillingham; all part of the great transformation that began in 1920 in the North Tyne and now has clothed more than 112,000 acres in Northumberland (over ten per cent of the total land surface), and another 36,000 acres in Roxburghshire and Berwickshire (about five per cent of the land), though these figures do not include private forests.

In the early years of this century, the Kielder district of the North Tyne was almost devoid of trees;[1] some scrub oak and birch woodland survived in sparse patches and the Duke of Northumberland had planted some Scots Pine and Norway Spruce on his estates. The Duke of Buccleugh had some plantations of Sitka Spruce across the Border in Liddesdale. Now the area holds the largest man-made forest in the British Isles, more than 80,000 acres of trees being already planted on what were once some of the bleaker, ill-drained slopes of the border hills between the road crossings at Carter Bar and Deadwater. The Forestry Commission started operations near Newcastleton in Liddesdale in 1920,

---

[1] *National Forest Park Guide: The Border* (H.M.S.O., 1958).

but the purchase of the Duke of Northumberland's 47,000-acre Kielder estate really got the process going. New roads, rides and fire-breaks were constructed, incidentally giving some new rock exposures, much to the delight of geologists, who find such evidence only too scarce in these hills. Extensive drainage was needed and gave rise to many complaints from lowland farmers who insist that floods have increased in volume and frequency since forestry operations began on the uplands. Then the young trees from the nurseries at Widehaugh near Hexham (where seven million trees are grown every year) and elsewhere are planted out on the upturned turfs and fenced in against deer and livestock grazing. On the higher slopes, the Norway Spruce and Sitka Spruce are favoured, with Scots and Lodgepole Pine on the heather moors. The deeper soils of the bracken slopes are dominated by Japanese larch, and these five conifers are the most important commercially. Intelligent mixed planting has added much to the visual amenity of these areas and there can be few lovelier sights for the motorists speeding along the A68 by the Catcleugh Reservoir and seeing the older plantations of mature trees by the roadside and beyond the varied ranks of spruce, pine and larch, especially in October when the larch needles are turning yellow and falling, in contrast to the dark green of the pine and the spruces, which seem in some conditions of light to have a purple glow. Some visitors prefer May time when the larch is putting forth its new needles of the lightest green. The forests need not mean a loss of visual pleasure. Other trees planted in fewer numbers include the hemlock, Lawson's cypress, Douglas fir and some oak and beech, though, with their slower growth rates, the hardwoods are a longer-term commercial proposition. Many of the stands of timber are now ready for thinning and a substantial economic return is being obtained for the enormous capital outlay over the last fifty years. Some of the timber goes to local fencing, or to the coal pits of the north-east, but more and more goes to new factories producing chipboard, wood wool and other processed timber products. Transport from the hill areas along the narrow, winding lanes of the rural areas poses a problem. New villages for forestry workers have been built at Kielder and Byrness, although they have not grown as was once envisaged, and some of the cottages are now being released for summer visitors. Many forestry workers (and six thousand people gain their livelihood from these forests) prefer to travel in from established villages such as Bellingham and Otterburn.

Planting in upper Lauderdale began in 1928 and now the Edgarhope Forests cover more than two thousand acres, mostly in areas that were traditionally 'forests' in the medieval sense, and the larch timber especially is widely used for local agricultural purposes.

The main forests, with their recorded areas in 1970, are:

| | acres |
|---|---|
| Chillingham | 4,000 |
| Chirdon (Wark) | 16,205 |
| Chopwell (N. and D.) | 2,233 |
| * Falstone (Kielder) | 17,179 |
| Harwood | 9,843 |
| Kidland | 6,405 |
| * North Kielder | 22,941 |
| * Mounces (Kielder) | 24,566 |
| Redesdale | 14,083 |
| Rothbury | 4,610 |
| Slaley | 3,067 |
| * Tarset (Kielder) | 9,401 |
| Wark | 24,199 |
| Craik (Roxburgh and Selkirk) | 10,922 |
| Duns | 1,797 |
| Edgarhope | 2,248 |
| Traquiar (Roxburgh and Selkirk) | 10,395 |
| Newcastleton | 8,652 |
| Wauchope | 21,005 |
| Stenton (Berwick and E. Lothian) | 2,284[1] |

* The old Kielder Forest area.

The great increase in forested areas has led to a revival of wild-life, especially of the roe deer, which was quite scarce at the end of the nineteenth century. Wild goats can be found on the hills bordering Wauchope and Newcastleton. The blue or mountain hare and the red squirrel are more abundant again.[2] The red squirrel is found throughout the region, being the native species and un-affected as yet by the invasion of the grey which has displaced it in Southern England. It eats pine seeds and litters the forest floor with dropped pine scales. The famous trio of fox, badger and otter are there, and salmon are sometimes reported as far up-stream as the Forest Park areas, especially in the last five years,

[1] Forestry Commission Statistics.
[2] E. Blezard, 'The Wild Life of the Border Forests', *National Forest Park Guide : The Border* (H.M.S.O., 1958).

possibly due to a decrease of pollution down-stream near the industrial areas of Tyneside.

Bird-life, too, has benefited: the red grouse and blackcock display on the moors, and pheasants have moved into the forest coverts. Most of the birds reported by Abel Chapman in his Wark garden find suitable habitats in the forest and the rivers. Small heronries can be found at Wark and in Redesdale. Many of the birds of prey find sanctuary here, with an increase of the short-eared owl and the long-eared owl. Buzzards, the hen harrier, merlin, sparrow hawk and kestrel, peregrine falcon and raven are all now regarded as regular visitors and some as residents. The rewards of bird-watching and the hope of seeing wild-life are amongst the many reasons for a great increase in visitors to the Forest Park areas, and new camping and picnic sites have been established. An information centre with a museum of natural history at Lewisburn helps to enrich the experience of visitors to the area. There is the likelihood now of a new reservoir in the forested areas of the North Tyne which will cause another change of the wild-life habitats.

Extensive afforestation is also taking place outside the main hill zones on the Fell Sandstone ridge. The lower slopes of this escarpment have long been fav-oured as suitable sites for large mansions and their parklands, such as Chilling-ham, Fenton, Callaly, and Cragside near Rothbury; much private forest has been planted on the thin, dry soils which only support poor grazing. Now the most impressive parts of the escarpment, below the crags of the Simonsides near Rothbury, are covered with the trees of the Harwood Commission Forest which is extending west and south along the dip slope. It is a pity that some rights of way have been impaired in the process but some of the new forestry roads give greater public access to the new landscapes. South of the Tyne, too, on the gritstone plateaux around Slaley, Commission and private forests clothe large areas of moorland, covering, as at Kielder, the scars of old quarries and small coal pits.

The whole region west of the A1 and north of Felton is classified by the county authority as of great landscape value and the lowland areas of the Border region are not without their interest in flora and fauna. The rivers are amongst the least polluted and most abundant in fish in the British Isles, though the best fishing stretches are usually in private hands (especially for salmon) or controlled by angling associations. Local inquiries usually make it possible for the enthusi-astic angler to indulge his patient passion. Inns, hotels and some shops can often supply a permit on behalf of the local angling club. The effort is worthwhile for the brown trout and sea trout available. Lauder in Berwickshire is contemplating fishing 'schools' as an added attraction to tourists. The local authorities are only too keen to make known the sporting assets of the region.

There is a nice legal point that complicates matters somewhat in that all tributaries flowing into Scottish rivers (and the Tweed is classified as a Scottish river) come under Scottish river laws. This has led, in practice, to fishermen on the Breamish, twenty miles south of the Border, appearing in Scottish courts. The salmon disease has also affected northern rivers in recent years. However, there are many inns on the rivers and near the coast that bulge with anglers during the season.

Catching salmon is more than a sport on the Borders: it is big business. The monks had interests in the fisheries and the Tweed rights were in the hands of the Crown by 1562. By 1725, salmon was a common food in the region:

The Largeness and Cheapness of the Fish make it much coveted by House-keepers who have large Families and so often cater that it is said that the Servants, when they are hired, do usually indent with the Masters to feed them with Salmon only some Days of the Week that they may not be cloyed with too often eating them.

The Berwick Salmon Fisheries, which now controls the rights five miles to seaward, seven miles to the south of the estuary and three miles to the north, grew out of the Old Shipping Company which ran regular coastal services to London. One great character, London John, used to take salmon down to London on horseback, but most fish went by schooner and, after the introduction of ice in 1787, the fisheries became more important than other aspects of the company business. New yards were opened at Meadow Haven in 1856 and finally were moved to the site of the old lifeboat station when the new one was built on the south bank of the Tweed. After many modifications, the close season was fixed from 14 September to 15 February and the minimum net mesh at $1\frac{3}{4}$ inches from knot to knot. About seventy fishermen are occupied on twenty-four boats, though numbers vary, and each boat has its special station in the deep water of the river where the fish run. One of the largest ever caught was of forty-six pounds weight in 1934. Up-stream are the 'shiels' and 'stells' of the river fishermen, and the preservation of the purity of the water of this and other Border rivers is one of the major factors when considering the development of new industrial activities. The remarkable 'cobles', most seaworthy of inshore craft, are still made on the south bank of the Tweed by the same family, I am told, who built the boat used by Grace Darling in her famous rescue off the Farnes.

The parklands, too, offer a variety of woodlands and shrubs to delight the eye and many are periodically open to the public. The gardens of some, such as Wallington, now National Trust property, and the Hirsel at Coldstream, are open to the public for much of the year.

The Hancock Museum of Newcastle upon Tyne initiated a series of 'nature trails' throughout the county of Northumberland with support from one of the oil companies, and visitors often come across a sign pointing to a new trail in this region of varied landscapes. The trails are not necessarily in the most exotic places, many being quite close to the major built-up areas of Tyneside. Indeed, one has been attempted on the Town Moor of Newcastle itself and another has been laid out in Jesmond Dene, a lovely nineteenth-century parkland to the north-east of the city centre. The wooded dene of Hartford within the coalfield, the Roman wall area around Crag Lough (visited by ten thousand people in one month), Hareshaw Lynn at Bellingham on the North Tyne, Dunstanburgh Point, the parks at Wallington and Callaly, the sandstone crags at Thrunton near Whittingham – these varied places have all been used in a most successful effort to enable the casual visitor to enjoy more fully the pleasures of flora, fauna and geology with the aid of specially devised notes made freely available. Each year, new trails are laid out and old ones revived to supplement the work of the National Park information centres and the publications of the Hancock Museum, the home of the Northumberland and Durham Naturalists' Trust.

A new nature reserve with trails is now well established on Harbottle Crags near Alwinton, a rugged sandstone moorland leased from the Forestry Commission by the Trust. Another trail established on the Inner Farne not only gives useful information to the ever-increasing number of visitors but helps to keep them off the vulnerable nesting sites.

The specialist and enthusiast can find even more pleasure and instruction by contact with this Trust which controls several nature reserves in the counties. Eleven more such reserves were handed over in 1970 by the Forestry Commission, three in the Coquet Valley and eight in unspoiled areas of mossy territory in the Roman Wall area. Two sites, at Big Waters, Wideopen, and the Throckley Ponds, both close to Tyneside, have been earmarked for development as special educational nature reserves, the forerunners of many more.

There is always the danger that excessive exposure of areas of especially interesting flora and fauna will lead to the destruction of the communities that the authorities seek to protect, so that many of the most interesting places can only be visited by permit. This is true of the many mosses such as those mentioned above near the Roman Wall north of Haydon Bridge and of Comb Rigg Moss, eighty acres of blanket bog, at 1000 feet, near the A696 as it passes Kirkwhelpington, a National Nature Reserve since 1960. Gordon Moss, Hule Moss, Bemersyde Loch and Hen Poo (a lake in the private parkland of Duns Castle) are an interesting group lying on the junction of the Merse and the Lammermuirs in Berwickshire, and some of the sites are under the care of the Scottish Wildfowl Trust, which shows the type of fauna to be expected there. Roxburghshire has the Yetholm Loch Nature Reserve just to the north of the border. Most of the mosses began forming after the decline of the ice sheets that covered much of the region and the study of their vegetation, past (by pollen analysis) and present, gives a measure of climatic changes since the Ice Age. The Nature Conservancy jealously guards its areas of special scientific interest but its protectionist attitude is understandable in view of the delicate ecological balance of some of the communities in the reserves. The famous alpine flora of the Upper Teesdale reserve has been damaged by visitors' boots as well as by the demands of the new reservoir.

For a glaciated landscape, the region is surprisingly deficient in natural water surfaces apart from the small lochs and mosses mentioned here, and the group that cluster under the shadow of the Whin Sill north of the Roman Wall. The largest water surfaces in the region are man-made, such as Catscleugh Reservoir in Upper Redesdale, opened in 1905, predating much of the forest that now hems it in. It is nearly a mile and a half long and seventy-eight feet deep at the maximum and its use is restricted to water extraction for the Newcastle and Gateshead Water Company, apart from local fishing rights for a private club. The new reservoir in the south of Northumberland, along the river Derwent, was opened in the late 1960s with recreational usage in mind as much as water supply and is already a focus of water sports. The siting of reservoirs understandably arouses passions and much debate is taking place over the projected reservoir to drown 2800 acres of the lower ground in the Kielder Forest below Falstone. Judging by results at Derwent, such a water surface would add even more to the tourist potential of the area but it would also displace two hundred people and lead to a series of subtle changes in the ecology of the valley with modifications in the wild-life habitats.

One of the best ways to enjoy the natural scene or, more properly, the semi-natural scene, is to follow one of the many courses run by the Adult Education

Department of the University of Newcastle or of the Holiday Fellowship at its fine centre at Alnmouth. The National Park authority has also initiated a series of guided tours (in the summer of 1971) to supplement the many Nature Trails.

# 3

# Briton and Roman

Well-wrought this wall: Wierds broke it.
The stronghold burst. . . .
Snapped rooftrees, towers fallen,
the work of the Giants, the stonesmiths,
mouldereth.

(*The Ruin*)[1]

Choose an April day: a dry, cool wind coming from the south over the Cheviots, the sky scoured, the hills bleached, too early in the season for much growth of grass. This is poor weather for the beginning of lambing but fine for the walker. A cool, late Spring is a common feature of the Border rhythm and the hills have a wide-open feeling about them with long visibility and no growth of bracken to clothe the flanks and hide the secrets that these hills hold in such abundance. A low sun brings out every wrinkle of the surface, every undulation of the ground having a story to tell of the past. History is something very much of the present on the Borders.

Leave your car at Whitton Edge where the map shows a sudden bend in Dere Street, the Roman road that has run straight south-east from the Tweed north of Jedburgh to this point and here starts to climb along a grassy track between stone walls over a moorland plateau at about 1000 feet. In the next hour's walking you will pass an Iron Age hill fort to your right on the summit of a low rounded hill, then five small stones of a standing circle from the Bronze Age, and two more cairns of the same period, and then drop down into the Upper Kale Water by the large Roman Camp in the trees before the school.

In the second hour, the track swings east to climb into the hill country, contouring round the outstanding knoll of Woden Law so as to make an easier ascent to the border ridge. Woden Law contains a fine assembly of earthworks, ditches, boundary walls and hut circles, some of the Iron Age Celts and others

[1] Anglo–Saxon poem translated by Michael Alexander in *The Earliest English Poems* (Penguin, 1966).

58

of the Roman investment works, a tribute to its strategic position, overlooking the lower ground of Roxburghshire. Then follow the track up to Blackhall Hill, past the Roman signal station, a fine green track still, just below the crest of the ridge, past Bronze Age cairns until it drops to the impressive and organized outlines of the great Roman camp at Chew Green, set on a broad hump of a hill, yet surrounded by the higher ground of Coquet Head, except where the view opens down-stream to the east, to Hedgehope and Cheviot. The last two miles have coincided with the Pennine Way, the new track for outdoor enthusiasts, but now the military tarmac begins rising to the artillery range to the south. Alongside the tarmac are the many grooves and tracks curving uphill, cut by man and chariot and livestock, for this was still a main stock route into England up to the early nineteenth century. Two hours' walking across four thousand years: and all the clues are still there, still clear in the shadows of the late sunlight.

Further exploration of the hills between this point and the Cheviot reveal one of the greatest concentrations of ancient routes, camps, hill forts, enclosures, cairns, standing stones and homesteads in the British Isles, a heartland of early peoples, an inner fortress of early British culture. The persistent interest in the Roman Wall and the comparative inaccessibility of this hill region, together with its long use as sheep-grazing land and the preservation of the evidence of the past, have produced the apparent contradiction of an area rich in antiquities which has received comparatively little attention. It is still possible to make real contributions to our knowledge of the past here, but more important to be able to appreciate it in an imaginative way, for so much is to be seen by even the casual observer in a superb setting. However, much is known, especially on the Scottish side, and the result of many digs in Roxburghshire can answer some of the riddles that the prolific earthworks pose.

To return to Woden Law: its site on a conical hill in volcanic rocks surrounded by steep slopes, commanding magnificent views, especially to north and west, is typical of the site of many such hill forts and camps. There is no particular evidence that the climate during the Iron Age was much better than now and life in such a difficult, exposed site must have been prompted primarily by reasons of security and defence. The site at Woden Law was excavated in 1950 and comparison with other nearby sites suggested three main stages of development of the site, the first being a simple single stone-walled enclosure using a quarry in the andesites immediately by the camp. This may date from the second century B.C. At a later stage, two further ramparts were added together with additional enclosures attached to the main camp. Sometime following this

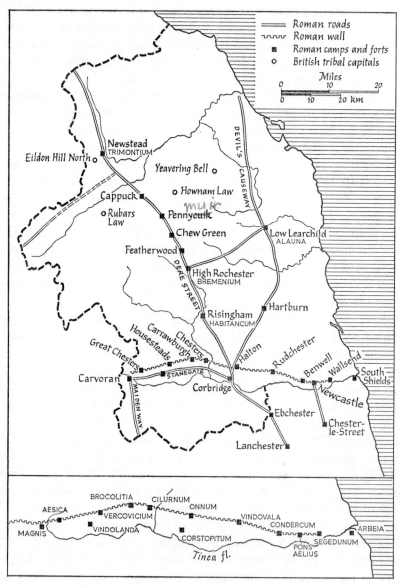

**Map 5** *Roman control of the Northern Border.*

the site was used for Roman investing works, being close by their major access road across the Borders, Dere Street, following a much older track (at least as old as the standing stones that we passed near Whitton Edge, the stones being as old to the Romans as the Romans are to us). Following the 'Roman period' a new rampart was constructed within the earliest alignment using materials from previous defences; these were supported by outer defences about twenty yards away, giving protection from thrown missiles. The sequence may be interpreted as adjustment to the instability of life before the Pax Romana and again after their withdrawal in the fourth century A.D. so that the hill fort would have a period of interrupted occupation from the second century B.C. to the Dark Age, giving a span of at least six hundred years.[1]

Within the earliest enclosure are at least four hut circles. This is a small number as compared with other sites, for example nearby Hownam Law which has 155 scoop huts, but the latter is one of the largest camp sites, 1500 feet by 800 feet as compared with Woden Law which is 400 feet by 140 feet internally and more typical of the Border forts. The attached enclosures or annexes may have been stockades for livestock and the scoop hut sites were the rocky bases for small wooden structures not unlike the kraals of the Zulu on the African veldt. One such hut circle has been cleared on Dod Law, near Doddington in north Northumberland, within the perimeter of another camp, and even the stone doorposts can be identified. On level ground such hut foundations would need to be dug about two feet into the ground to support pliable branches, but on slopes the same platform could be produced by using the material scooped from the hillside to make the platform extension, reducing the labour.

On the ground it is often impossible to see any significant difference between a 'camp', a 'hill fort' and an 'enclosure' but, generally speaking, the Ordnance Survey uses the description of 'hill fort' 'wherever circumstances justify its use', those circumstances being the siting of the earthworks on a hill summit or other physical feature where security seems to be major consideration.[2] There is such a close relationship between hill summits and camp sites that a close inspection of hill-tops where no camp is mapped often reveals the type of uneven ground that suggests such a settlement did exist there.

The mature conical shape of many of the Border hills gives rise to quite simple camp structures – often a single embankment of earth and stones tracing a circle round the summit. But, as with Woden Law, the earthworks follow the contours of the ground and the shapes vary according to the terrain. Even the

[1] Cf. R.C.A.M., *Roxburghshire* (Scotland).
[2] 'Field Archaeology', Ordnance Survey Professional Papers No. 13 (H.M.S.O., 1951).

most complex are basically variations on the circular pattern and seldom show the rigid uniformity of the later Roman camps.

Throughout Roxburghshire, there is a close association between the volcanic outcrops and camp sites. On nearly every conical hill on the andesitic lavas, on nearly every volcanic plug, occurs a camp site of the Iron Age, though, of course, the sites may have been occupied even earlier. Some of the camps are so large that they have been called 'oppida', possibly tribal capitals of the Ottadini, the Celtic people who occupied the whole region from the Tyne (their name may signify 'north of the Tyne') to the Lammermuirs. The boundary between their territory and that of the Selgovae to the west is difficult to establish though it was certainly in the Upper Tweed area.

Eildon Hill North (the backcloth to Melrose Market Place), Rubers Law, Hownam Law and the Dunion in Roxburghshire, and Yeavering Bell in Northumberland are all on prominent sites overlooking the Tweed lowlands. Rubers Law, with its distinctive knobbly silhouette, is particularly dominant in its setting on a high oasis of wild in the farmlands of Teviotdale. The earthworks (which include a fragment of Roman masonry) are less impressive now than the site itself but enough remains to suggest a major defensive settlement. The prominence of the site means that other contemporary camps would have been in view and, perhaps, in communication. Minto, Bonchester, Hounam, Southdean, even Woden Law, twelve miles to the east on the edge of the main hill zone, are all visible from Rubers Law.

The unusual size of the fort on Hownam Law, enclosing an area of twenty-two acres, with a total of one hundred and fifty-five huts identified, make it of particular importance, though at least three hundred hut circles have been identified in Eildon Hill North fort, with an estimated population of two to three thousand people, as many as in many Border burghs today.[1] The great oppida indicate an organized society, but they are few in number; much more widespread are the small forts and camps which may have been either the outer 'villages' of tribal organization or of a different period in Celtic history (the decline of Roman power, for example) when a fragmented society needed defence against other groups and wild animals (a familiar story on the Borders to be repeated a thousand years later under different circumstances).

The thirteen acres of the hill fort on Yeavering Bell are situated on a fringing summit of the Cheviot Hills commanding views not only over the Cheviot Massif but the entire Milfield Plain and the Tweed. The enclosure is one of many that

[1] R. W. Feacham, 'The Hill Forts of Northern Britain', *The Iron Age in Northern Britain*, ed. A. L. F. Rivet (Edinburgh University Press).

lie on the hills surrounding the plain, especially along the Fell Sandstone escarpment facing the Cheviots. The evidence of place names, such as Fenton, suggests that the entire plain, even after the post-glacial lake had drained away to the north through the Till Gorge, was forest and fen. These summit camps, such as Ros Castle above Chillingham (now a National Trust property), give the finest panoramic views of the whole Cheviot range.

It is on this ridge of Fell Sandstone that many Iron Age enclosures remain at lower levels, even at 300 feet. I can remember seeing such a camp just below Flodden Farm, clearly visible in pastures at 250 feet, which was obliterated in three years of ploughing, though the air view would probably still reveal it. One of the most exciting and picturesque sites in the whole Border country is one such lowland camp situated near the waterfall at Roughtinglinn, a name suggesting roaring water; though the waterfall itself is not quite so imposing, it is memorable in an area where such falls are rare. The camp here is situated at the junction of two burns and uses their natural gorges for two sides of its defensive system, the perimeter being completed by four high earthworks running in a broad arc from burn to burn. The interior enclosure is now wooded and overgrown but gives a quite different perspective on the settlements of the Iron Age Celts from that imagined on the windswept ridge at Woden Law.

Another important lowland site is at Greaves Ash, in the Breamish valley above the farm at Linhope. This has been described by George Jobey (who has been called a one-man Royal Commission) as 'the largest accretion of huts and courtyards in the whole county [of Northumberland] ... where there are 27 extant huts in one group and a further 13 no more than a hundred yards distant'. The outer walls of this settlement at Greaves Ash are notable for their construction with many very large boulders. The occurrence of such large boulders in groups on many of the slopes nearby enlivens the imagination. Many of them are locally derived, judging by the erosion of the rock outcrop upslope to the north by Long Crag. Some of the standing walls are six feet thick. Excavation has revealed huts with a diameter of about twenty-five feet, with paved floors and low stone thresholds, with a simple internal division. Simple models of such huts can be found in the Museum of Antiquities in the University in Newcastle.

A simple field system, identifiable with the familiar Celtic fields of the south country, may be seen at another excavated site up the Calroust Burn in the Upper Bowmont, south of the hamlet at Mow. Here, at 1000 feet, are two circular enclosures down by the burn side, both again constructed with outer walls of large stones. The outer enclosures are both about one hundred feet along the longest axis and sixty to seventy feet along the shortest axis. Within the east homestead is 'a single large circular stone-built house with central post-hole ... set on a platform or terrace occupying about half an oval area enclosed by a massive wall'. Here too were found paved courts, querns of various sorts, native pottery, stone axes, a bronze brooch with an iron pin and a fragment of Roman glass. There are three parallel lynchets on the slopes to the north-west which *may* be contemporary but may be later. The finds suggest a period of occupation between the second and seventh centuries A.D. – that is, from the Roman period until the Dark Age before the coming of the Anglo-Saxon invaders. Similarities have been noted between this 'homestead' at Crock Cleugh and the 'cell' that St Cuthbert made for himself on the Farne Islands in the seventh century.

The general distribution of Iron Age forts shows a concentration on the foothills of the Cheviot Hills and of the Southern Uplands, especially in the valleys of the Upper Bowmont and the Upper Kale, and then a second major group in the Teviot Head area of the Slitrig and Borthwick water. The lower land near the main rivers is avoided. This may be only because the evidence for lowland settlement of this period has been obliterated by later farming, forestry and settlement, but it is likely that the lowest ground was heavily forested, especially on the thick boulder-clay lands, and that fens and marshes were much more extensive then than now. The best grazing lands would be on the lower hill slopes with an extension to the upper slopes during summer, while some cleared land could supply limited grain crops, though there is a paucity of evidence of the Celtic field systems which are such a feature of the chalk downlands of southern England. The rare finds of querns show that grain was grown near the camps. Lynchets or shelves cut in hill slopes often occur throughout the Cheviots near camps and forts, but there is none of the evidence such as that found in the south to associate them with early settlement, excepting their geographical proximity.

One of the surprises of Border archaeology is Edin's Hall Broch. It is unique in the region, though it is possible that other such structures did exist but have been pirated for their stone. It is fairly inaccessible, in a shelf above the deep-cut valley of the Whiteadder in Berwickshire in the hills north of Duns. This may account for its remarkable state of preservation, its great dry-stone walls up to twenty feet thick, broad enough to be honeycombed with steps and chambers, still quite intact up to the height of a man. This is one of the most southerly brochs in Britain, the structures being most prolific in the north, in the Orkneys and along the east coast, in association with the regions of Pictish influence.

3. St Abb's Head, where the contorted rocks of the Southern Uplands meet the North Sea: a fierce coast, haven of seabirds, guarded by the lighthouse.

4. The Whin Sill breaking through the carboniferous rocks creating a north-facing escarpment utilised by the Roman Wall; the Roman camp of House-steads in the foreground; the gallows pointing east towards the plain of south-east Northumberland.

Linguistic links have also suggested pockets of Pictish settlement on the Lammer-muir perimeter[1] and this broch confirms the suggestion and may be linked with a period in which Picts were in alliance with the Ottadini against a common enemy. The broch is now signposted from the road to Abbey St Bathans and is in the hands of the Department of the Environment.

Another unique antiquity in Berwickshire is the hundred-yard long mound of stone boulders known as the Mutiny Stones (earlier called the Mitten o' Stanes or Meeting Stones). They are believed to be the remnants of a long cairn, though the original structure has been obscured by wall collapse and the use of the stone for adjacent sheep stells. Set on a fellside near the bleak, level summit of the Lammermuirs east of Longformacus, they make an impressive pile.

On many hills in the region can be found straight embankments and ditches, often quite short in length, cutting across spurs and ridges, usually in the proximity of hill forts and camps, suggesting some form of territorial division, or outer defence. But there are some longer earthworks that run for long distances across country which defy analysis and which may be linked with the Iron Age settlements, though current opinion suggests a later period – the Dark Age or the beginnings of Anglo-Saxon colonizations. The most famous is the Catrail, which early maps showed as running for many miles from the headwaters of the Slitrig south of Hawick west and north to the Gala near Galashiels. (A short stretch of dyke is still mapped west of Bowden.) At present it is mapped more cautiously and is confirmed only in the section west of Robert's Linn Bridge on the road over to Liddesdale. It is difficult to follow, being discontinuous and mixed up with modern drainage ditches across the bleak moorland. But the central ditch with bank on either side is still impressive, aiming across the lower ground to the north of Maiden Paps. The Catrail 'could as well mark the limit of the Northumbrian earldom before Carham when its relationship to the Strath-clyde Britons required definition'.[2] Another rather shorter dyke, but more pleas-ant to explore, is Heriot's Dyke which cuts east-west across the heather moors two miles north of Greenlaws in Berwickshire. This is a single ditch and bank and is very clear. The Black Dyke of the North Tyne is much more difficult to follow, being mixed up with the forestry west of Wark. Another interpretation of these long dykes is as boundaries marking the upper limit of good cattle pasture, perhaps of Anglo-Saxon vintage.

So far, these comments on the archaeology of the Border region have been almost entirely concerned with the Iron Age people, the Celts, the Ottadini

[1] See Chapter 4.
[2] R.C.A.M., *Roxburghshire*.

c

group of the Britons who settled in the region before the Romans came, endured their occupation, and survived into the Dark Ages which followed the collapse of the Roman power and the establishment of new kingdoms by new invaders from the east and the north. The present evidence of this period is by far the most prolific in the region but there is evidence of early peoples, though they are best seen now in the various local museums, in the Museum of Antiquities of Newcastle University and especially in the National Museum of Antiquities of Scotland in Edinburgh's 'New Town'. There are the Stone Age micro-flints found at Dryburgh, Neolithic hammer-heads from Oxton, and many stone axe-heads of the Neolithic people (perhaps about 2000 B.C.) from many parts of Berwickshire and Roxburghshire. Nearly one-third of such axes found in southern Scotland have been traced to the great stone-age 'factory' in Great Langdale in the Lake District and are known as 'Cumberland clubs'. But there is little evidence on the ground of these early antiquities and it is not until the Bronze Age, following the Neolithic cultures, that field evidence is available. But much of that is quite remarkable.

Lying just outside the perimeter of the camp at Roughtinglinn is one of the great riddles of Border archaeology. The Fell Sandstone outcrops through the grass in the form of an enormous tilted boulder nearly six feet high. Its surface is covered with carvings, some in the shape of cups and surrounding rings, others as simple circles joined by grooves, others looking like a bunch of flowers. On one vertical surface is a complete arch of three grooves and ridges. Although the sandstone does weather to lovely patterns, these markings are too regular to attribute to natural causes and have teased the imagination of travellers ever since they were first recorded by the pioneers of local antiquarian societies in the nineteenth century.

Such sculptured rocks occur in many parts of the Fell Sandstone ridge, the one on the Simonsides above Rothbury being marked by a plaque. They vary considerably both in form and in degree of perfection. Those on Dod Law are mostly crude rectangles and rough circles quite different from those at Rough-tinglinn. They are less in evidence in Roxburghshire but are found as far south as Ilkley Moor, where at least one such stone appears in a local park.

The similarity in shape of the cup and ring marks to the outline of the adjacent camp sites led some local antiquarians to suggest that they were a primitive form of map, and great efforts were made in the Wooler area to correlate the maps with the distribution of camps; some of the rocks have deep clefts in them which have a rough east–west alignment and these added to the hypothesis of a map.

Detailed work done on similar carvings in south-west Norway and southern Sweden, as well as the appearance of similar carvings on the lids of burial cists known to be of an earlier period, confirms a Bronze Age origin. Many examples can be seen in the Museum of Antiquities in Edinburgh. Their significance has not yet been elucidated. If of the Bronze Age, as seems likely, these sculptured rocks are contemporary with other evidence of the Bronze Age which are scattered through the Borders, especially the burial cists of the Beaker Folk with their characteristic crouched position of the skeleton, often found under cairns, or piles of stones, that are such a feature of many ancient trackways across the hills. Periodically, such burial cists are turned up by the plough and are found on the low ground as much as the high.

Other striking relics of the Bronze Age are the many standing stones, single monoliths and stone circles. Many of the standing stones have attracted new names associated with later events, such as the King's Stone (north of Flodden Field) and the Battle Stone near Humbleton associated with one of the many battles between the Douglas and Percy families. The stones were often used as rallying points before border raids. The Stob Stones in Halterburn may mark the medieval border agreed in A.D. 1222 but there is little doubt that, although some stones may have been erected in medieval times, the vast majority belong to the Bronze Age and have been standing in the landscape for more than three thousand years. Some have been cut in half and have to be hunted for in gateways and farm buildings and many have fallen and are covered by soil. Many of the place names have the element 'stone' in them; this is sometimes merely a corruption of the Anglo-Saxon 'ton' but is frequently a reference to a standing stone that was on the site when the English settled, as antique to them as they are to us. The Biddlestones can still be found in a hedge near the hamlet of Biddlestone near Rothbury.

Anyone expecting another Stonehenge will be disappointed. The stone circles that remain are small and crude by comparison, suggesting a much lower level of culture than that existing farther south and west, judging by the stone circle near Keswick. One of the best is at Duddo, five stones about six feet high (mapped often as Duddo Fourstones for some reason) each smoothed at the base by sheep rubbing themselves against it and each grooved by running water. They look like clenched fists or rotting teeth.

Another group that must once have been most impressive are to be found in the newly-forested area of Threestone Burn. The 'three stones' are set in the middle of a bleak basin at 1000 feet in the Cheviots west of Ilderton. The Forestry Commission from Chillingham are now busy transforming the scene but the stones are readily accessible on the low ground at the junction of two burns. The stones are seldom more than six feet in height, and a little searching will soon reveal at least fourteen stones, most of which are half-buried in the loose glacial debris that fills the valley. They are only reached by a long and rather tedious walk. Much more dramatic and perhaps the most rewarding in the entire region are the Brethren Stones, the two tall angular stones standing on the summit of an outcrop of the Kelso volcanic trap rocks within sight of Smailholm Tower. They are quite unlike the other stones in the region, but down the long slope to the east stands another stone, smaller, rounded and much more like others in the region.

The Bronze Age cannot be left without mention of the three superb bronze shields, dating from the eighth century B.C., which were found in the marshes at Yetholm in Roxburghshire and now have pride of place in the National Museum of Antiquities of Scotland. Whereas the stone circles and even many of the sculptured rocks suggest a fairly low level of culture as compared with Bronze Age relics elsewhere, these shields show craftsmanship and artistic invention of the highest order. In the Black Gate Museum at Newcastle are other Bronze Age finds, including the 'Whittingham Sword' found at Thrunton Farm.

There is no clear-cut line to be drawn between the two major periods of pre-history in the North; the comparative cultural lag as compared with the south and the lower level of achievement, if comparisons between the Duddo Circle of standing stones and that of Stonehenge are a pointer, may mean that there is no major break between the Bronze Age and the Iron Age.

The hill forts and enclosures of the Iron Age Celts, then, were in occupation before, during, and after the Roman Occupation, and the complex development of their defences was related to the varying fortunes of the Romans' north-west frontier: and so it is from Roman sources that we can find written evidence of the people, their organization and lives. Tacitus, for example, in his study of the early British campaigns, writes, 'Their strength is in their infantry. Some tribes also fight from chariots. The nobleman drives, his dependants fight in his defence. Once they owed obedience to kings; now they are distracted between the jarring factions of rival chiefs. Indeed, nothing has helped us more in war with their strongest nations than their inability to cooperate.'

The Celtic and Roman contributions to the Border landscape are, to a large extent, contemporary, and a study of the Roman period casts further light on the Celtic tribes who inhabited the inhospitable moorlands and whose relics add so much to the variety and excitement of the present landscape.

## The Roman Occupation

Many travellers heading west from Newcastle upon Tyne, leaving from West-gate Street along the A69 trunk road to Carlisle, choose the right fork at Heddon-on-the-Wall and follow the B6318 to Chollerford, Greenhead and thence to Carlisle. It is a narrow but very straight road and of great scenic beauty, much favoured by the weekend motorist. Having passed places with names such as Walbottle, Heddon-on-the-Wall, Rudchester, Wall Houses and Walwick, he can hardly be unaware that he is following a road with unique significance.

This is the so-called General Wade's road, actually supervised by a local man called Allgood, constructed, following the Jacobite rebellion of 1745, as a convenient way of moving troops and trade from east coast to west coast to either of the major routes into England. He followed the example of engineers who had an eye for country and strategic considerations more than sixteen hundred years before him and used the alignment of the Roman wall as the basis for his road, only leaving it when it made its determined way over the crags of the Great Whin Sill west of Chollerford. The wall materials themselves acted as a fine quarry for road stone. Yet for the first thirty miles of his journey, the traveller will not see the Wall itself. Fragments do remain, even within the suburbs of Newcastle and at various points along the road, as on Brunton Bank, but they are not obvious from the road.

Stagshaw was once called Portgate, and is still marked as such on the Ordnance Survey maps, one of the major Roman gates to the north where the key road of Dere Street left the base at Corbridge and penetrated the major wall defences. Road changes here had to be a matter of compromise between the ministries concerned with traffic problems and those concerned with the conservation of a unique heritage, one of the greatest monuments to Roman civilization in Europe, the Roman Wall, eighty Roman miles long, spanning the narrow neck of England, the frontier zone more than one thousand miles north-west of Rome itself.

Throughout much of the eastern part of the journey, the most obvious features of interest to the motorist are the two ditches that flank his route, the one to the north close by the road, the one to the south rather farther off, cutting through pastures and heaths parallel with the road. The former was the ditch fronting the Wall, the latter is called the Vallum and its origin has been the subject of discord, though it seems most likely that it marked the southern limit of the military zone and enabled access from the south to be policed efficiently.

In fact, much of the Wall lies not only under the existing road but especially in the farmhouses and mansions in the vicinity. Many of these buildings date from the late eighteenth century, when the common lands on the fells over which the road runs were enclosed and the improvers of the time used the Wall as an excellent quarry. It was men like William Hutton, who walked the length of the Wall (at the age of seventy-eight) in 1801 who used their influence on the local gentry and helped to preserve some sections, such as that by Plane-trees on the top of Brunton Bank.

John Clayton, the owner of Chesters, the estate occupying a strategic part of the Wall area, was another Roman enthusiast and wealthy enough to buy up as much land as he could on which Roman remains stood. Excavator, collector and preserver, he became one of the leading Romanologists in the mid-nineteenth century and contributed many papers to the early editions of the *Archaeologia Aeliana*.[1]

From Chesters westwards are found some of the most spectacular monuments to Roman military might and organizational skill to be found anywhere in Britain. The Wall in its real glory, as one of the most important archaeological features in Europe, stretches from the great camp at Chesters on the North Tyne to the vicinity of Brampton, though there are fragments even as far as Bowness on the South shores of the Solway Firth. There is now an excellent map published by the Ordnance Survey devoted entirely to the Roman Wall, which makes an unrivalled guide.

When the Military road deserts the Wall at about 800 feet for easier ground the Wall itself strides on over the highest crest of the crags, reaching heights of over 1200 feet in its search for the best defensive line, though the patrolling soldiery must have found it a very tiresome business indeed. Even here, in the superb stretch that lies between the Roman camp at Housesteads and Melkridge Common, much renovation has been carried out by the various authorities responsible for its maintenance and one cannot be sure that the stone courses one sees are the same as those constructed by the Roman engineers.

It was, according to Tacitus, in the year of his campaigning that Agricola 'opened up new nations, for the territory of tribes as far as the estuary named Tanaus was ravaged. . . . No fort of his was ever stormed, ever capitulated or was ever abandoned. They were protected against long protracted sieges by supplies renewed every year.'

This would put the date of Agricola's advance to the Tyne at about A.D. 79.

---

[1] E. A. Wallis Budge, *An Account of the Roman Antiquities Preserved in the Museum at Chesters, Northumberland* (Gilbert & Rivington, 1903).

Having conquered the Brigantes, he reached the territory of the Ottadini, whose land stretched nearly to the Forth. (The name Ottadini still appears somewhere about the Cheviot Hills in eighteenth-century maps.) To their west was the territory of the Selgovae, whose name is recalled in the name of the Solway Firth. The basic pattern adopted by Agricola was built on and modified by later Roman generals, but not fundamentally altered. His fourth season of campaigning 'was spent in securing the districts already overrun. . . . Clyde and Forth, carried inland to a great depth on the tides of opposite seas, are separated only by a narrow neck of land. This neck was now secured by garrisons and the whole sweep of country was safe in our hands.'

The keystone of this early military occupation was a series of forts, at Corbridge (Corstopitum) and Chesterholme (Vindolanda), linked with the supply route of Stanegate. From Corbridge, the main military route lay north between the lands of the Ottadini and the Selgovae, on the line of the later Dere Street with forts at High Rochester (Bremenium) and Chew Green on the Cheviot summit ridge. A second route went north towards the Tweed's mouth, now called the Devil's Causeway, with a fort at Low Learchild, at the junction of another road from High Rochester.

Chesterholme, in its pastoral calm on the steep bankside of Brackie's Burn, is one of my favourite sites. From the Roman signal station on Thorngrafton Common, one can look down on the fort and the straight track of the Stanegate rising over the low moors. In the valley itself, in a small grove, is a Roman milestone, still standing intact. On the skyline to the north is the craggy silhouette of the Great Whin Sill, utilized fifty years after Agricola by the readvancing Romans under Hadrian as the line of their major defensive barrier, known as Hadrian's Wall.

The Wall, seventy-two miles long, had the advantage of the shortest crossing of the island, abundant good stone available locally, the supply route of the Stanegate and the early Agricolan forts. The wall was generally over ten feet in width and over fifteen feet high, faced with well-shaped ashlar work and filled with rubble core in puddled clay. Forts and garrisons were attached to the Wall, such as Rudchester, Chesters, Housesteads, Brocolitia and Greenhead. Between the main forts were mile-castles at regular intervals and between them smaller turrets. The whole length was fronted where necessary by a deep ditch and to the rear was the vallum, a broad ditch delimiting the military zone. Causeways across the vallum were policed, for the land to the south, the territory of the Brigantes, was often hostile.

71

The Wall was in effect a raised patrol route and a barrier against which attacking forces could be driven and trapped. The supply route was the Stanegate linking the west coast to the east, to the main bridge across the Tyne at Pons Aelius (present-day Newcastle upon Tyne) and on to Wallsend. Even as early as Agricola, great attention was paid to suitable harbours for supply by sea. A typical fort guarding the sea routes is found at South Shields, well preserved amongst the terraced houses of this seaport with streets bearing Roman names, but an integral part of the Border defence system. Several mile-castles may still be seen, and an excellent example of a turret occurs conveniently near the main road at Brunton, near Chollerford.

It is, of course, the great garrison forts that have occupied much of the time and interest of archaeologists. They are often sited on weak points of the Wall system, where natural routeways, such as the North Tyne, cut north–south across the defence line. Much visited and very well organized for visitors are the main camps at Chesters, north of Hexham, Housesteads on the west road, and Corbridge. Chesters covers nearly seven acres of parkland on the west bank of the North Tyne while Housesteads covers three acres of moorland above the South Tyne. The regularity and organization of their layout is in marked contrast to the Iron Age camp sites and hill forts, suggesting the higher civilization represented by the Roman invaders. The gates and turrets of the surrounding wall enclose an area laid out with military precision: the headquarters building in the centre, commandant's house and bath-house; workshops and granaries; then the barracks for the legionaries and stables for the horses of the cavalry units.[1]

Modern excavation techniques have shown that each of the camps is the result of many periods of modification, a long adjustment to a changing frontier situation. By the third century the Roman garrisons had moved north, using the Wall forts as their supply base, and the main routes north over the hills became the site of further impressive camps and signal stations into the valley of the Jed and up Lauderdale over Soutra to the Antonine Wall to the Forth–Clyde 'neck'. In the comparatively settled conditions of the Tyne area, civilian settlements, 'vici', grew up in the shelter of the forts as embryo trading towns. The evidence is most clearly seen in aerial photographs, and the civilian settlement at Chesterholme is now being investigated. Meanwhile, the great north roads became the bases for the frontier rangers, the *exploratores* who kept an eye on dissident Celtic groups.

[1] Detailed descriptions are available in many sources, especially the handbooks of the Department of the Environment and J. Collingwood Bruce's much republished *Handbook to the Roman Wall*.

The line of Dere Street from High Rochester right over the Cheviot summit ridge into the headwaters of the Kale and then aiming straight as an arrow to the three outstanding peaks of the Eildon Hills is one of the most interesting stretches of Roman road in Britain and much of it can still be walked. Since 1971, the Roxburgh stretches have been signposted. The alignment is quite clear as far as the river-crossing over the Tweed near Melrose, but the route beyond, following the right bank of the Lauder up to the Soutra Pass over the Lammermuirs, is not shown on modern maps and is still in dispute, though it seems likely to have followed the ridgeway between the Leader and Allan Water, certainly to the old Channelkirk, perhaps the same route known in later medieval times as the Girthgate and Malcolm's Road (after the Scots king of that name).

This great road slicing across the centre of the entire region from its base at Corbridge, across the Border hills, the Tweed Valley and the Lammermuirs, was the main thread of the Roman military presence and along it was constructed a sequence of great camps: High Rochester in Redesdale, close to the present military camp, then to that most bleak and dramatic of places, Chew Green, set in a high basin of the Cheviot range at about 1400 feet. If ever there was needed a tribute to the determination and endurance of the Roman conquest, this is it. The enormous ground plan of the two rectangular camps, side by side, covering more than a quarter of a mile, strikes even the eye jaded by too much sight-seeing with dramatic force in the incongruity of its setting, particularly if you approach it from the Scots side. A world of wide skies, sheep, skylarks and then this. Pevsner calls it 'the most remarkable visible group of Roman earthworks in Britain'. But Chew Green is now accessible from the military tarmac that leads up from the Alwin valley and is available to the public when the red flags are not flying, indicating no firing on the range. Chew Green itself, being below the rim of the hills, has no view to the north and so was supported by a signal station on the ridge. The visible remains of the camps at Pennymuir on the Kale, at Cappuck, east of Jedburgh, and that of Newstead, known as Trimontium after the three peaks of the Eildons, are very sparse. The great camp of Trimontium covering nearly seventeen acres, three times the size of Chesters, is marked only by an inscribed stone by the roadside. But the finds from excavation there dominate an entire room of the National Museum of Antiquities of Scotland in Edinburgh, a marvellous display of Roman and native weapons, tools, house-hold goods and sundry items of the daily round two thousand years ago in the green meadows where the Tweed meets the Leader Water, this key point of Roxburgh, still the focus of its life, at the junction of main routeways. It began as an Agricolan fort and had successive rebuildings culminating in an Antonine fort, with bath-houses as usual outside the main camp towards the river, a much more pleasing prospect for the soldiery than the windswept walls of Chew Green. Much of the stonework was used in the later buildings of the great Border abbeys, and the excellent small museum in the Commendator's house alongside Melrose Abbey has many Roman fragments on show.

The setting of Trimontium is reminiscent of the great camps of the Wall area along the Tyne Valley, and there the visible relics are much more abundant and impressive, with enough of the lower courses of the walls, fragments of standing columns, roadways and bath-houses, houses, stables and hypocausts to make imaginative reconstruction much easier, especially with the aid of the excellent museums on site. Chesters is the best example of a cavalry fort visible not just in Britain, but in the entire territory of the Roman Empire. Its standardized plan is based on two parallel streets (one on the line of the Wall) cutting the interior into three sections – two for barracks and stables, and the central area for headquarters' buildings, the commandant's house, granaries and workshops. The four gateways, approximately east and west along the Wall, north and south through the wall-zone, are still intact. The fort at Housesteads, an infantry fort, is based on the same layout of buildings but with the long axis being east–west instead of north–south as in the case of Chesters. At 750 feet on the open ground of the Whin Sill, guarding one of the many deep gaps through that natural defence, Housesteads has a much bleaker outlook than Chesters; the land to the south, now large grassy pastures, must have seemed scarcely less hospitable to the Roman than the ground to the north, which is broken by small glacial lakes and the advancing columns of new afforestation. But this is one of the favourite stretches of the Wall and a new National Park information centre has opened up at Twice Brewed.

The museum at Housesteads includes material found at near-by Chesterholme, but the museum at Chesters is the more important, containing 'one of the most important collections of Roman relics in Britain'.[1] Among the inscribed stones, altars, statuary and household goods is a copy of a diploma (the original is in the British Museum) showing the grant of Roman citizenship to an auxiliary soldier, who settled in the area when he had served his time and thus held a small stake, as it were, in maintaining the Roman power on the northern frontier.

Corstopitum, or Corbridge, set on the north bank of the Tyne three miles

[1] Department of the Environment *Guide*.

behind the Wall, differs from the layout of the other two camps, at least in its visible remains, which have been contorted by slumping in the underlying gravels, giving a most odd corrugated appearance to the site. Fragments of Antonine, Severan, Constantian and Theodosian buildings remain, especially storehouses, workshops and the living quarters of officers and other ranks. Fragments of five temples remain in the south-east corner. The museum contains many fine examples of sculpture and bas-relief, most famous of which is the Corbridge lion, depicted devouring a stag. Another pediment shows another popular Roman subject, Romulus and Remus being suckled by a she wolf.

Many of the bas-reliefs in the museums give evidence of the various deities of the Roman garrisons, but from the religious point of view few sites are more remarkable than that of the Mithraeum near the earthworks of the Roman camp on the Wall at Brocolitia, half-way between Chesters and Housesteads. The signed footpath leads from the road down over the pastures and there tucked away in the shelter of a small burn is the complete outline of a Mithraeic temple, unseen from the road but commanding a fine view to the south over the Tyne valley. A complete reconstruction of such a temple has been attempted, together with lights and taped commentary, in the Museum of Antiquities at Newcastle.

This impressive array of the remnants of a great empire is, perhaps, the most important feature of the antiquities of the Border country but, in perspective, it is only a part of the widespread visible evidence of the Iron Age peoples who colonized the region before the organized conquerors came from the south, who endured their occupation, sometimes with battle, sometimes with trade, and continued in their own pattern of life, changed as it may have been, after the withdrawal of the frontier cohorts. By the end of the fourth century, the barbarians from north and east had combined against the Roman power, and the final breaching of the frontier defences by Picts, Scots, and Saxons meant the end of a military occupation that had lasted for more than three centuries. In the chaos that followed it is probable that many of the hill forts and camps were reoccupied, and the Roman roads became raiders' paths. The Border country awaited its new wave of invaders and colonizers and the next stage in the formation of its human landscape.

The Wall itself and the great camps became the quarry for later builders, and Roman stones and columns are to be found in mansions and farms in the vicinity, and especially in the churches of the Tyne valley where entire arches, as at Corbridge, or columns, as at Chollerton, have been incorporated into Saxon churches. Many a Roman altar became the base for a Christian cross, as at St Oswalds on Heavenfield. But the most moving link with the new colonizers, that symbolizes the historic change, is the crypt at Hexham Abbey, built in the seventh century entirely with large blocks of stone taken from the camp at Corbridge. In the semi-darkness of the Christian crypt, Roman inscriptions can still be deciphered on the stones hewn and shaped nearly two thousand years ago.

STONE CIRCLE NEAR ꝺuꝺꝺo.                                    p.ꝼ.c.ա.

# 4

## Church and village and rural scene

O the broom and the bonny bonny broom,
    And the broom of the Cowdenknowes!
And aye sae sweet as the lassie sang,
    I' the bought, milking the ewes.

*(The Broom of Cowdenknowes)*

A gentle walk up the track from the village of Doddington to the shepherd's house and all about you on the open moorland is the fragmentary voice of the distant past: earthworks of Iron Age enclosures and camps; bared outcrops of the Fell Sandstone carved with rings and cups and snaking grooves from the art gallery of an even earlier age. Over by the stone wall and the gate leading to Horton Moor stands a six-foot monolith, with others of its once-companions prostrate in the heather.

But these are marginal aspects of the present rural scene. Looking west over the broad river haughs of the Milfield Plain where the Till meanders north to the Tweed, the essential element of today's landscape is the ring of villages and hamlets that circle the plain, avoiding the areas liable to flooding, linked with lanes that thread a route along the foot of the hills. Doddington at our feet, then Nesbit, Fenton, Kimmerston, Ford and Etal. Across the vale are Wooler, Humbleton, Akeld, Yeavering, Kirknewton, Lanton, Coupland, Milfield, Flodden, and Crookham. The most recent edition of the one-inch map of the Ordnance Survey marks two small crosses in this area, one near the farm at Old Yeavering, marked 'Gefrin', the other to the east of Milfield, marked 'Melmin'.

For a long time, earlier editions marked the farm at Old Yeavering in Gothic lettering as 'Edwin's Palace', the supposed site of the inland capital of the seventh-century Anglo-Saxon king of Northumbria. But aerial photography in the 1950s revealed unusual crop-markings in the field to the north of the farm, a field that was being quarried for sands and gravels. The urgency led to a three-year dig under the aegis of the Ministry of Works, which resulted in Brian Hope-Taylor and his excavators revealing the original timber post-holes of a succession of Anglo-Saxon halls, each built on or near the site of the previous one, spanning most of the seventh century. Nearby was a wooden amphitheatre, a most unusual feature, and this may have been the site of some of the earliest conversions of the Heathen English to Christianity under the missionary Paulinus on his journey from Rome by way of Kent. The classic encounter of Christian and pagan priests and the description of the life of man, 'as a sparrow's flight through the hall . . . in at one door and tarries for a moment in the light and heat of the hearth fire, and then flying forth from the other vanishes into the wintry darkness whence it came',[1] might well have taken place at this historic spot.

After repeated destruction by fire – for the acceptance of a new god did not take place without bitter struggles – the royal hall was moved to near-by Melmin, the ancient name being corrupted through time into the present Milfield (Melmin's field). In a similar way, 'Gefrin' became corrupted into 'Yeavering' and the study of place names as shown by Ekwall in his *Dictionary of English Place Names* suggests that most of the village names in the area have Anglo-Saxon origins. A study of the earliest known spellings in monastic rolls and royal tax rolls gives a clearer possibility of interpretation: Crookham from 'crucum' at the bends of the river; Coupland, the bought land; Lanton, the long 'tun'; Kirknewton, the 'new tun' by the church; Akeld, by the slope of oak trees; Etal as 'Eata's haugh'; Ford, the main crossing of the river Till; Kimmerston, the 'tun' of Kimmer; Fenton, the 'tun' by the fen; Nesbit, on a spur or 'nose' of higher land sticking out into the plain; Doddington, the 'tun' perhaps of people belonging to a chieftain called 'Dod' or named after the Celtic hill.

The seventh and eighth centuries A.D. were the heyday of Anglo-Saxon power in the north, under the kings of Northumbria, developing out of the earlier kingdoms of Bernicia (according closely with the region under study) and Deira to the south. Following Edwin's acceptance of the Christian faith, his successor King Oswald defeated the heathens under Cadwallon at Heavenfield by the Roman Wall north of Hexham, in 634. The site is still marked by St Oswald's chapel (heavily modernized, though, with a Roman altar serving as the socket for a later cross) and a huge wooden cross by the roadside. In the following year, Aidan was invited from the Celtic church of Iona off the west coast of Scotland to help Oswald and found the monastery on Lindisfarne. At this time, Northum-

---

[1] J. R. Green, *History of the English People.*

brian power reached north as far as the site of present-day Edinburgh (the name may be derived from the Northumbrian king).

'The Celtic world had the advantage that it had no towns. It was, therefore, forced on conversion to find a type of ecclesiastical structure suited to its needs. The solution was the tribal monastery.'[1] It was the monasteries then founded at Lindisfarne, Old Melrose, and Coldingham that were the source of Christianization, and the earliest 'parish priests' were supplied from the nearby monasteries.

Finan succeeded Aidan and was successful even to the point of baptizing Penda of Mercia, the slayer of both King Edwin and Oswald, in the Tyne near Benwell. But the latter half of the century is most closely associated with the name of St Cuthbert, the border shepherd boy who became a monk at Old Melrose and later Bishop of Lindisfarne, 'wonder worker of Britain', who ultimately chose solitude in a cell on the isolated rocks of the Farne Islands, at home with the sea birds and the seals. His name is perpetuated in many wells and caves, known locally as Cuddy's cave or Cuddy's well, even Cuddy's tups, a reference to local sheep and Cuddy's beads, sections of the fossil crinoid stem. It was the removal of his body from Lindisfarne after the Danish raid in A.D. 793 that symbolized the decline of Northumbria and its relegation to a tributary earldom of the Danelaw.

Much of our knowledge of this period is derived from the writings of the Venerable Bede, who followed the monastic life at the nearby monasteries of St Peter at Monkwearmouth (founded in 674) and St Paul at Jarrow (founded in 681). His *History of the English Church and People* was finished in A.D. 731. At both these places are the physical remains of original stonework that give the present a direct link with the Anglo-Saxon past. The earliest church buildings, as with Edwin's palace at Yeavering, were built with timber. Finan rebuilt the church at Lindisfarne, for example, 'after the Scottish fashion, of oak plants thatched with reeds'.[2] But such buildings soon gave way to stone, especially where readily-shaped stonework was available, for example, in nearby Roman camps and on the great Wall. Three of the most complete examples of such early churches are south of the Tyne, at Jarrow, Monkwearmouth, and Escomb in present-day County Durham. The setting of each is now disturbing, all three being locked against the possibilities of vandalism. St Paul's stands solitary among the creeks, dumps, and timber yards overlooking the melancholy mud flats of Jarrow Slake, while St Peter's at Monkwearmouth is insulated from the

[1] Eric John, 'The Social and Political Problems of the Early English Church', *Agricultural History Review*, Vol. 18, 1970.
[2] Attwater, *Dictionary of Saints*.

flats and shipyard cranes of Sunderland's north bank by a green cordon. Escomb, one of the finest surviving examples of an Anglo-Saxon church in Britain, is now surrounded by a new, quite imaginative layout of council housing. It is the simplicity of architectural style with the richness of the decorative work that suggests a highly-cultivated society that founded these works of aspiration and art.

Perhaps the most exciting and most moving site of all, however, is the crypt of Hexham Abbey, founded by St Wilfred in A.D. 670 and destined to be the finest building of its kind north of the Alps until its destruction by the Danes, marauding up the Tyne two hundred years later in A.D. 875. The crypt is built entirely of Roman stones taken from nearby Corbridge, some of the stone bearing inscriptions of the third century and one bearing the erased name of Gita who was struck from such inscriptions in A.D. 212. It is laid out as a simple sequence of steps and passages to lead the faithful through to a display of relics, and it is not difficult to imagine the expectant single file of weary feet shuffling through the semi-darkness, marvelling at the great stonework taken from the 'work of giants'.

Parts of the old floor of the nave have been revealed in the abbey, but the other magnificent survival of the earliest foundation of the Abbey is a seventh-century throne – a simple seat, carved from one piece of stone, standing beyond the screen, the centre from which the one-mile of sanctuary radiated. Several fragments of early crosses and decoration have been built into the later walls of the nave, making an art gallery of early workmanship.

Outstanding is Acca's cross, dated about A.D. 740, which is now in the Cathedral Library at Durham. Cross fragments remain at Birtley, Bywell, Kirkhaugh, Nunnykirk, Ovingham, Simonburn, Warkworth and Woodhorn as well as in the museums in Newcastle and Edinburgh and attached to the major abbey sites under the Department of the Environment. One of the most important fragments now supports the font in All Saints church in Rothbury, the shaft showing the typical foliage scrolls and animals that seem to carry a hint of the Mediterranean. Christ and the Apostles appear on the reverse side. The head of the shaft is in the Black Gate Museum in Newcastle. The crosses had a variety of purposes, sometimes being used by estate owners to hallow a cemetery, to mark a preaching station or to mark the centre of an itinerant administration. Most are now found in churches but cross bases and even standing shafts can still be found at Warden, Thockrington, and Whittingham. One of the best wayside crosses, with its slender, simply carved shaft and circular capping cross, still stands in the hedgerow by Crosshall Farm near Eccles. It is possible to find, with effort, a cross base in the

5a. *Scrub oak woodland near Rothbury.*

5b. *Remnant alders in Calroust Burn.*

5c. *A grassy ride through the plantations of Kielder Forest.*

6a. *Seal and calf on the Brownsman, Outer Farnes.*

6b. *Guillemots and kittiwakes nesting on the whinstone cliffs of Staple Island.*

7a. *Typical Iron Age hill fort on Blackbrough Hill, near Hownam.*

7b. *Passages and chambers in the drystone wall of Edin's Hall Broch, near Duns.*

7c. *Direct aerial view of the Iron Age hill fort on Woden Law with Dere Street descending from the hills to cross Kale Water; early cultivation terraces on the lower slopes.*

8a. *Roman camps at Chew Green, 1400 feet up near Coquethead; Dere Street crossing from left to right.*

8b. *Housesteads: three Roman deities.*

8c. *Corbridge: terracotta plaque of the Celtic god, Taranis.*

hedgerows leading from Hexham to Chesters, one of the group that marked the sanctuary rights that radiated from the Frith Stool in the Abbey. The tradition was continued in later market crosses, several of which remain *in situ*. That at Ancrum in Roxburghshire, one of the earliest, has recently been restored. All crosses are now 'listed buildings' of the Department of the Environment.

The physical survivals of the Anglo-Saxon heyday, fragmentary as they are, are enough to indicate a highly organized civilization based on village and small-town communities. They represent the culmination of a period of colonization that had proceeded for many decades prior to the victory over the invaders at Heavenfield.

The traditional starting-point (comparable with the tradition of Hengest and Horsa in Kent) is the reign of Ida, beginning about A.D. 547 at Bamburgh, otherwise known as Dinguardi. This area has also been associated with the Arthurian cycle of resistance by the Romano-Britons to the invading Anglo-Saxons. These earliest invaders found 'a land of Celtic traditions whose scanty pastoral population still lived largely on the moorland and mountain fastnesses from which the Roman armies had but temporarily and partially dislodged them',[1] the people who constructed the camps and enclosures on Dod Law where this chapter began.

The confrontation must have been warlike on some occasions, on others that of an uneasy peace with the gradual subjugation and possible enslavement of the native 'Britons'. Bede reported that Aethilfrid 'laid waste the nation of the Britons, for no one before him had rendered more of their land either habitable for the English by the extermination of the natives'. And surely it cannot have been mere coincidence that Edwin's 'villa regalis', the administrative centre at Yeavering, was sited at the foot of the hill on which stood the largest British camp site in the region, on Yeavering Bell. Another authority suggests that 'a British strain in the personal names of the Anglo-Saxons especially visible in Northumbria is witness to a certain amount of intermarriage'.[2]

It is in the difficult study of place names that other evidence may be adduced for this 'dark age' between the fall of Roman power and the emergence of the Anglo-Saxon Kingdom. The earliest element agreed by most students of place-name analysis is that of 'ing' and 'ingham', which are frequently associated with a personal name, suggesting the early family groups which sought new homes in this foreign land beyond the Frisian Sea. Only two names with the 'ing' ending are certain in Northumbria – Birling, near the mouth of the Coquet, and

[1] Collingwood and Myers, *Roman Britain and the English Settlement* (1945).
[2] D. Whitelock, *The Beginnings of English Society* (Penguin).

Yeavering itself. But there are several villages with 'ingham' endings, grouped around Alnwick, along the Tyne as far up valley as Bellingham on the North Tyne, and, in the extreme north of the region, Coldingham.

As their numbers increased, the Anglo-Saxon invaders took over more land from the native population, and with their superior tools, especially the axe and the plough, progressively made inroads in the lowland forests for their agricultural pursuits. By A.D. 670, eleven farming settlements in the valley of the Bowmont south and west of Yetholm, which can still be recognized,[1] were included in a grant of properties to the monks of Lindisfarne by King Oswy of Northumbria. There is archaeological evidence that even earlier sites, of the Dark Age, may be identified, at Sourhope and at Crock Cleugh, and were used as the model for St Cuthbert's lonely retreat on the Farne, a roughly-circular court and a hut circle with an enclosing wall. There is even an indication of the type of agriculture at this time in that, after the failure of his wheat crop, Cuthbert succeeded with barley, and the name of barley or 'bere' may be in the name of Berwick.

Most of the names of physical features such as rivers and hills are British and were retained by the Saxons, such as Tweed, Till, Tyne, Cheviot, Eildon. But the vast majority of names of settlements are Anglo-Saxon, their 'hams' and 'tuns' covering all the lowlands, the most accessible and agriculturally worthwhile land, penetrating up the valleys in the hill areas such as the Cheviots and the Lammermuirs. Their sites avoided both high ground and the marshy fenlands of the river bottoms and preferred well-drained areas on river gravels and light glacial soils.

Place names are a specialized study for, often, they are not what they seem. 'Cornhill', for example, seems obvious enough, but it derives its name from two elements, one meaning 'crane', the other 'haugh', the whole name meaning 'the low-lying ground where cranes are'. 'Ashington' suggests a typical early Anglo-Saxon name with the ending 'ington', yet in earlier documents it is shown as 'Essenden'.

'Den', together with such endings as 'ley' and 'field', are indicative of later movements from main settlements into the new forest clearances and are prolific, for example, in the difficult area south of the Tyne, Shotley, Whitley, Slaley, Painshawfield, Stocksfield and many others appearing in a group up on the high ground contrasting with the older settlements like Ovingham, Ovington, Wylam and Eltringham on the low ground near the river. Another frequent ending, 'wick', is indicative, also, of an outlying 'farm' attached to an earlier

---

[1] Thornington, Mindrum, Shotton, Halterburn, Yetholm, Staerough, Clifton, Morebattle, Whitton, Gateshaw and Sourhope.

'township'; an interesting group is found on the shore near Lindisfarne: Goswick, the goose farm; Cheswick, the cheese farm; Fenwick, the farm on the fen; Berwick, either the barley farm or the demesne farm.

Even later are the 'granges', outlying farms attached to post-Norman monasteries, the 'shiels' and 'steels' indicating temporary settlements often connected with summer grazing of the hill pastures or on poor ground near the coasts. The name was transferred also to other temporary shelters for fishermen, for example. Some of the shiels along the Tweed come in this category and, perhaps, the shields near the mouth of the Tyne.

The process of colonization of the wild, the clearance of the forest, proceeded with the need for new land certainly until the thirteenth and fourteenth centuries, until only fragmentary areas of the original forests remained, largely as privileged hunting areas for game, either for the Crown or by licence of the Crown. The word 'forest' in this context indicates the open ground beyond the cultivated area, as much moorland as woodland. The Cheviot 'forest', for example, had little woodland cover and is better known as Cheviot Chase.

The word 'shiel' has been interpreted by some writers as indicative of Scandinavian influence. Such influences are surprisingly rare in view of the known Danish 'occupation' of the region, but the main area of Danish place names, indicated especially by 'by', 'thorpe' and 'biggin', lies well to the south towards the Tees in the southern areas of the Northumbrian kingdom. The element 'holm' is often indicative, too, of Scandinavian settlement, meaning 'island', but the frequent occurrence of 'holm' north of the Tweed is a variant of the English 'ham', as at Smailholm, Denholm, and Yetholm. Two names in Tyneside – Walker and Byker – both share the 'ker' or 'carr' element, the Danish word for marshland. Byker starts with the familiar 'by', which is so prolific farther south.

Another interesting name is Morebattle, spelt in early documents as 'Mereboda'. The first element is obviously indicative of the lake or 'mere' that stands near the settlement (now silted up but easily identified). 'Boda' is very close to the Norse 'booth' that occurs so frequently in the Pennine Dales.

J. B. Johnston, in his study of Berwickshire place names, 'the most English county in Scotland', records at least sixty-six non-English or Anglo-Saxon names, many of them associated with rivers and hills but some connected with settlements. Auchencrow, for example, means 'the glen with trees' in the Celtic (British) tongue. There is some confusion between Celtic, Welsh, and Gaelic elements and it may be better to think of them as 'British' (i.e. connected with the Iron Age people) as distinct from the predominant English names as in the cases of Duns, a hill; Longformacus, the church in the field; Carfrae, the camp on the border; Primrose, the tree on the moor; Melrose, the bare moor; Mow, a hill; Penmanshiel, height with the great rock; Prendergast, the priest's deep glen; Cambus, the crooked place.

The general pattern revealed by the place-name evidence, however, is not disputed. It shows a colonization of the coastal region north of the Roman Wall by Anglo-Saxon groups who, as they gained strength and further accessions of emigrants from the continent, pushed inland at the end of the sixth century, establishing settlements on the lower grounds favouring well-drained sites near watercourses, penetrating deep inland along the main waterways and along the old Roman roads, right up to the foothills of the Cheviots, the Lammermuirs and the Upper Tweed Basin. It was not until much later, after the formation of the political frontier, that the linguistic homogeneity of the region broke down.

In the early Middle English period there is a continuous dialect area from the Humber to the Forth, but since 1157, the eastern end of the border had followed the Tweed and its presence led to the progressive division, linguistic and otherwise, of an area that had previously been homogeneous.[1]

Even when the Lothians were lost to the emergent Scottish kingdom, the region was allowed 'to retain its own laws and customs and its English language'.[2] This English language and the predominant English place names were the product of an amalgamation of the various Anglo-Saxon colonizing groups into a cohesive 'nation', that of Bernicia (later to be merged into Northumbria with its focus farther south, in York), with its centre of power at Lindisfarne and Bamburgh and its total area very similar to the region covered by this study.

The economy of the early settlements became based on large, open arable fields producing corn crops, on hay meadows, and on associated common grazing on poorer hill land. The township and parish boundaries that evolved frequently ran from river to hillside, incorporating these varying types of land, making the rural communities to some extent self-supporting. The boundaries often used physical features such as rivers, burns, and hill crests, but also distinctive human features such as the then ancient Roman 'streets'. This is noticeable even today, along the Roman Wall and especially along Dere Street.

The Domesday survey did not include the Border region, so that a most valuable record in that point of time is missing, but the frequent references to townships being laid waste in the northern parts of England suggests that the Border country itself suffered a similar fate.

[1] B. Strang, *A History of English* (1970).
[2] J. Murray, *Dialect of the Southern Counties of Scotland* (1873).

The high administrative and organizational power of the Normans – a conquering *élite*, rather than a new peopling of the land in the sense of the previous Anglo-Saxon invasion – meant that new patterns were superimposed on the existing rural organization. The new Norman castle strongholds, the revival of monasticism and the imposition of severe forest laws were grafted on to the existing groundplan of rural life. Indeed, in Teviotdale, for example, the land was still administered by 'thegns and dregns' in the Saxon fashion until the twelfth century.

The Norman marcher lords carved out estates for themselves and were reinforced by the expansionist bishops of the newly-revived church, the greatest being the Bishops of Durham who held much land along the border including territories that still bear the name of separate shires, though now submerged within modern counties. Norham and Islandshires, stretching from Norham on the Tweed to the Farnes, was one such, as was Bedlingtonshire on the east coast, and Hexhamshire on the Tyne.

Monastic settlements were re-established on old Anglo-Saxon sites at Lindisfarne, 1093, Coldingham, 1089, Melrose, 1130, Jedburgh, 1118, Tynemouth, 1083 and Hexham, 1113, while new establishments were set up in deep-wooded valleys at Brinkburn on the Coquet, Newminster on the Wansbeck, Blanchland on the Derwent, Hulne on the Aln, Kelso and Dryburgh on the Tweed and Abbey St Bathans on the Whiteadder. There were in addition many small cells as, for example, the Benedictine ones at Amble and Warkworth and on the Farnes, a Cistercian nunnery at Eccles and a concentration of monastic houses in the largest town of the region, Newcastle, where Benedictines, Dominicans, Whitefriars, Blackfriars and other groups were all represented.

Most of the monastic buildings that have been the source of inspiration to endless topographical artists, painters and photographers in the last two hundred years date from this post-Norman period, which saw also the rebuilding of hundreds of churches, reaching its climax in the thirteenth century when Alexander III of Scotland and Henry II of England were reigning. The comparative prosperity and peace of the time is reflected in the fact that there is scarcely a church in the region that does not bear the imprint of architecture of the period, the 'Early English' style.

The greatest concentration of abbeys and priories is in the basin of the middle Tweed where the great Border Abbeys were founded, largely under the influence of David I of Scotland. The Cistercians settled at Melrose, the Benedictines at Kelso, the Augustinians at Jedburgh and, in the thirteenth century, the Premonstratensians at Dryburgh, coming from Alnwick. All suffered acutely from periodic depredations during the long period of Border wars, culminating in the raids of the Earl of Hertford in 1545, and further damage was done by the Scottish reformers themselves.

All the major abbey ruins are under the control of the Department of the Environment, and the sites beautifully laid out for the enjoyment and appreciation of visitors. At Jedburgh, Melrose, Dryburgh and Lindisfarne, small museums adjacent to the abbeys and priories greatly add to the enjoyment, with many evocative fragments rescued from the ruined parts of the splendid buildings.

Jedburgh Abbey stands in the heart of the town and its fine south doorways of the Norman and Early Decorated period dominate the scene on the approach along the main road from Carter Bar, the A68. There, above the river's broad sweep, stands the roofless silhouette of the nave and the tower on massive Norman pillars. On the river bank, the foundations of some of the conventual buildings have been uncovered and labelled, but some of the loveliest Celtic and Anglo-Saxon work is to be found in the small museum by the great west doorway, one of the outstanding examples of Norman work in Scotland.

The remnants of Kelso Abbey, too, are an integral part of the town which grew by them, but it suffered more than any other abbey and, in effect, only the west tower remains, with all the appearance of a fortification in which it is said some of the monks fought against the English onslaughts.

In contrast is the Gothic splendour of Melrose, standing within its precinctual area to the north of the market place. Much of the choir, the presbytery and the transepts remain, with Perpendicular windows rising against the low, flat foothills beyond. The large red-sandstone blocks have weathered to a delicate rose colour, made for sunsets and nostalgia, but they also attracted local builders who used this as a convenient quarry for good stone for years. The cloisters, fraters, dorters, drainage ditches and wells have all been uncovered, and enough stonework remains to give a good impression of monastic life. Beyond the great ditch lies the Commendator's house, a very fine tower house, which now holds an extensive and most attractively-organized museum, showing links with Old Melrose, which lay to the east by the Tweed, and with the Roman camp at Trimontium.

At Dryburgh, the conventual buildings are the most complete of all the abbeys – cloister, chapter house, dorter, frater, and a gatehouse over the water channel to the south of the site. The choir, presbytery and transepts of the main building are more ruinous than at Melrose but house the burial tombs of Sir Walter Scott and the Haigs of Bemersyde, including the first Earl Haig. What makes Dryburgh memorable, however, is the quietude – a setting of sylvan calm with the greenest grass and the panoply of magnificent trees as if designed specifically to enhance the romantic appeal of the ruined abbey.

The abbeys are not evenly spread throughout the region, nor in what are now the most isolated areas. The least accessible, even today, is possibly Blanchland, that most attractive of villages which was rebuilt in the eighteenth century, using much 'monastic' stonework from the ruined Premonstratensian Abbey, the pattern of which may still be maintained in the present layout with terraced stone cottages grouped round a paved square, which is approached by a fifteenth-century gatehouse. The local inn still serves refreshments in a barrel-vaulted room which was perhaps part of the monastic storehouse. The hotel itself may perpetuate the monastic guest house. A local story suggests that the monks once pealed their bells for joy at having escaped the attention of a marauding band of Scots, the sound of the bells immediately giving the Scots a method of finding their prey and robbing it. But the same story is applied to other sites, including Dryburgh and particularly Brinkburn, which is even more hidden by the wooded banks of a meander in the Coquet, a delightful, restful site recently opened up to the public. Only the priory church remains, but it was restored with more than usual good taste by a recent owner and offers one of the most complete buildings of its type in the region. The organ has now been restored and windows replaced after recent gales (surprising in so sheltered a site), and musical recitals are now held there.

At the other extremity lies Coldingham, with little beyond the church standing, except one or two fine arches. Excavations are now taking place here to establish the outline of the monastic buildings. The present church is in the old choir, with fine decoration on three walls and the fourth plain. The graveyard stands on the site of the great nave. Its site near the marvellous shoreline of Coldingham Bay and St Abb's Head gives particular pleasure, especially when a north-easter is beating across the North Sea, but no site is more dramatic from that point of view than Lindisfarne itself, the priory buildings torn apart not only by raiders and stone-pirates but by the weather. Some of the columns have been weathered to a paper thinness. But the great piers of the nave, so reminiscent of Durham Cathedral, still stand and support the slender 'Rainbow Arch' that so romantic-ally frames the view of the castle beyond. One of the first Ministry of Works sites, the priory building foundations have been exposed, well labelled and filled with lush green turf. There is a ready-made vantage-point for the whole site on the 'heugh', a steep outcrop of igneous rock just to the south on which stands the lighthouse and was believed to be the early fortified site before the present castle, which is Elizabethan in foundation.

At Newminster there are very few fragments; at Hexham, enough to make a pleasant backcloth to Beaumont Street which was driven through the site of the monastic buildings, though here the whole town is embellished by the Seal, the open space now public, once the private enclosure for monkish contemplation. The east end that confronts the market place is largely a Victorian restoration by John Dobson, replacing a varied medieval structure that was screened by housing. But the interior is complete, a basically Gothic building that is still in use not only for regular services but for the annual festival of medieval music and art that takes place now late in September – an ideal setting. Even in the restored nave, many fragments of earlier Roman and Saxon work are set like a living museum, as well as part of the original floor adjacent to the seventh-century crypt described at the beginning of this chapter. The chancel lying beyond the fifteenth-century painted wooden rood screen contains Wilfred's throne, a seventh-century stone chair, the delightful carvings of Prior Leschman's Chapel portraying a gallery of border characters, and a small Anglo-Saxon chalice only three inches high, made of gilt-bronze, set in a special alcove. The north transept is a fairly complete example of the Early English style whilst the south transept is broken by the night stairs, one of the finest examples in the country of medieval stairs leading over the slype, processional in size and, apart from the lowest steps, worn into the subtlest of shapes, most pleasing to the eye. At the foot is a Roman tombstone of Flavinus riding down a barbarian, presumably of the local Ottadini.

Little remains of the cloister, though the area recently tidied up by Beaumont Street brings thirteenth-century stonework into public view. The paths through the Seal lead to a twelfth-century gateway that gives access to Gilesgate.

Another spectacular coastal site is at Tynemouth. Here, at the end of an elegant high street leading towards the sea, there is firstly the moat, and then the fortified gatehouse that leads into the priory proper situated on a rocky promontory dominating the entry to the Tyne estuary, with cliffs on three sides, one of which is now giving problems because of instability in the Magnesian Limestone. Here is a splendid variety of views, along the sandy bay towards Whitley Bay or across the Tyne to South Shields, inland along the shipping quays and fish docks of the Tyne, but best of all in the late afternoon when the big ships are leaving for Oslo and Bergen, the peaceable link with the Scandinavian lands that was once so bloody when the priory was ravaged at least three times in the ninth century by Danish invaders. Enough remains of the Norman church and the monastic foundations to make the site well worthy of a visit, quite apart from the superb setting.

Many of the churches north of the Tyne bear Romanesque features, some incorporating Roman work directly into their fabric such as the arch in Corbridge linking nave to tower, the Roman columns in the nave at Chollerton, probably from nearby Chesters, and a Roman altar used as a cross-base in St Oswald's near the Wall at Heavenfield where the Northumbrian Christian armies defeated the pagan Mercians. Roman stonework is found in many churches, especially in the lower courses of towers, and Pevsner attributes many of these to the period of comparative peace following the subjugation of the Northumbrians to the Danes after A.D. 950. St Bartholomew's at Whittingham shows 'the best quoining work in the county'[1] with large rectangular stones alternately up-ended in the corner-work. At Bywell, in the quiet pastoral flats of the Tyne, is the unique feature of two early churches within a bow-shot of each other – St Andrews and St Peters – known locally as the 'white church' and the 'black church'. At this point on the Tyne, two Norman baronies met: Walter of Bolbek gave the advowson of St Andrews to the 'white' canons of Blanchland, while the Baliols granted that of St Peters to the 'black' monks of the Benedictines. The former has a Saxon tower, the latter a twelfth-century tower, but both are essentially of the thirteenth century, and the small, calm, shadowed interiors are typical of the atmosphere generated by the best northern churches. The township that once thrived alongside them, busy with the manufacture of woollens, is only recalled by early prints and the market cross that still stands alongside the meadow sloping to the river.

Another lovely tower is that of Bolam, now reached by a narrow curling lane that gives the church a sense of privacy and retreat. This church, too, was once the centre of a settlement of two hundred houses and a castle, with rights of market and fair. A great deal of renovation has been done recently to archways and roof but nothing has been done to spoil the sense of rightness that the church interior presents. The small windows in the tower throw light on to the font in the tower base and several of the columns have good decoration. Warkworth, in contrast, surprises by its sense of size and space, a fine Norman church, with its tower making the culmination of the main street running down from the Castle in one of the best small townscapes in Britain. The interior is remarkable for its ribbed vaulting in the chancel, with zig-zag decoration showing close architectural similarities with Durham.

Other Anglo-Saxon work can be found at Ovingham and Heddon-on-the-Wall, adding to the fine group that lie along this sheltered area of the Tyne, within reach of the Roman 'quarry' of the Wall. It is not easy to draw a temporal

[1] Pevsner and Richmond, *Northumberland* (Penguin, 1957).

line between the Anglo-Saxon work and the Norman churches: the styles merge. Examples of Norman work range from the rural calm of Old Bewick to the bustle of St Andrews in the heart of Newcastle, both preserving their Norman chancel arches and other early medieval workmanship.

In its setting and atmosphere of melancholy, one of the most extraordinary churches is at Thockrington, lying on the edge of the limestone moors, beyond the farm group, with a great buttress like a broken nose running the whole length from belfry to ground, giving the church the appearance of a blind face gazing over the moors towards the west and the raiding dales. St Aidan's church is set in a neglected churchyard, with the base of an old cross near the porch, and all around it the evidence of the village that was destroyed by the cholera in 1847. A Romanesque arch remains at the east end of the nave.

One of the oddest towers is that of St John at Edlingham on the moorland road to Alnwick. It looks as if it was finished prematurely but its strength and squareness are reminiscent of the fortified tower at Ancroft, which has as much right to be considered as a feature of military architecture as of ecclesiastical. But its major interest is in the rare Norman tunnel-vaulted porch. Equally interesting vaulting can be seen at Kirknewton where both the chancel and the south transept show this unusual building style. In fact the chancel has no perpendicular wall at all and makes a dramatic backcloth to the lovely and rare carving of the Adoration of the Magi, showing the three wise men with short beards and something like kilts. The date of this is uncertain and has been attributed to the twelfth century, but a remarkably similar composition appears, on a much smaller scale, on the Frank's casket, a seventh-century Northumbrian ivory carving now in the British Museum.

Not far from Kirknewton is the church of St Michael's at Ford with its bell-cote, with three apertures, taller and more elegant than that at Thockrington. Other fine bell-cotes are found at Elsdon, at Bothal and at St Mary's on Holy Island.

Impressive in its size and decoration is the south arcade of St Cuthbert's church at Norham, of fine Norman work, probably associated with the Bishops of Durham who built the adjacent castle, one of the cornerstones of early Border defence. Only a mile away, across the Tweed in Scotland, is Ladykirk church, erected in 1500 in gratitude for the rescue from drowning of James IV, who was to die only three years later on Flodden Field. It is one of the last entire examples of a pre-Reformation church in Scotland.

Early churches north of the Border are rarer than in Northumberland, though fragments remain at Smailholm, at Linton, St Mary's, Hawick, St Boswells and the western door of Maxton church. The Royal Commission report on Roxburgh says, 'the medieval parish churches that survived are neither numerous nor important'. Ecclesiastically, the Border glory rests in its ruined abbeys. But there are two small but fascinating Norman buildings close together near Duns in Berwickshire. At Bunkle by the existing church is a complete apse standing alone looking rather like an oratory in a Breton churchyard. It has been restored recently. Nearby in Edrom there is yet another Norman fragment, this time of the western part of the old church complete with decorative door.

Of the rural landscape that evolved from the time of the early Anglo-Saxon settlement to the new administration, an organization of firstly the Danish Conquest and then the northernmost borders of the Norman Conquest, several basic features still remain and underlie the present rural pattern. Firstly, there are the settlement sites themselves and the church buildings that in many cases were the central feature of those settlements or 'townships'. The fortified sites, such as castles, remain in abundance and need a chapter to themselves.[1] As the land associated with each township grew, the boundaries cut into the wasteland and met the pressures of other townships. Parish boundaries evolved and many of the present boundaries follow alignments set out over a thousand years ago.

But there are other less obvious and less distinct features that survive from the early human landscapes that link up with the pattern of the settlements themselves and the way in which they organized their agriculture, their arable fields, their common lands and the great forests that were preserved outside the cultivated land for the privileged minority of nobility and church. Much of the evidence derives from estate maps and documents of a much later time, at the end of the medieval period, from the sixteenth century and later, and it is only the assumption that many of the features recorded then had been in existence for many decades or even centuries before that can help unravel more secrets of the past. Such, for example, are the old 'riggs', the high-backed ridges that swing across many a parkland, meadow and golf-course today and give the grasslands a corrugated appearance when the sun is low or an extraordinary striped effect after a light flurry of snow.

A single car journey or a trip up the main line to St Abb's is enough to show that these high ridges in the fields are a very common feature, and the view from the air is even more convincing, for whole areas are covered with them. The riggs run under the later field boundaries, showing that they must be older

[1] See Chapter 5.

than the present field system. Writing in 1794 on Northumbrian agriculture, Culley and Bailey called these riggs 'old plough', and in different parts of the country a comparison of air photographs and early estate maps has shown that there may be a very close relationship between the riggs that still exist so widely in the region and the early form of strip cultivation in commonly-held open arable fields. Many present-day rights of way and footpaths still follow the old tracks along the head-riggs, the access route to individually-held arable strips. The land in the township of Chatton was reported in 1566 as being allotted 'rigg upon rigg as is the custom in every husband town'.[1] The 'husband towns' were the rural communities that worked the 'husbandlands'; for example, 'every husbandland a man if they be not too highly rented'.[2] A husbandland was that amount of ploughland needed to keep a man fully equipped for Border service, with horse and harness.

Detailed surveys of the townships of the Border carried out on behalf of the Tudor monarchy during the sixteenth century give details of the number of 'ploughlands' or 'husbandlands' in each township. Ridges were still being made even up to the eighteenth century for drainage, but such ridges are reasonably easy to distinguish, being straight and low-backed.

In many parts of the region where arable farming is dominant, new ploughing has obliterated the old ridges, but in pastoral areas and the hill fringes they remain in abundance, varying from five to ten yards across, usually with a reversed S-shape, the result of ploughing by ox-teams. A straight furrow was unknown until the agricultural improvers of the eighteenth century brought up ploughmen from Norfolk. The very high ridges suggest that they were the result of a long period of cultivation, and their association with the townships indicates that they were of Anglo-Saxon origin. Such old ploughing can be seen high up on the hill slopes of the Cheviots even at 1000 feet, where bracken and poor grasses now thrive. Climatic improvement, as in the tenth and thirteenth century, and land hunger may have 'pushed' the plough up the hills. Some of the steeper slopes in the Border hills show terraced features, marked on the O.S. maps as 'lynchets'. Such stepped hillsides in the south country have been dated to pre-Roman periods, but on the Borders no such claim can be made. Above Hethpool and above Clifton in the Upper Bowmont the lynchets appear in conjunction with rigg and furrow which is certainly medieval. It seems that lynchets (which are much more widespread than the maps suggest and usually face south) are the furthermost extension of medieval plough to otherwise un-

[1] County History.
[2] Calendar of Border Papers.

productive hill slopes. Again the Royal Commission of Ancient Monuments on Roxburgh (where more than seventy-nine areas of lynchets have been recorded) concludes that 'their dates – in view of the facts at present known – are probably to be found in the long span of the Middle Ages'.[1] One of the incentives to give them greater antiquity is that they often occur near Celtic hill forts and encampments, but there is no archaeological proof so far that they have any connection.

By mapping the riggs and even the lynchets (they occur together, for example, in the old township of Mow, south of Morebattle) we may get some idea of the medieval field systems. The frequent occurrence of groups of names such as Eastfield and Westfield hints at the pre-existence of at least two township fields, and the two-field system is recorded in at least four surveys from the sixteenth and seventeenth centuries in Northumberland. But the field systems show great complexity. A recent study[2] of 115 late-medieval surveys shows the three-field system to be dominant, at least thirty-six townships using this method, whilst ten townships showed four-field systems, and others showed five and six fields in very complex arrangements. The variations would naturally relate to the type of terrain, townships on the Cheviot fringes having a quite different problem of land organization from those on the broad boulder-clay plains of the east coast. This study suggests that 'almost 90% of the arable was both common and open and was located in large fields which were greatly subdivided into small elongated parcels'. These small elongated parcels may link up once more with the riggs discussed earlier.

Some of the surveys refer to 'infields' or 'ingrounds', which in some cases may be a reference to a system then prevalent in Scotland, the infield-outfield system by which certain lands near the township, i.e. the infield, was improved with all the available manure and thereby made fertile enough to support a crop rotation, whilst marginal land, the outfield, was only brought into cultivation periodically and then left to recover its fertility. The infield was divided into strips separated by baulks, subject to reallocation on an annual basis and more rarely on a biennial and even triennial basis. This system of reallocation was known as 'run-rig'. The main crops grown were bere or bigg (an early type of barley, the name of which is still used in the Bigg Market in Newcastle upon Tyne), especially on the infield, and oats on the outfield. This system continued well into the seventeenth century, until the 1695 laws permitted the division of run-rig land into enclosed blocks.

[1] See also R. Eckford, 'Terrace Groups of Southern Scotland', *Hawick Archaeological Society Proceedings*, 1931.
[2] R. A. Butlin, 'Northumbrian Field Systems', *Agricultural History Review*, Vol. 12, 1964.

Another aspect of medieval farming that has made its mark on the landscape was the occasional use of the hill pastures for summer grazing, involving the large-scale movements of livestock and people to temporary settlements, the 'shiels', in the summer months. An account written in 1542 said the people of the townships near the hills 'will about the beginning of April take the most part of their cattle and go with them up into such high lands and waste grounds towards the border of Scotland and there build them lodges and sheales and remain still with their cattle in such hopes and valleys where they can find any pasture for them until the month of August'.[1] They called this transhumant pattern 'soming' or 'summering' or 'shieling'.

More details of this movement are gleaned from a court case in Redesdale in the 1630s when the men 'divide up their lowlands by the land itself and they do not divide up the lands of their highlands but only the rents and eat the lands in common'. This form of 'eating the land in common' is still the basis of 'stint' grazing used in unenclosed highland commons which remains only on the moorland plateaux around Allendale and Hexham, though it is still common in the Lake District. The Redesdale folk went up to their summerings to the west of Redesdale after the bere was sown. The Tynedale men had grazing on the south side of the Coquet, whilst the upland-grazing in the Kidlandlee area was in the hands of the monks from Newminster Abbey. This upland grazing on the fringes of the old Cheviot Forest was of 'much brushwood and some oak, ground overgrown with ling [heather] and some with moss', according to Leland. His account also gives us some indication of the reason why no rural architecture of the period exists today; unlike the stone churches and castles, the ordinary cottages were shaky structures, for the woodlands of the hills 'serveth much for the building of such small houses as be used and inhabited by husbandmen in those parts'. A report from the Scottish side confirms this type of building: 'if the English do burn our houses what consequence is it to us? We can rebuild them cheaply enough for we have only to require three days to do so, provided we have five or six poles and boughs to cover them'.[2] These structures may have had some resemblance to the 'black houses' that may be seen, usually in a ruinous condition, in the north and western coasts of Scotland today. Our knowledge of 'shielings' has been increased by a recent survey carried out by the Royal Commission on Ancient Monuments[3] which has recorded the physical

[1] Calender of Border Papers: Bowes & Elleker.
[2] J. Borland, *Border Raids and Reivers*.
[3] R.C.A.M. (England), *Shielings and Bastles* (H.M.S.O., 1970).

evidence of no less than fifty-eight sites in the Liberty of Tynedale alone, including a group near the Roman Wall in the vicinity of Greenlee Lough. The management of summer pastures has 'left a variety of remains, huts, cottages, and houses,
including the occasional pele tower and bastle house,[1] in various stages of ruin,
and the ruined enclosures of fields, gardens, yards, folds and stack stands, and
traces of cultivation'. The shielings were still in general use into the seventeenth
century and, in some isolated places, survived until the 'improvements' in farming in the eighteenth century.[2]

The names of these upland grazing areas can still be identified in the names
of present-day farms. For example, the sale of part of the Cheviot Forest to
Sir Ralph Grey in 1611 mentions the 'shiels, granges or grounds commonly
known by the names of Twishope, Trowupp, Fleeup, Shorthope, Hethpole,
Loftwyere, Losthill, Swickside, Penleswyers . . . the Harrowbog, Platewell,
Faucett, Roughside'.[3] Several of these names can be traced today up the College
Valley south of Kirknewton. Settled upland sheep-holdings now occupy the
grounds which were once summer grazing areas linked with lowland townships.


Hardly any of the present buildings in the 'townships' or present-day villages
date from the medieval period, except for churches and castles – the stone
buildings. It is possible that the actual shapes of the settlements recall the earlier
days, but this is a region in which armies and raiding bands have been active
for at least three hundred years where townships have been laid waste time and
time again, and where many of the border villages were effectively rebuilt in the
seventeenth and eighteenth centuries. Old estate plans of villages often show a
quite different picture from that of today.

There are many village greens in the region and, though some of them are of
quite recent origin, especially north of the Tweed, others may be related to
early defensive needs, especially in the use of the green as a defensive stockade
for livestock. There is a particularly fine group of village greens in the south of
Northumberland at Kirkwhelpington, Matfen, Stamfordham, Kirkheaton, Heugh
and Wall (where raiding was slightly less persistent than the Border country
proper). The greens tend to be rectangular in shape, longer on the east–west
axis, and in one of them at least, a farmer still retains the title of 'Guardian of

[1] See Chapter 5.
[2] See Chapter 6.
[3] County History.

the Green'. The full extent of some greens is obscured by later cottages built on them; traditionally known as squatters' cottages, they resulted from someone squatting on the land who, having no objection raised in twelve years, was able to establish rights on that common land. Many of these central greens are common land with established rights for those with frontages upon them. A recent survey of common land comments that 'the Roman Wall marks approximately the northern limit of common land in Britain if one excepts the village green and coastal sand-dune commons of the Northumberland coast'.[1] The forty such village common greens add up to about fifty-four acres in all, giving an average size of just over one acre. One of the largest of the greens is that of Elsdon, which covers over seven acres, a broad, sprawling green roughly the shape of a spindle with the church sited on the green and buildings grouped irregularly round the perimeter. But Elsdon was once the territorial capital of Redesdale and the green may reflect the Norman organization of the time. The strict pattern of greens such as those of Wall and Kirkheaton suggests organization, either by mutual cooperation or by imposition from above – e.g. the Norman overlord.

Some fine greens still survive along the Tweed, especially at the two Yetholms – Kirk Yetholm and Town Yetholm (the 'gate' towns). This twinning of names occurs quite frequently on the Borders – Kirknewton – West Newton, Kirk Harle – West Harle – and makes an interesting link with the division of Scottish settlements into 'kirktouns' and 'ferm-touns'. Other good examples of the triangular-shaped green exist at Norham, and at Ancrum, both complete with market crosses, whilst smaller examples survive at Bowden and Maxton. A shopkeeper at Ancrum told me that she held common rights on the green 'according to my feus'. Some very regular rectangular greens are found in Berwickshire, though at Swinton and Gavinton these may be related to planning at a much later period.[2] Similar types are found in Roxburghshire at Denholm and Midlem. Many of the village greens are associated, on the Scottish side, with settlements that once bore 'burgh' status, and held market rights.[3]

A deterioration of climate that set in during the early fourteenth century, leading to a series of poor harvests, led to the desertion of some marginal settlements.[4] Sometimes, townships were deserted through monastic overlords want-

---

[1] Hoskins and Stamp, *Common Lands of England and Wales* (Collins).
[2] See Chapter 6.
[3] See Chapter 7.
[4] H. H. Lamb, 'Britain's Changing Climate', *Geographical Journal*, December 1967.

9a. Melrose Abbey, founded by David I of Scotland in 1136, seen from the north-west with Eildon Hill North in the background.

9d. Norman west door of Lindisfarne Priory.

9b and c. Anglian carving, c. A.D. 700, on St Boisil's tomb, Jedburgh Abbey museum.

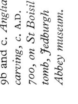

10a. *Village green at Ancrum with sixteenth-century market cross.*

10b. *Etal: typical estate village with rare thatched roofs; gatehouse of ruined fourteenth-century castle in the background.*

10c. *Eighteenth-century houses grouped round the green at Stamfordham with cross and lock-up on the green; thirteenth-century church overlooking the fen land.*

ing to establish new modes of farming, especially related to the introduction of sheep. For the monastic establishment and to some extent the royal houses were the early propagators of agricultural 'improvement'. 'Under David I, who founded monasteries and agricultural establishments, there was a period of plenty and landlords were stimulated by his example,'[1] with attention both to crop and livestock husbandry. Mills were established and the first dairy recorded was at Melrose.

Land was cultivated often by the monks themselves from outlying granges (the name still exists in many place names, such as Horton Grange, once attached to Newminster Abbey) and it may be contemporary with this movement that some of the fine medieval farm buildings still surviving in Allendale were established, particularly that group lying to the west of Allendale Town with names like Burnlaw, Westside and, most significant, Monk. This area was under the control of Hexham Abbey, and farms were established in the wild by 'the enclosure and clearance of rough land by individuals who were accepted as manorial tenants by the Abbey, mainly on copyhold tenure'.[2] By the sixteenth century, 150 farms had been established, many of which can still be identified. In many deserted buildings, such as Steel and Ninedarg (an interesting name suggesting nine-days' labour), fine old medieval doorways can still be found. These farm buildings have a rather less military appearance than those north of the Tyne.

Further details of monastic activities can be obtained from the many legal wrangles between monastery and monastery, or monastery and crown, in defence of what they regarded as their privileges. The old Roman Dere Street, for example, running along the ridge to the west of Lauderdale, linking Melrose with Soutra, was the boundary between estates granted to Melrose (to the west) and Dryburgh (to the east). Forest grazing rights were hedged about with restrictions. Malcolm IV's grant to Melrose of permission for a 'house' for sheep and cows in the Threepwood area was followed by further permission to house sixty cows. Then they were granted the right to a house for 120 cows and a hay-shed at Whitelee in the Gala. The Earl of Dunbar granted pasture rights to Dryburgh for 500 sheep and 140 oxen but no 'lodges' could be built nor land ploughed. 'Nor shall the cattle of the aforesaid earl or he himself or his house or men go across the aforesaid road and the cattle of the aforesaid earl shall return each

---

[1] A. Meiklejohn's Essay on Agriculture in *Scientific Survey of S.E. Scotland* (British Association, 1951).
[2] R. Clark, 'Handbook on Catton', Northumberland Education Authority.

D

night to the villa of Hercheldune, unless storm or inundation should prevent.'[1] The monks' cattle were to have 'free entrance to the pasture from their nearest cow or sheep house'. Such temporary 'lodges' and 'shiels' became the established farms of a later period.

This active movement of the agricultural frontier in the 'wild' led to the progressive diminution of the ancient hunting forests, some of which were preserved in the early deer parks. Leland, in his famous survey, wrote, 'as I heare say be no Forests [in Northumberland] except Chivet Hills and there is a greate plenty of Redd Dere and Roo Bukk'. But this was certainly not a full survey, for Chillingham was established in the thirteenth century and in its enclosure was preserved not only deer but the herd of wild white cattle which are still such a feature of the place. In fact, several ancient parks are recorded in Saxton's Survey, and Speed's map of 1610 shows at least five. The principal ones were at Hulne and Cawledge (Callie), both connected with the Earls of Northumberland at Alnwick. They held nearly 1400 deer between them.[2] The former park still remains in part, though the old Callie park is identifiable only by the names of farms in the area – Cawledge, East Park, Middle Park and the West Park farm on the A1. Hulne Park was disparked but restored in part in 1829. Acklington Park, associated with Warkworth Castle, is also identifiable by farm names – High Park, Low Park and Acklington Park Farm. Others existed at Widdrington, Cockley Towers, Bothal and Mitford and, one of the biggest, at Dilston, ancient seat of the Radcliffes, south of the Tyne.

Johan Blaeu's map of Teviotdale shows three early emparkments along the Slitrigg south of Hawick, another near Ancrum and Drygrange north of Old Melrose. Others existed at the Hirsel in Berwickshire, at Eccles, two at Polwarth, one at Coldingham and six along the Whiteadder. Several are associated with old monastic establishments, as at Drygrange, Coldingham, Eccles and Coldstream.

Such was the rural landscape of the Borders, village and field, church and abbey, forest and deer park, that was to be ravaged by more than three hundred years

---

[1] Quoted by Hardie, *The Roads of Medieval Lauderdale* (1942).
[2] E. Shirley, *Deer and Deer Parks* (1867).

of warfare along the political frontier that divided two nations, Scotland and England; two nations that had developed from the earlier kingdoms of Anglo-Saxon and Scot. To that frontier and that warfare we shall now turn our attention.

Saxon quoin work. St Bartholomew's. Whittingham.

99

# 5

## The evolution of the Border

And he has burn'd the dales of Tyne,
  And part of Bambrough shire;
And three good towers on Roxburgh fells,
  He left them all on fire.

*(The Battle of Otterbourne)*

With the great hump of the Cheviot to the east, the intrepid, but, no doubt, weary walker of the Pennine long-distance walkway, taking a breather by Auchope Cairn, has the final satisfaction of knowing that the last eight miles to his ultimate destination at Yetholm are nearly all downhill; he can enjoy following the undefined track as it wanders along the line of the marcher dyke, the Border fence, heading north and west between the two countries, the hill country largely lying in England and the deep burns feeding down into the Bowmont from Black Hagg and the Schil. Here is the full pleasure of walking, especially in April when the bracken is yet to cover the fells with its wet greenery and the brisk dry winds follow down from Cheviot. The low sun picks out all the history of man's occupation in ancient farms, enclosures and encampments like an ever-changing map. Down past Red Cribs and White Swire, the ancient passes lead through the hills beloved of 'mosstroopers', the early raiders seeking the quiet ways, along Steer Rig and Whitelaw, past the two Stob stones and ancient tumuli, dropping into Halterburn where the Scots once diverted the river in order to lay claim to the pastures on the river 'haughs'. They were even accused of ploughing 'English ground' during the sixteenth century, ploughlands belonging to the English townships that they had devastated. Much of the ground here was still marked as 'disputed ground' as late as Armstrong's map of 1769, a device carried over into early-nineteenth-century maps. The grassy slopes on the east side of Halterburn were grazed by the Faa gypsies centred on Yetholm, 'the gate town'.

Another area of disputed ground remained at the northern end of the Border line where it met the Tweed at Carham, following the mouth of Redden Burn. Much of what is now Wark Common lying to the east of the Border was claimed by the Scots. Two other areas marked as 'disputed ground' lay on either side of the Border crossing at Deadwater in Upper Tynedale.

The nascent kingdom of the Scots, emerging in the Forth lowlands under the leadership of Kenneth Macalpin, laid claim in the ninth century to all the land between the Forth and the Tweed. This, according to James Logan Mack, whose study of 'The Border Line', written in 1926, is the finest work on the subject, was the first indication of the river Tweed as the 'natural frontier' to which the Scots aspired. The claim took another 150 years to become reality with the defeat of the Earldom of Northumbria by the Scots armies under Malcolm II at Carham in 1018, which effectively confirmed the eastern section of the Border,[1] apart from the precarious future of Berwick-upon-Tweed and the territories of its 'liberty' which were to change hands fourteen times in the next four hundred years.

The Norman Conquest of the south of England introduced a new, organized military aristocracy and, after laying waste much of the northern marches, the Norman barons and bishops carved out large estates or baronies from the frontier zone and brought a new disciplined force against the expansionist Scots. Malcolm III invaded northern England five times during the late eleventh century, but it was the great king David I, founder of many Border burghs and abbeys, who gained the Earldom of Northumberland for his son and for a while established the river Tees as the southernmost limit of Scottish power, during the reign of Stephen. By 1157, under Henry II, the earldom was restored to the English crown and William II's futile claim, supported by invasion in 1174, fizzled out in his capture at Alnwick, from which time the Tweed became the undisputed frontier, with Northumberland as the northernmost outpost of the English crown.

The Tweed is really no great barrier for much of the year, for at low water it is easily fordable in many places and meetings sometimes took place at mid-stream on gravel banks. Major fortified sites had to be established to protect it, at Berwick-upon-Tweed, at Norham and at Wark. Nevertheless, it was less liable to dispute than the hill frontier that ran from the Tweed at Carham to the western limit of the Middle March (the middle section of the frontier, which was divided into three 'marches') at Kershopefoot, in Liddesdale, the westernmost

[1] G. W. S. Barrow, 'The Anglo-Scottish Border', *Northern History*, Vol. II, 1966 (School of History, Leeds University).

Fast

✿ Walled Towns
⚔ Castles

Berwick-upon-Tweed

Norham

Lindisfarne

Heaton
Wark
Etal
Ford
Bamburgh

Roxburgh

Wooler
Cheviot
Chillingham
Dunstan-
burgh

Alnwick

Edlingham
Warkworth

Harbottle

Hermitage

Tarset
Dally
Morpeth

Mitford
Belsay

Wark
Chipchase
Thirlwall
Haughton
Tynemouth

Blenkinsopp
Langley
Aydon
Featherstone
Prudhoe
Newcastle

**Fortified Towers:**

| | |
|---|---|
| 1 Cockburnspath | 24 Langshaw |
| 2 Houndwood | 25 Hillslap |
| 3 Billie | 26 Darnick |
| 4 Bunkle | 27 Fatlips |
| 5 Mordington | 28 Lanton |
| 6 Edington | 29 Timpendean |
| 7 Hutton | 30 Cessford |
| 8 Nisbet | 31 Morebattle |
| 9 Bite-about (near Fogo) | 32 Whitton |
| 10 Evelaw | 33 Queen Mary's House, Jedburgh |
| 11 Wedderlie | 34 Bedrule |
| 12 Cranshaws | 35 Fulton |
| 13 Carfrae | 36 Pele-house |
| 14 Thirlestane | 37 " |
| 15 Whitslaid | 38 " |
| 16 Corsbie | 39 " |
| 17 Greenknowe, (near Gordon) | 40 Southdean |
| 18 Mellerstain | 41 Branxholme |
| 19 Smailholm | 42 Larriston |
| 20 Bemersyde | 43 Hartsgarth |
| 21 Cowdenknowes | 44 Mangerton |
| 22 Rhymer's Tower (Earlston) | 45 Ancroft |
| 23 Colmslie | 46 Duddo |

| | |
|---|---|
| 47 Barmoor | 77 Bothal |
| 48 Lowick | 78 Cambo |
| 49 Kyloe | 79 Wallington |
| 50 Fenton | 80 Elsdon |
| 51 Doddington | 81 Otterburn |
| 52 Chatton | 82 Hole |
| 53 Howtel | 83 Simonburn |
| 54 Lanton | 84 Swinburn |
| 55 Hethpool | 85 Cocklaw |
| 56 Akeld | 86 Willimoteswick |
| 57 Lilburn | 87 Staward |
| 58 Ilderton | 88 Hexham Moot Hall & 'Prison' |
| 59 Preston | 89 Corbridge |
| 60 Beadnell | 90 Halton |
| 61 Embleton | 91 Welton Hall |
| 62 Craster | 92 Bywell |
| 63 Crawley | 93 Fenwick |
| 64 Whittingham | 94 Ponteland |
| 65 Lemmington | 95 Burradon |
| 66 Shilbottle | 96 Ferniehurst |
| 67 Alnham | 97 Bellingham |
| 68 Biddlestone | 98 Pele-house |
| 69 Clennel | 99 Pele-house |
| 70 Hepple | 100 Ninebanks |
| 71 Tosson | 101 Dilston |
| 72 Whitton | 102 Hepburn |
| 73 Longhorsley | 103 Hefferlaw |
| 74 Widdrington | 104 Littledean |
| 75 Cresswell | 105 West Beechfield  106 Shortflatt |
| 76 Cockle Park | |

**Map 6**  *Castles and fortified towers in the Frontier Zone.*

point of present-day Roxburghshire. And of that hill frontier no area was so vulnerable as the comparatively low ground that lay to the south of the Tweed between Carham and Whitelaw, the drumlin-country between the Tweed and the Bowmont giving an east–west grain to the landscape with heights seldom over five hundred feet, not ideal for a border to be organized with a basic north–south orientation. When you cross the Tweed at Coldstream, you can have the sense of passing a real frontier, as you do again when stopping the car at Carter Bar to gaze at the two quite differing landscapes lying to north and south of the pass. But travelling on the B6352 road that follows the Bowmont from Yetholm to Mindrum gives no such visual sensation. The signpost to Scotland or England comes as a surprise.

From Whitelaw south to the Cheviot and thence west to the head of Redesdale, the Border line follows the watershed, generally from summit to summit, dividing the waters that flow north and south. On Kieldermoor the Border lies to the south of the summits of Carlin Tooth and Hartshorne Pike which lie entirely in Scotland. From here westwards until it follows the Kershope Burn, the Border has no clearly defined topographical basis – one of the reasons, no doubt, why it remained 'disputed ground'. But even the summits of the Cheviot Hills are rounded and, in most cases, merely great flat humps of hills that lack a well-defined peak. The difficulties that have been encountered in high mountain ranges, such as the Himalayas and the Andes, in establishing acceptable political frontiers were not dissimilar to those that caused contention on the Scottish Border.

By 1222, Henry III commanded the Sheriff of Northumberland, the Bishop of Durham and other 'discreet knights to proceed to the marches between England and Scotland, at Whitelaw, and there by their view and advice, settle the said marches as they used to be in the time of King John and his predecessors'. Later in the century, in 1291, another English king, in succession to the Scottish throne, Edward I, gave his support to John Balliol, and initiated a further three hundred years of even more bloody and contentious raid and counter-raid across the Borders, culminating in Flodden Field.

Flodden and its destructive aftermath, with the centralized power of the Tudors confronting the Scottish Crown, led to even more active surveys of the Border, and the names mentioned in these surveys (most of them available in the Calendar of Border Papers) are more familiar than those of the earlier reports and more easily identified with place names on present-day maps.

The most important and complete surveys of the Border were carried out in astonishing detail by Sir Robert Bowes and Sir Raufe Elleker for Henry VIII in 1542 and again in 1550, when even individual fields were mentioned. The Border on both sides was divided into two marches – the East March and the Middle March – the third, the West March, lying on the Cumberland border outside the region covered by this book. On the Scots side, the East March was much the same area as that covered by present-day Berwickshire, and the Middle March was almost the same as Roxburghshire, although Liddesdale, the worst of all the raiding areas, was often under special control of the Keeper of Liddesdale, based at the castle of Hermitage.

On the English side, the East March ran from the Liberty of Berwick-upon-Tweed along the Tweed and south into the Cheviot Hills to what is always referred to as 'the hanging stone', a massive outcrop of rock to the south-west of the Cheviot summit (which is entirely in England). There began the Middle March which extended up and down the hills as far as Kershopefoot in Liddesdale.

> First beginning at the Hanging Stone which is the very uttermost part of the said middle marches towards the east the said border stretcheth and goeth westward to the Butt Road and from thence to Hexpathgate head and so still west to the Windy Gyle, and from thence to the Black Brae. And so westward something inclining toward the south by Gugges Grave to Hindmars field and from thence to Brown Hart Law and so to Gamelspath. From Gamelspath to the Almodes roads and so to the head of Spithope and from thence to Phillip's Cross and so to Ramshopehead and by the Black Roads to the head of the water of Rede.

Many of the points of identification were the Border 'gates' or crossings, which were also the meeting-points for knights responsible for the maintenance of Border peace, often at the 'head' of burns that rose near the watershed. These 'gates' are still marked by Border paths that were used more recently for cattle-droving and have been in use since antiquity; they make magnificent walking routes today. The present edition of the One-Inch Ordnance Survey still marks Butt Roads, Windy Gyle, Black Brae, Brown Hart Law and Gamel's Path (which is another name for the Roman 'Dere Street' crossing the border at Coquet Head). Phillip's Cross is marked too, two miles above Catscleugh Reservoir, as is the Reediswyre, the Carter, the Wheel Causey and Kershopehead, all of which are mentioned in the 1542 report.

This Border zone was, to some extent, isolated from the central sources of royal power, in the English case being more than 350 miles from London, and even in the Scottish case being isolated by a rim of high hills from Edinburgh, linked by routes such as Soutra (across the Lammermuirs) and the Fala gap, which could be very difficult in winter. The defence of the Border, therefore, depended on the local nobility and their retainers and the custom was established of royal appointment of one of the leading Border lords as Warden of the Marches, to maintain the fragile peace of the Borderland, to negotiate for justice and the redress of grievances, to prevent raids from his own side yet to organize retaliation when necessary.

On the Scots side, the social pattern was based on feudal tenure and kinship groups, the same names occurring time and time again throughout contemporary records. The position of the Wardens became almost a family affair, although they were royal appointments: the Humes of Cowdenknowes, of Manderstone and Wedderburn dominated the wardenship of the East March, whilst the Kerrs of Cessford and Douglas of Cavers were the main guardians of the Middle March. At the west, the clans owed allegiance to the head of the 'family' in the defence of their part of the Border; isolated by hills, bad roads and constant danger, they were a law unto themselves. At the worst, they degenerated into bands of brigands feared by English and Scots alike, led by such men, made famous or infamous in ballads, as Jock-o'-the-Side and David the Lady. Their power may be judged by the promises made by the notorious Johnny Armstrong, whose activities at last attracted the wrath of his own king.

> Grant me my life, my liege, my king
> and a bonny gift I'll gie to thee . . .

which included twenty-four milk-white steeds, much Irish gold, twenty-four ganging mills and all the rents between Langholm and Newcastle town. Perhaps he exaggerated in a vain attempt to save his life, but he was powerful enough to be a thorn in the flesh of both nations.

Inter-clan feuds were as frequent as antagonism across the frontier and were one of the main sources of concern to the central royal powers. The enmity of the Kerrs of Cessford and the Scotts of Buccleugh was matched by the hatred of the Carrs of Etal for the Herons of Ford, which divided the whole of north Northumberland into warring camps and led to an ambush in which the Mayor of Berwick and his treasurer were slain. 'In these parts almost no person rideth unarmed, but as surely upon his guard as if he rode against the enemy of Scotland.'

Some of the most famous skirmishes became identified in popular accounts with the clan leaders. The Battle of Otterburn, for example, which took place near the banks of the North Tyne in 1388, became a heroic encounter between Hotspur and Douglas.

> It fell about the Lammas tide
> When the muir-men win their hay,
> The doughty Earl of Douglas rode
> Into England to catch a prey.

His two thousand or so horsemen, spearmen, and archers swept south along the Tyne into County Durham, laying waste the land, and eventually, before the wall of Newcastle, Douglas met Henry Percy in single combat, and won. But before he could return across the Border, the private armies met again, at nightfall at Otterburn. Before it ended, Hotspur had gained his revenge.

> This deed was done at Otterbourne,
> About the breaking of the day;
> Earl Douglas was buried at the braken bush,
> And the Percy led captive away.

The panoply of chivalry cloaked ruthless conflict. Royal armies marched along the coastal routes or along the so-called Kings' Highway, which skirted the eastern flanks of the Cheviot Hills, the line of the present A697 from Coldstream to Wooler, and it was along this route that most of the great battles of the Border Wars took place, including the most celebrated of them all, the Battle of Flodden Field.

It was on a wet September day in 1513, on the ninth by the new calendar, that the Scottish army under the command of their forty-year-old king, James IV, left its camp burning on Flodden Edge and moved down the muddy slopes northwards towards the homeland across the Tweed. In the dull afternoon, Lord Home and his Borderers came upon a group of English soldiers struggling through the marshy ground between the hillocks around Branxton, dispersed them after a brief encounter, and moved on to Coldstream. By dusk, which fell early, the main body of the Scottish army was engaged in one of the greatest battles ever to take place on English soil. The tired armies under the Earl of Surrey, perhaps twenty thousand in number, had been marching since breaking camp at Barmoor at 4 am, crossing the Till to the north (probably by Twizel Bridge which still stands) and approaching the Scots from an unexpected direction.[1]

[1] The facts of this battle are still in dispute but there are interesting accounts in Elliot's, *The Battle of Flodden* (1911); W. M. Mackenzie's *The Secret of Flodden* (1931); and especially in Henry Weber's *Battle of Floddon Field* (1808).

During the preliminary cannonades, the Scottish guns, with pieces like Mons Meg (still to be seen in Edinburgh Castle), reputedly the best in Europe, proved ineffective and the master-gunner was slain.

The English fought in their stockinged feet, the better to advance over the slippery slopes, while the Scots formed a phalanx armed with eight-yard pikes. In the close combat that followed, the English 'bills', the more flexible weapon, 'did hew and cut them down'. The Scottish king dismounted and fought on foot 'as a mean soldier' with sword and dagger. But all went one way and by the next dawn the remnants of the Scottish army had left the field to the English victors. Lord Dacre, long inured to Border campaigns, went through the corpses and recognized the broken body of the King of the Scots, which was then taken to Berwick and finally to Shene in Surrey by command of Henry VIII.

The campaign which had begun so gloriously in Edinburgh in August, with about two hundred thousand men laying waste the English Borders on behalf of the French Crown, foundered in the mud of Branxton Moor with the death of a king, an archbishop, and the flower of Scottish chivalry. The Merse and Teviotdale lay open to the English avengers and the Border burghs mustered their young men for a desperate defence. But both the Scottish and English camps had been plundered by the Borderers on both sides, for whom this had been just one more round in the perpetual brutality that had been part of their lives since time out of mind.

In the hindsight of four and a half centuries, Flodden was the culmination of the Border conflict that had festered and erupted for five centuries before. But to contemporaries, it heralded a century of even bloodier conflict, the destruction of the great abbeys, the periodic devastation of village, farm and crop, the proliferation of defensive towers, all of which have left their marks on the present landscape.

It was the quiet, difficult ways through the hills that were favoured by the Borderers themselves, the mosstroopers, small bands of raiders seeking revenge, cattle, sheep, horses to drive on the hoof, crops to burn, timber to steal and any 'insight'[1] gear worth the taking. The nature of these raids is brought out in the terse sentences of reports from a Warden, Sir Robert Cary:

In Hethpool in daylight by the Davisons, Yonges and Burns of 40 kyen and oxen and hurting Thomas and Peter Storey in peril of their lives. Another there by daylight by the Kerrs, Yonges and Taits of 46 head of neate, shooting

[1] Literally, anything in sight.

John Gray with a piece in peril of death and hurting one of the Brewhouses following and taking his horse.

The Wardens of the Marches attempted to counter the raiding bands by organizing all the townships to keep nightly watch on the 'passages' across the Border, supervised by 'setters and searchers' to make sure the watches were maintained. At least they could raise the alarm if not prevent raids. The constant skirmishing led to the gradual evolution of a code of conduct, the Leges Marchiarum, the Border Laws, the enforcement of which lay in the hands of the Wardens. They are extremely complex, but perhaps the most striking was the law of the Hot Trod by which the victims of theft were allowed 'to follow their lawful trod with hue and cry, with hound and horn and a burning peat on the lances end' to regain their property. The guilty person could seek sanctuary in the first church he came upon by ringing the bells, or he could avoid conflict by driving the stolen livestock to the midstream of the Tweed or other appointed places. The sale of horses across the Border was forbidden. So was marriage between Scots and English unless with the consent of both wardens, which was rarely given. Not the least important item was the establishment of days of truce during which grievances could be aired and the laws administered by a meeting of the Wardens and a jury of twelve – six Scots and six English. These meetings usually took place at the 'gates' or passes mentioned earlier in this chapter, and the occasions were not always peaceful. Russell's Cairn is named after Lord Russell who was killed by his father-in-law's side, Sir John Forster of Bamburgh, then Warden of the Middle March.

The reports of the Warden of the East March, Sir Robert Cary, quoted above on the 'slaughters, stouthes and reafes' committed within his wardenry by the Scots, not only give an indication of the types of livestock upon which the farming communities depended but also on the importance of the fortified dwelling house or tower. Two of the accounts suggest that the livestock were taken after 'breaking' the tower or smashing its wooden door in; in other words, the livestock were kept in the base of the tower for safety. Safety on the Border depended not only on a weapon to hand and the support of the kinship group and the power of the Warden but on the construction of strongholds. One of the dominant features of the human landscape of the eastern Borders even today is the existence of an extraordinary variety and number of fortified strongholds, from the major stone castles of Norman barons and bishops such as Norham and Alnwick and later royal castles on the grand scale such as Bamburgh and

Lindisfarne to the fortified manor houses that grew especially out of the Scottish war of independence under Bruce and Wallace in the early part of the fourteenth century.

Castle-building began in earnest with the assertion of Norman power in the northern counties and its confrontation with the Kingdom of the Scots to the north, which by the eleventh century encompassed the whole of Strathclyde and Galloway as well as the main centre of power in the Lothians. Yet no distinctively Norman military structures exist north of the Cheviots. Of the great castle of Roxburgh only earthworks remain; of Jedburgh Castle, only the name remains; of Liddel Castle, only earthworks from the twelfth century. The reasons for the paucity of early military structures may be hinted at by a report by Lord Dacre during one of his many punitive expeditions against the Scots after the defeat of Flodden, when he wrote that 'little or nothing is left upon the frontiers of Scotland without it be parts of old houses, whereof the thatch and coverings are taken away by reason whereof they cannot be burnt'. In such raids, some of the main targets were the major strongholds, which were attacked time and time again. Indeed, the castle at Jedburgh was destroyed by the Scots themselves in 1409 so as to give less cause for English attacks. It was a source of weakness rather than strength, often occupied by the enemy. In 1528, the King and Council of Scotland insisted 'that any man intending to erect any strength or fortalice upon the Borders near to England was to desist until King and Council decided whether it would cause trouble between the nations'.

Of the early motte-and-bailey 'castles', probably of timber construction initially, which numbered between eleven and twenty on the Northumbrian side, the best examples extant in terms of the outlines of the earthworks are at Elsdon, Alnwick, Harbottle, Mitford, Morpeth, Wark-on-Tweed, Wark-on-Tyne and Warkworth. Some of these have been covered by later structures, but Elsdon and Wark-on-Tyne are comparatively unaffected. Wark-on-Tweed and Harbottle have fragmentary remnants of stonework, melancholy ruins of once-great castles that dominated the Border crossing of the Tweed and of Coquetdale respectively. Harbottle was the keystone of the Middle March, frequent home of the Warden of that military zone, now hardly noticed by the traveller passing through the small village. Wark-on-Tweed was the reputed origin of the Order of the Garter during the famous occasion when Edward III picked up a lady's garter during a ball. The castle was finally destroyed after the Union of the Crowns but still commands a magnificent view over the broad sweep of the Tweed and the small islands in midstream, situated on an isolated hump of glacial sands and boulders.

Mitford retains the shell of a fine thirteenth-century keep on its Norman foundations, another picturesque aspect of this delightful village on the Wansbeck, home of the Lords of Redesdale. What remains of Morpeth Castle is now a private residence. Alnwick and Warkworth both have their original Norman layout obscured by later developments, and both offer superb examples of fairly complete fortifications, that of Warkworth, now under the Department of the Environment, being much favoured by film work, with its unique flanking towers, and superb setting at the head of an almost complete medieval town, set in a meander of the river Coquet, a coastal outpost of the Percy family, the Earls of Northumberland. Pevsner describes this as 'one of the rare cases where the military engineer happened to be a great architect', and the keep is a place of beauty far removed from many of the grim stone walls of earlier building. The views inland over pastoral scenes, to the east over the mouth of the Coquet and Amble, north down the main street to the market place, church and unique medieval bridge and gatehouse, make this one of the most pleasant historic sites on the Borders.

At Alnwick, stronghold of the Percies, decorated everywhere by the stiff-tailed lion, the castle, once painted by Canaletto from the north side, still retains its sheer impression of size and grandeur, though much of the building owes more to the decorative sense of eighteenth-century taste than to the need to deter the Scots, including the statues of soldiers who stand guard on the battlements. The Barbican that fronts on to the tortuous course of the old Great North Road is separated from the main Gatehouse by a moat, which leads in turn to the Outer Bailey and the Keep and other towers and courtyards. This is still the residence of the Duke of Northumberland, though much of the building is occupied by a College of Education. Parts of the building are open to the public on occasions. The whole precinct is surrounded by a flanking wall. It is almost a town within a town, intended to withstand long siege even after the loss of the civil town outside its walls.

The line of great defences along the vulnerable frontier of the Merse lowlands in Berwickshire marked by Wark-on-Tweed to the west was completed by Norham and Berwick-upon-Tweed. The great hall and most of the outworks of Berwick were removed by the railway builders of the 1850s, and a plaque on the main platform records the site, but towers and walls do remain and are part of the unique military fortifications of the Border town which deserve detailed treatment in their own right.

Norham controlled a fording place of the Tweed; its earlier name was Ubbanford. The early shires of Norham and Islandshires, covering the eastern part of the East Marches, were under the control of the Bishops of Durham and remained part of the County of Durham until the nineteenth century. Here, Bishop Flambard built the first castle in 1121, probably a wooden structure. With the return of Northumberland to the English Crown, Henry II started the rebuilding of many of the Border castles, and Bishop Hugh of Puiset started the construction of the complex fortification, some of which still stands under the supervision of the Department of the Environment. The Keep, the Inner Bailey, the Outer Bailey, and the West Gate stand above the neat village of Norham, grouped round its triangular green. The castle was constantly besieged and rebuilt, and every century until the sixteenth is represented in the present stonework. Such was its strategic importance in the 'front line' as it were, that it was even rebuilt after its taking by the Scots armies under James IV, dragging Mons Meg, the greatest cannon in the country, all the way from Edinburgh to batter its garrison into submission, before he proceeded on his way south to defeat and death at Flodden. The great keep, ninety feet high, eighty-four feet by sixty feet round the base, was soon rebuilt and stands today. From it is a fine view south to the Cheviot.

Other Norman keeps remain at Prudhoe, west of Newcastle, now undergoing restorative work by the Department of the Environment, at Bamburgh, and in Newcastle itself, the great square tower built by Henry II in 1172 blackened by industrial smoke and passing trains that greets travellers crossing Stephenson's High Level Bridge. It has been cleaned and restored and is now a city museum.

The great keep stands in the Castle Garth completed by a curtain wall, with a fine arched gateway still giving access to the riverside and the fortified Black Gate guarding the northern access. Beyond this inner fortification lies the medieval town (it became a city only in 1882) enclosed by a two-mile wall with eight gates and twenty-four flanking towers, amongst the strongest in Europe, and never breached during the whole period of the Border Wars. The wall, long submerged beneath nineteenth-century warehouses and offices, is being restored as a visual feature of the city. The walls owe their origin to a grant of murage from Henry III in 1256, but were rebuilt in successive periods up to the Napoleonic danger. Only fragments remain, and renewed interest has been shown in their preservation by clearances of old properties in the wall zone by war and redevelopment. Part of the wall has been renovated west of the castle by Forth Street but the best continuous section, flanked by a grim little alleyway and the barred windows of red-brick warehouses, is in the north-west, running from Westgate Road to the junction of Gallowgate and Newgate Street. Several turrets remain on this stretch, including the Morden Tower, which has achieved new fame as a centre of a new poetry renaissance in Tyneside, and the Plummer Tower in the north-east, which is in effect an eighteenth-century house now used as a museum attached to the Laing Art Gallery. The Wall Knoll Tower and Sally Port near the City Road to the east also has civilian additions but the lower stonework is unmistakably military. A plaque on a large stone wall running along the Close, west of the bridge, also announces the ancient wall; this section may follow the original alignment and may even use some of the original material.

One of the most delightful corners of the wall is in the heart of the city on the north side of the churchyard of St Andrew's, a medieval structure that certainly antedates the wall and the West Gate that stood at its east end. In this small oasis of green among the shops and warehouses is a good exposure of the inner stonework of the wall, with stone steps rising to its parapet which is now surmounted by red-brick structures which continue the motif by means of metal fire-escapes. The destruction of the City Wall was piecemeal, for the present road-pattern, except for the north and north-west, is unrelated to the wall alignment.

Bamburgh is one of that remarkable chain of coastal fortresses that owe less to the Norman Conquest than to the Tudor sensitivity to the alliance between France and Scotland and the need to protect the long eastern coastline against invasion from the sea. Berwick, once more, with its magnificent Elizabethan walls, was the corner-stone of this defence, but down the coast in turn lie Holy Island, Bamburgh, Dunstanburgh, Warkworth (though this lies a half mile from the shore) and Tynemouth. What makes them remarkable is not so much their interest as military features but their settings on rocky outcrops and headlands. The eight-acre site of Bamburgh is almost entirely surrounded by the steep cliffs of the Whin Sill overlooking the sandy shores, and the difficult channel running between the mainland and the Farne Islands offers a spectacular and naturally defensive site. The immense pile of stone is most impressive seen from the village to the west, but much that is now visible is little to do with potential warfare. The ruined buildings were partially renovated in the eighteenth century for use as a school, an infirmary, a granary and a home for mariners, and further rebuilding by the industrialist, Lord Armstrong, in the 1890s made it a modern residence now divided into flats.

Much the same might be said for the castle on Holy Island. Its setting on a volcanic dyke against the backcloth of the North Sea, flanked by the sand dunes to the north and Ross Links to the south within bowshot of Lindisfarne Priory, is so much more impressive than the structure itself, with twentieth-century modifications transforming the original Elizabethan fortress, an impressive mass of stonework but not of great architectural or historic interest. It is the ruined shell of Dunstanburgh farther south that really captures the imagination. Whether seen from Embleton inland or approached by the coastal footpath from Craster, a lovely green way across lush turf overlying the gently shelving Whin Sill adding greatly to the final aesthetic pleasure of the great gatehouse of the fourteenth-century castle, Dunstanburgh is majestic. The effect of wind and weather on the stonework produces remarkable patterns, and the curtain walls stride perilously close to the cliff's edge with the sea surging into the joints of the rock.

Almost as remarkable in its own way is Fast Castle at the northernmost extremity of the region, in sight of the Firth of Forth. Here at the foot of the cliffs, the sparse masonry, approached by a gangway across a rocky chasm, seems to grow out of the sea itself. The remains are too fragmentary to give any concept of its greatness for the site is a personification of isolation and was an impregnable prison for many a famous hostage.

Protected by this perimeter of great fortresses stand the many other fortified dwellings of the interior. Following the raids of Bruce and Wallace in the early fourteenth century, the so-called wars of independence, many landowners gained royal licences to 'crenellate' their manorial residences. For example, the ten years between 1330 and 1340 saw the erection of three courtyard-type castles in close proximity at Ford, Etal, and Chillingham. The masons' marks on the older stonework suggest that many of these castles were built by groups of itinerant masons taking their skill from place to place. Ford is now a field centre, Etal a ruin, and Chillingham an empty shell. If the main defences were breached or by-passed, the individual estates needed protection against marauding bands and against each other. Their castles were not intended to withstand attack by armies. Almost every manorial residence built on the Borders shows some evidence of fortification, although often disguised by later demands for peaceful elegance and good taste. Amongst other impressive tower houses of the fourteenth century, dominated by corner turrets, are Langley, Haughton, and Feather-stone.

One of the most perfect specimens of castle-building at this time lies in the remote dale in the extreme west of the region – the home of the Keeper of Liddesdale, called the Hermitage, for the site was originally a small hermitage for monks from Kelso. Fragments of monastic buildings may still be seen to the west of the main structure of the castle which, with its ground plan of a capital H, bears some resemblance to Northumbrian structures such as Haughton. It is a different world from Teviotdale; approaching from Hawick, one is aware of a major divide being crossed. It lies beyond that rim of hills that encloses the Tweed basin, the road reaching a height of 1182 feet before dropping into Whitrope Burn. The geology changes, the climate changes, and the dull grey stonework is a surprise after the rich red sandstones and black volcanics of the Tweed area. The architect was English and the castle was frequently garrisoned by English troops, and much of the building took place during the occupation by the English family of Dacre. But the place is more closely associated with the name of Douglas and, ultimately, with the Duke of Buccleugh, from which family it passed to the Ministry of Works in 1930. Its setting on the moorland edge and its links with the ill-fated Mary, Queen of Scots, and her visit to the Earl of Bothwell, surround it with a romantic aura which a visit does nothing to dispel. The tree-lined burn to the south adds just the right touch of softness to the scene.

One of the most attractive fortified buildings in the entire Border, both in its setting and in its completeness as a building, is Smailholm Tower. It can be seen for miles (and could be seen from for miles in the event of raids), perched on the summit of an outcrop of the Kelso Trap rocks, the scoured surface of the volcanic rock making just the right foundation. The red and black walls (masoned sandstone and irregular volcanic boulders) seem to grow out of the bedrock. The walls are nearly nine feet thick at the base, and the access to the upper storeys is by way of a spiral staircase in the corner. The vaulted ground floor also links with the upper hall by way of a small aperture in its apex. At least four storeys can be identified, and catwalks survive on the north side which may also have been used for a warning beacon. The enormous double key is always available at the nearby farmhouse of Sandyknowe, where the young Walter Scott spent much of his childhood gathering together the images of war and landscape that were to be the inspiration of his romantic novels.

The tower-houses, such as Smailholm, are one of the definitive features of the Border region and their occurrence marks its geographical unity, although similar features do occur on the west coast on either side of the Solway Firth. They mark a response to physical and historic conditions that are unique in the British Isles. Many of them are hidden in farm buildings, as at Castle Heaton, at Akeld and at Howtel. Others are lost beneath the later structure of manorial residences and the great houses such as Wallington. Some have found a new lease of life as unusual inns where refreshments can be had in the coolness of a tunnel-vaulted basement, such as at Ponteland, Craster, and Blanchland. The tower at Tosson confronts you as the car drops down the forestry road from the

Simonside Hills, and that at Hole dominates the skyline on the approach from West Woodburn to Bellingham. But one of the finest examples of the fortified core so typical of Border settlements is in the farm at Welton Hall, near the Military Road that follows the Roman Wall west from Newcastle. There the courtyard of the farm with its later byres and steadings and its fine seventeenth-century hall are grouped around the great hulk of a fifteenth-century tower built from Roman stones. The pastures to the west of the hall show the marks of a now-deserted village and the whole setting symbolizes the endurance of the people of the north against the tribulations of living in a frontier region.

Tower-houses were still being built late in the sixteenth century, as at Doddington in 1584, its ruin still dominating the centre of the village. A recent study[1] records at least 306 fortifications in Northumberland alone, many with no physical evidence remaining. A new edition of Hugill's classic work[2] records 109 well-preserved sites on both sides of the eastern borderland.

It was the absence of major fortifications on the Scottish side that led to the great increase of tower-houses after the defeat at Flodden. An act of 1535 ordered every Scottish Borderer having land to the value of £100 to build a 'barmkyn' and tower, sixty feet square, as refuge for himself and his retainers. The towers were usually built with a vaulted basement for stores and a walled enclosure (the barmkin) 'for save guard of cattle'. Usually, there was no internal link between the basement and the upper storeys, except by a narrow hole in the apex of the vaulting, but access to the living quarters was by an outside stairway to the main hall on the first floor with an intra-mural stair spiralling up to the domestic quarters. They were copies on a small scale of keeps and corner towers of the major castles. There are several accessible groups still to be seen and marvelled at. In the vicinity of Smailholm, for example, are Greenknowe, just to the west of the village of Gordon, and Corsbie, two miles farther west, situated on a hillock of firm ground surrounded by a broad bog which would have proved a formidable barrier to anyone unfamiliar with the ground and is still a disincentive to the modern visitor searching for this isolated and excellent site.

Another fine tower is near the junction of Kale Water and the Tweed, the ancient home of the Kerrs of Cessford, now a gaunt L-shaped ruin amid trees and fragments of a barmkin away from the present farm settlement. Many towers are isolated from the main settlements. Whilst this is due in some cases

---

[1] Brian Long, *Castles of Northumberland* (Harold Hill, 1967).
[2] R. Hugill, *Borderland Castles and Peles* (Frank Graham, 1970).

to the destruction of the villages that once surrounded them, in many cases it was intentional, as if to lead off the raiders or to show that their main function was to protect fighting men rather than property. The much-quoted report of Aeneas Sylvius in 1448 emphasizes the point, the men and children of a Border village leaving after a supper of pulse, poultry and geese (Aeneas supplying the white bread and wine which caused much excitement) to go to a tower 'a great way off for fear of the Scots', leaving the future Pope Pius II with 'two servants, a guide and 100 women' who sat all night dressing hemp.

Along the old road from Melrose north by Allan Water are three tower-houses in various stages of decay and showing variations on the same defensive theme. Colmslie is attached to a modern farm group whilst Hillslap lies in the fields to the south. Langshaw, the most ruinous, retains an enclosing wall that may be part of the medieval barmkin, to protect stock. These towers bear mostly sixteenth-century features, and it says much for the depth of English raids during that century that they are forty kilometres from the frontier.

Near Southdean, on the especially vulnerable route from Redesdale into the Upper Jed, are a cluster of small towers, often standing in complete isolation in fields of vegetables and oats, easily mistaken at first for derelict barns and only recently recorded as the simplest type of pele-house.

The tower-houses were not confined to the rural districts vulnerable to raids. Many such towers were grouped in the towns – three at Lanton, three at Darnick, six in Jedburgh and several in Hawick. The town house associated with Queen Mary in Jedburgh, open to the public, is an excellent example on the Scottish side, as are the Moot Hall and Prison at Hexham on the Tyne, from the fourteenth century. The main tower extant at Darnick, west of Melrose, is still occupied, little modified, and can be admired from the road. The Hexham towers make no concessions to refinement, with large plain stone walls, whilst that at Jedburgh with its turrets and ornamented windows of the sixteenth century speaks of later aspirations towards better living conditions.

Another group of towers of distinctive interest are the so-called 'parsons' peles' – fortified houses built for the protection of a largely catholic priesthood. The tower of St Anne's at Ancroft, built as part of the church, is a case in point. The Norman doorway leads into a tunnel-vaulted room with a spiral staircase in the corner giving access to the upper storeys and another door leading into the nave. Other fine examples standing free from the church but close by are at Elsdon, Embleton, Corbridge, and Alnham. The fragments of several others remain, as at Ford and Ponteland.

A recent survey of part of the Borders has identified many more 'bastle houses', small fortified farmhouses with accommodation for human beings on the upper floor and livestock below. They are exceptional buildings in that 'with one or two exceptions, all the surviving examples are within about twenty miles of the Border'.[1] This was the very distance within which an Act of 1555 required castles and forts to be repaired. They tended to be in clusters, presumably for mutual help during alarms. About sixty-two bastles have been recorded, but the authors of the study consider that they are merely the survivors of several hundreds of these 'poor man's tower and barmkin in one'. Two examples survive at Gatehouse near Tarset on the North Tyne, one ruinous but the other in a good state of preservation. With ground dimensions of about twenty-four feet by thirty-six feet, the four-feet thick walls are grimly devoid of windows, and outside stone steps give access to the upper storey. There is no vaulting in the lower room, just support timbers. Other fine examples occur in the same vicinity, such as Black Middens, isolated in a pasture, and Hole, an integral part of a farmstead.

The different names given to the defensive towers, such as pele, bastle and fortellet, are confusing, but the social distinctions of the time are shown by Sir Robert Kerr's advice, regarding alterations to his 'house' near Jedburgh:

By any means do not take away the battlement for that is the grace of the house, and makes it look like a castle, and hence so noblest, as the other would make it look like a peel.

The pele-tower was for the lesser gentry, whilst the castle was the home of the greater landowners.

The number of peles that have survived is very great whilst many of the castles have almost vanished from the scene. The very size of the castles would make them difficult to maintain and to restore and they would make excellent quarries for building stone. The smaller towers were more easily adapted to other uses and could be incorporated into later houses, as is the case at many mentioned above, together with those at Whitton, Halton, Proctor Steads, Lemmington, Shilbottle, Little Harle, Rock, Lanercost, and Clennell.

[1] Royal Commission on Ancient Monuments (England), *Shielings and Bastles* (H.M.S.O., 1971).

Of all the settlements in the region only four were of sufficient importance to merit the construction of surrounding walls – Roxburgh, Berwick-upon-Tweed, Alnwick and Newcastle upon Tyne. The walls of Roxburgh, medieval centre of administration for the county, moulder unnoticed in the fields to the west of Kelso. Apart from the Percy Gate, virtually nothing remains of the Alnwick walls, although they can be traced in the alignment of the present road systems Those of Newcastle are fragmentary, much being quarried for new purpose. during the improvements of the late eighteenth and early nineteenth centuries. Melrose records a mantel wall on early maps, though this was likely to be merely a statement of monastic enclosure, as at Hexham, rather than a military construction.

Yet, in Berwick-upon-Tweed, in contrast to the decline and fall of all the other examples, is a town that still thrives within its medieval walls and bears them like a halo. They represent the apex of the art of fortification and are unique in Europe, being modelled during the sixteenth century on the latest military fashions from the Continent, as exemplified by Antwerp and Verona. Small wonder that alarm is current over the schemes of developers, road builders and other modern 'improvers' to make great holes in the complete circuit of the Elizabethan ramparts to smooth the traffic flow up the Great North Road and even, by some local 'interests', to remove the Cowport, the best remaining gateway, to give visitors easier access to the shore. Fortunately, Ministerial approval has so far not been given to such schemes, but these unique ramparts will not be safe until the decision is made to by-pass the town, adding another to the existing three bridges. It was a tragedy that the 1928 road bridge was taken into the town centre and the opportunity lost to follow the line of the railway bridge, which reaches the high left bank of the Tweed north of the Elizabethan town. The railway builders did their own mite of destruction, for the railway station is on the line of the original Norman walls that enclosed a substantially larger area than the later wall. But the famous White Wall still remains guarding the approach from up-stream, together with the later Henry VIII gun-tower by the water's edge. Further fragments lie westwards along the ramparts to Lord's Mount at the north-east corner, with the Bell Tower still standing intact overlooking the 'glacis' zone. The withdrawal of the new walled line may have reflected the comparative decline of the town following the Border Wars, but the Norman walls enclosed fields and gardens as well as the urban area. The Elizabethan wall alignment was shorter, cheaper and easier to maintain, and still defended the sea entrance and the approach along the land peninsula from the north, leaving the Magdelen Fields open to the cliffs, easily raked by gunfire from the bastions. It was the alliance between Scotland and France which prompted Elizabeth to bring up Sir Richard Lee to rebuild the walls with their bastions, flankers, and parapets, the costliest undertaking in the Queen's reign.

Cowport is the only surviving gateway of the period, though modified gateways still give access to the harbour and to the North Road. To walk the walls of Berwick is one of the great experiences, a quiet stroll round the busy heart of the market town, in sight of the great river and of the North Sea, with green open spaces, tree-lined walks and grazing sheep bringing the rural scene lapping against the northern fortress.

The constant raiding which came to a climax in the sixteenth century had a devastating effect on Border life and led to an effective depopulation of many of the more vulnerable areas that may yet account for the comparative emptiness of the Border scene, the lack of large, prosperous villages, and traditions of hostility and lawlessness that remained until this century. Some of the parishes are amongst the largest in the countries, consisting of as many as fifteen 'townships', now represented only by farm hamlets.

The deserted village is a common feature of the Borders and the evidence can be seen everywhere. So often one comes across a church without a village, or a churchyard mouldering under the grass as at Fenham or Downham, Linton or Fenton Demesne. Air photographs or the observant eye, especially with low sunshine or a sprinkling of snow, bring out the outlines of cottages, gardens and roads such as at Ogle, Shilvington, and Belsay, all grouped together north-west of Newcastle. Yet the desertion which caused such concern to the Tudor monarchy, partly because it undermined the defence of the frontier, was put down at the time to many other reasons. A report of 1580 on reasons for the decay of Border service by which a tenant supplied horse and harness and gear at his lord's or warden's request suggested that the reasons were largely due to the actions of landowners making excessive exactions from their tenants and converting much of the arable land into sheep-walk, to the sale of horses daily into Scotland, to deadly private feuds and, most unexpected, to the 'long peace'. This is a reminder that the backward look tends to telescope events; the wars and raids merge into one unbroken succession and the intervals of peace are not recorded.

The dispersal of monastic lands, the onset of the new speculators in land so typical of this period, the expanding demands of the woollen industry and the comparative vulnerability of the Border tenant all contributed. It was not only the sheep that 'ate' the men in the region but the deer, too, for many a land-owner 'emparked' his estate and drove off the tenants. 'Sir Thomas Grey of Chillingham in the latter end of Queen Elizabeth's reign expelled 17 score men and women and children, all upon one day as the reports of the inhabitants have it.' Clennell and Biddlestone, situated near Kidlandlee, due to raids one of the most difficult valleys to maintain tenants, were both emparked at this time.

Throughout the region, the only reminder of a complete medieval township may be a farm or a hall still bearing that township's name. The deserted, or rather, contracted village, in the sense that some buildings remain on the site, is the rule rather than the exception.

Such was the situation when James VI of Scotland rode with his retainers to the Liberty of Berwick-upon-Tweed, where

> he was received with every demonstration of joy and respect by Sir John Carey, then Marshall, accompanied by all the officers of the garrison, at the head of their several bands of horse and foot. While these saluted his Majesty in passing with a discharge of vollies from their muskets, they were returned by the thunder of cannon from the ramparts and the air resounded with acclamations of joy.

This was a much more pleasant confrontation than Berwick's walls had usually witnessed and the potential peace of the Borders was emphasized by a report on the same day that three hundred 'banditti' were raiding on the West March, whence the King sent some of the garrison from Berwick who blew up the habitations of the bandits and some of the bandits too. Those who escaped were overtaken and 'afterwards suffered the just punishment of their crimes'. Better still, the old timber bridge did not please the King and he gave orders for a new stone bridge to be built. Twenty-four years later it was completed and there it still stands with its fifteen fine arches and mellowed stonework still carrying some of the town's traffic.

With such peace and the same king ruling both nations, the Borderers faced the problem of adjusting to a new situation, when castles could become mansions and a tenant farmer need not carry his sword near his plough, and his livestock could graze the Border hills in comparative security. The adjustment was long and hindered by the events of the Stuart fall and the restoration that began in the heart of the Border country at Coldstream, where a plaque in the old market place still marks the beginning of the Coldstream Guards, when General Monk marched south to overthrow the Commonwealth.

GATEHOUSE BASTLE.
NEAR BELLINGHAM.

# 6

## The landscape of improvement

God save our King, and blesse this land
  With plentye, joy, and peace;
And grant henceforth that foule debate
  Twixt noble men may cease.

*(The Ballad of Chevy Chase)*

The dark, angular stonework of Smailholm Tower, standing in bold isolation on its volcanic crags, symbolizes the warring frontier. But now it stands in an oasis of moorland in the rich, arable fields of Berwickshire. That rich, lowland landscape that stretches on all sides symbolizes the time of peace that slowly followed, of restoration and union.

The present rural landscape bears the overwhelming imprint of one particular period, of the passion for 'improvement' that had its origin in the comparative calm of the late seventeenth century and reached its climax in the late eighteenth century, sweeping away the medieval landholding system and subsistence farming in favour of large-scale commercial agriculture geared to the vastly extended markets, and the ability to organize in the expectation of a long peace that was only jolted by the Jacobite rebellions. The last army marched over the Border from Kelso in the final romantic flurry of Bonny Prince Charlie and the '45. Garrisons were strengthened, walls rebuilt, new military roads constructed, and the Duke of Cumberland marched north. But it was only an echo of other days and the gentry soon settled down with their ambitious plans to use the fruits of their foreign travels and the new status as the centre of a growing commercial empire to construct a new landscape in place of the old.

The 'great rebuilding' which transformed the southern parts of England in the late Tudor and early Stuart periods was delayed in its effect on the north by the troubled and impoverished state of the region, but changes were taking place even during the turmoil of the late sixteenth century. The old medieval ploughland, the 'husbandland', was being enclosed by some landowners, such as the Ogles and Greys, for sheep-walks, with the consequent expulsion of the peasantry, much to their distress and that of the Bishop of Durham, whose Border towns were receiving an influx of landless people, as well as of those responsible for the defence of the Border who were losing many of their potential defenders. But the loss of tenants due to the instability of the Borders did facilitate enclosure, and no anti-enclosure cases were heard in the Tudor Exchequer for Northumberland.[1] Some of the tower-houses and castles were being rebuilt, with the needs for fashionable living almost as important as those of siege. The Duke of Northumberland was introducing glass, and fires with chimneys, and many of the decorative windows and doors spoke of peace rather than war. Tudor manor houses (such as Black Heddon and Fenwick Hall) appeared, especially along the Tyne valley. Many fine houses such as Wallington and Thirlestane developed around defensive towers, and the appearance of the great castle of Alnwick owes as much to the imagination of Adam as to the medieval supremacy of the Percy family.

New houses were built alongside the old 'keeps' at Belsay, Walton, and Chipchase early in the seventeenth century, Ponteland tower was converted, and a new hall was built outside the shelter of Newcastle's walls at East Denton in 1622. This has a certain irony, as the great town walls which had never been breached during the five centuries of Border war were finally taken by the Scots in 1644 in league with the Parliamentary party against the Royalist inclinations of Newcastle's burghers. But soon the work of local architects such as Robert Trollope was adding renaissance scrolls and pediments to Newcastle Guildhall, to Capheaton and Callaly. Hexham Grammar School (still standing behind the old Moot Hall) was built in 1684. But, of that century, one of the great Border historians wrote:

> architecturally the most numerous monuments are yeoman's houses, or small manor houses, composed of a long, narrow front building and a back wing . . . huge stone buildings projected from back and ends of the house, windows were mullioned and sometimes of oak instead of stone.[2]

Many such buildings with dated lintel stones appear in the vicinity of Allendale; the village of Wall, grouped impressively around its square green, is almost entirely of this period.

By the early eighteenth century the Borders were in close touch with the

---

[1] M. Beresford, *Lost Villages of England*.
[2] H. Honeyman, *Northumberland* (R. Hale, 1949).

aspirations of the metropolis, and Morpeth Town Hall was built to a design by Sir John Vanburgh. At nearby Seaton Delaval, the same architect produced one of his major works, the Great Hall which was the scene of some of the liveliest activities of the 'Gay Delavals' and still acts as a great attraction, complete with 'medieval' banquets. To Vanburgh, too, is attributed at least some of the responsibility for the great palace built near Kelso for the first Duke of Roxburgh, Floors Castle, which Sir Walter Scott regarded as 'altogether a kingdom for Oberon or Titania to dwell in'. The present structure is largely the result of later rebuilding but still has one of the finest settings of any great house in the North. The approach to Kelso, either by way of Rennie's bridge or from the ruins of Roxburgh Castle on the south side of the Tweed, is dominated by the extraordinary battlements of Floors and the great sweep of the lawn and pastures right down to the river. Most of the great houses open their gardens and even their portals once a year for the public pleasure, and some of the most famous, among them Mellerstain and Abbotsford, Wallington and Seaton Delaval, are open throughout the summer season.

The Palladianism of another local architect, James Paine, was paramount in the mid-eighteenth century at Gosforth, Bywell, Belford and Wallington, and the Italianate influences on interior decoration were linked with a group of Italian 'stuccatori' houses at Cambo. Many of the nearby mansions, and there are many grouped in this part of mid-Northumberland, were embellished with Tuscan columns and Venetian windows at this time. The architectural culmination of this period was the work of Robert and James Adam, whose plans and sketches suggest that they contributed to at least fourteen mansions in Roxburghshire and Berwickshire as well as working at Alnwick Castle in 1769 for the Duke of Northumberland. Their father, William Adam, had already started to rebuild Mellerstain House in the 1720s and the two wings show his early work, quite different in style and material from the main body of the house, the grey stonework of which seems almost out of place in a region dominated by the warmth of red sandstones and dark volcanic rock, still used in the older parts of the building. The interior of the house, especially the library, shows the full flowering of the sumptuous Adam style.

Most of these mansions have equally fine settings, in parklands laid out with tree clusters, tree-lined drives, artificial lakes and carefully diverted watercourses, with statuary and other such embellishments of the Enlightenment. Classic fervour and romantic imagination produced many acres of carefully fashioned landscape. There are few approaches to a great house to equal the 'Mellerstain Entries', the long, leafy lanes that were such an attraction to the

Border gypsies based at Yetholm, and that still produce a sense of excitement. Another fine view is that obtained from the old Corn Road from Hexham to Alnmouth as it winds over the ridge from Bavington and skirts the southern boundary of the Kirkharle estate. The pleasure of parklands is one of the surprises that the Border counties offer to visitors from the south, in whose vocabulary the north is equated with hardness of landscape and utility of expression. It should not be a surprise, for it was on the Kirkharle estate that Launcelot Brown was born in the same year as the Jacobite rebellion and later achieved fame as one who saw the 'capability' of improvement here in Northumberland before perfecting his landscaping skill farther south. Nearby Wallington is one of his early essays in landscape design.

At the very time that new parklands were being laid out and old castles were becoming new mansions, William Roy, a British military surveyor, carried out his great survey of Scotland and produced a large-scale map of the Border region, a unique document that shows the landscape still dominated by the old open-field system, with the run-rigs clearly dominating most of the lowlands, but with the new enclosures taking shape in the vicinity of Kelso and the bold outlines of the great estates transforming the 'waste'. Pennant's tour of Scotland in 1769 noted the new enclosures round Kelso and compared them with 'the work of a new colony in a wretched impoverished country'. In only another thirty years, a later traveller could call Berwickshire 'a district in which agriculture has been happily carried to perfection', an example to the rest of Scotland. This comment was made at the time that two great innovators of new farming techniques, John Bailey of Chillingham and George Culley of Fenton, were writing their *General View of the Agriculture of Northumberland* for the Board of Agriculture and Internal Improvement. Their task was to collect and summarize the new ideas on farming that had been carried out in the county, to encourage their emulation. Many of their references were to pioneers north of the Tweed and all the writing of the time shows close contact between English and Scottish landowners and farmers. The Tweed lowlands were a pioneering area. It seems strange that William Cobbett, engaged in his rural rides in the 1820s, could be so scathing about the north, although politics rather than observation may have coloured his views, as a good Tory in a Whig stronghold.

Much of the initial impulse for improvement came from the large landowners. The Earl of Marchmont (the Marchmont estate still shows his handiwork) introduced a variety of new techniques to his Polwarth holdings. He drained the land with new ditches, enclosed it with hedgerows and stone dykes, limed it, brought trees and seeds from London and planted large areas of woodland. He introduced Ayrshire cattle, and sowed wheat, barley, oats, peas, turnips, carrots, clover, hay-seeds, potatoes, artichokes, asparagus, strawberries and other new crops. Nearby, Lord Kames, one of the initiators of the Board of Agriculture, was the first to raise turnips with drills and to plough up the ground for potatoes, then a new crop. Dr Hutton, the geologist, brought Norfolk ploughmen to his estate near Duns.

But it was the influence of the lesser gentry, local farmers like George and Matthew Culley of Fenton, and William Dawson of Frogden, near Kelso, which had most effect. The pioneer work of the Culleys in introducing new livestock breeds, as a result of their association with Robert Bakewell in Leicester – the new Shorthorn cattle, the New Leicester sheep (known then as the 'Culley' breed) – in the drainage of low-lying ground in the Milfield Plain, and in new rotations of crops, was successful in the large farms that they controlled (at least ten in north Northumberland) and made them nationally respected. The County Report for the Board of Agriculture, written by George Culley and his neighbour, John Bailey of Chillingham, was regarded by contemporaries as one of the finest of all the reports.[1]

Working with more limited means, William Dawson produced such results that the commemorative plaque in Linton Kirk calls him 'the benefactor of his country'. The process was cumulative. John Rutherford used two-horse teams for ploughing straight furrows on his farm near Melrose. John Small of Blackadder Mount invented a new plough, and 'Old' Rogers of Cavers, near Hawick, adapted Dutch ideas to a new winnowing machine. In twenty years the rents of land in the Kelso area doubled and the improvers set up the 'Border Agricultural Society', holding exhibitions and fairs in the region for the dissemination of the new ideas.

The accounts written by local clergymen in the monumental Statistical Account of Scotland are full of references to the new agricultural improvements, and especially to the improvement of health resulting from the draining of the marshier lands. Much of the best land we now see is on glacial deposits that were marshy and ill-drained well into the eighteenth century, a region of difficult passage even to the Border raiders of a previous age.

Arthur Young, during his extensive travels in the second half of the eighteenth century, reported, of the million and a quarter acres of Northumberland, that 'there were at least 600,000 acres waste and great tracts were covered in broom

[1] J. D. Rowe, 'The Culleys, Northumberland Farmers, 1767–1813', *Agricultural History Review*, Vol. 19, Part II, 1971.

and gorse'. John Grey of Dilston spoke of his father who 'took his axe, and like a backwood settler, cut away the broom and cleared for himself a space in which to begin his farming functions'.

Many of the estates in Northumberland in the late eighteenth century were 'lying open and unenclosed'[1] and this was equally true of the area north of the Border, judging by Roy's survey.

This area had been dominated by the run-rig system, in which there was an annual or biennial reallocation of strips according to need. Coherent blocks of farmland were rare. The best land was the infield close to the township in which 'bere' (barley) was the dominant crop. Even today, many farmers still refer to the infield or 'in-by' which receives most of their effort and to the outfield or 'out-by', the poorer ground. Each township had its common 'muir' or its links by the seashore for common grazing of poor livestock.

In 1695 a law was introduced in Scotland permitting the division of run-rig land, a process which was slow to get under way but suddenly accelerated in the mid-eighteenth century. At Smailholm, for example, 'in this parish in the year 1739–40, 1800 acres of lands in run rig were divided up into large farms'.[2] But the results were not beneficial to everyone. For 'the village and homes formerly possessed by the smaller farmers have fallen down and the lands are let to a sixth part of the former number of tenants'. The other five-sixths were presumably dispossessed of their land and drifted to the new towns and the new factories for employment. Many of the entries in the Statistical Account of Scotland repeat the pattern of new integrated farms being set up and the dispossession of many peasants. At a later period, in the 1820s, Bewick, the great Northumbrian wood-engraver, inveighed against the enclosure of the common lands along the Tyne valley and the loss of common rights to the peasantry.

Common to both sides of the Border is the presence of small, neat estate villages which mark the replacement of earlier 'townships' by a new settlement for estate workers. Some of the gentry destroyed whole villages in order to lay out parks, such as Clennell and Belsay, re-erecting planned groups of cottages at a 'suitable' distance from the big house. The planned villages of the Merse and Teviotdale, like Swinton, Bedrule and Gavinton, are part of the same pattern. Gavinton, for example, was the creation of David Gavin, a self-made man 'of low birth and obscure',[3] who purchased the estate of Langton in 1757 from the traditional owners, the Cockburns. The village he planned in 1768 has not been

---

[1] Mackenzie, *History of Northumberland* (c. 1840).
[2] 'Old Statistical Account for Berwickshire'.
[3] T. H. Cockburn-Hood, *The House of Cockburn of that Ilk* (1888).

altered fundamentally by Victorian additions and a recent housing estate. The largest venture in planning was the creation of Newcastleton in Liddesdale by the Duke of Buccleuch in 1793 as a weaving centre. It is now the unrivalled centre of a large rural area, still complete with the main Douglas Square and two flanking greens bisected by the straight main road, the basic grid plan still looking rather stark in contrast with the earlier pattern of 'natural' villages. The process continued throughout the Victorian period, each new heir to an estate introducing his own building fashion, with many cottages bearing the date and initials of the laird.

The topographical writers and artists who proliferated at this time, under the impetus of a new readership, the landed gentry and commercial groups, were enthused with the new changes. Mackenzie wrote that 'the memory of Sir John Hussey Delaval is highly honoured in Northumberland. The country around Ford which was one continued sheepwalk, he divided and enclosed with excellent hedges, and clothed the bare hills with fine plantations.' Physically, this involved the construction of ninety-two miles of quickset hedges and stone walls, keeping four men busy for thirty years. Thirteen entirely new farms were built away from the village centre, out on the enclosed land, apart from the reconstruction of old buildings. New higher rents were charged and, to give greater incentive to good farming, longer leases granted, which prescribed certain injunctions on the type of crops grown and techniques 'not to plunder the earth'. Rotations were laid down – oats, wheat or barley, then turnips, another grain crop and then grass leys for up to three years. The 'clothing of the bare hills' involved no less than the planting of 1,870,000 trees.[1] The landscape produced then is still recognizable as that of Ford and district today.

By the mid-nineteenth century little of the region was left unenclosed. Even the extensive sheep-walks of the Cheviot Hills were parcelled up with the long, straight stone dykes that still stand as a tribute to the craftsmanship of dry-stone walling. On the Scottish side, these were known as 'Galloway dykes', named after the region where they had been traditionally used for cattle enclosure. Much of the stone for the dykes was taken from the many Iron Age camp sites and hill forts, for good stone exposures are not abundant in the hills, much to the loss of our understanding now of their archaeology.

The only large area of unenclosed land was left on the poor moorland pastures on the high plateaux around Allendale, where 23,000 acres of stinted pasture still remain today – Hexhamshire Common, Whitfield Moor, and Allendale

[1] Delaval Papers, County Record Office.

11a. *Hermitage Castle, once the fortress of the Keeper of Liddesdale, bloodiest of the Border dales.*

11b. *Ruins of the fourteenth-century castle at Dunstanburgh, guarded by the cliffs of whinstone.*

12a. *The White Walls of Berwick-upon-Tweed, remnant of the defences built by Edward I.*

12b. *Corsbie, typical sixteenth-century tower house in an isolated site near Gordon.*

12c. *Queen Mary's house, Jedburgh: sixteenth-century fortified town house of the Kerr family, now a museum devoted to Mary, Queen of Scots.*

Common and Actor Moor where the farmers of more than one parish share stint rights – that is, the right to keep a certain head of livestock on the rough grazing land.

Although many of the Cheviot sheep-holdings have names which occur in early medieval records, their architecture on the whole is rather disappointing as compared with the Dales to the south and with the Lake District, being mostly Victorian buildings with little evidence of local inspiration. Visually the most exciting farm buildings are those of the Allendales, which have a quite different cultural tradition from the other hill areas, using the gritstones and flaggy sandstones of the Pennines to great effect. The Cheviot volcanics have rich coloration which is often obscured by pebble-dash and wash.

The final act of union between the nations greatly stimulated the droving of black cattle from north to south and the drovers returned with the evidence of better farming and better breeds of livestock; the new Shorthorn breed intro-duced by George Culley quickly spread throughout the Borders, whose farmers wanted 'quick feeders that lay their fat upon the most valuable parts'. The Galloways had then been tried by only one or two farmers but were to gain later popularity for fattening stock. The improvers knew that breeding from the best stock would produce only slow change; 'there is little doubt but that this may be accomplished by proper selection; and probably the best kind of Cheviot sheep, from their hardiness, and producing a portion of fine wool, are the properest stock'. Such improvement of the native Cheviot breed was largely the work of Robson of Belford, who crossed the ewe with the Border Leicester ram to produce a 'half-bred' sheep suited to lowland 'in-bye' grazing. In turn, the half-breed was crossed with a Suffolk ram. The resulting cross is still amongst the most popular in the region. The Border Leicester, introduced by Culley in 1766, was also crossed with the native Black-faced ewe to produce the 'mule' or 'grey-faced' sheep. By such selection, a breeding stock was developed with much better fattening possibilities, yielding a heavier fleece and yet retaining the hardiness that would enable them to flourish on the poor hill grazing and in the extremes of a Cheviot winter, when farms can still be cut off by snowdrifts for up to three months. Generally, the Black-faced sheep dominate the 'black' lands, the heather-dominated slopes, while the Cheviots prefer the somewhat softer land, the 'white' lands, dominated by grasses. The Border hills are still amongst the greatest reservoir of sheep breeds in the country – indeed, in the world.

Sheep trials, sheep-dog training and the annual shows in the hill towns are still amongst the high spots of Border life, and the first sheep-dog trials in the country were held at Otterburn in Redesdale in 1866. Thomas Bewick spoke with admiration of these dogs which were 'preserved in the greatest purity in the northern parts of England and Scotland'.[1]

The older townships and steadings grouped around the pele-towers and bastle houses no longer needed to be confined, and new farms, simple, stone structures, sprang up on the newly enclosed land, using the best freestone available. Existing Roman walls and camps and old castles were one of the best sources of readily cut stone and many suffered more in this way than from the Border Wars. This is especially true along the line of the Roman Wall in the Tyne Valley where only the pleading of early enthusiasts for antiquities saved the remnants that we now admire and enjoy.

The vast increase of building necessitated the opening of many new quarries for freestone and road stone. Lime pits were opened up and many kilns are still to be seen, especially in Northumberland. Some of the kilns, as at Beadnell Bay and on Holy Island, are structures as worthy of interest and preservation as the more favoured castles. Coals to burn the lime, drive the engines and heat the houses were mined wherever they were found not too far from the surface; there was a great traffic in coal and lime from Northumberland, where they were plentiful, into Berwickshire and Roxburghshire, where they were less abundant. Marl occurred in many of the bogs and silted-up glacial lakes of the region and made a great contribution to the fertility of the soil. Both lime and coal were worked even on the bleak moors by Carter Bar, and much of the moorland zone is pock-marked by the early industrial endeavours associated with agricultural improvement. Many of the larger farms used coal to drive the threshing engines, and the tall chimneys of the big grain farms, though no longer in use, are still widespread, especially along the line of the Great North Road. Smaller farms, or those farther from coal supplies, used horses to drive the threshers, giving rise to a characteristic circular or hexagonal building adjacent to the threshing barn known as the 'gin-gang', 'gin' being short for 'engine'. Some farms, especially in the hills, had water-wheels incorporated into their structure and elaborate dams built up-stream to take off the water through a special channel direct to the farm. In some cases, these large wheel-houses have been converted into drying plants for barley; the dams can be seen in many of the Cheviot valleys and in the burns of the other hill ranges.

It was usual for the farm-labourers, the 'hinds', to live on the farm, and rows of hinds' cottages are still a feature, standing 'in a long row or an open square

---

[1] T. Bewick, *History of Quadrupeds* (1790).

and are all one-roomed except perhaps that of the steward who often has the privilege of two houses knocked into one, or "two ends" as the two rooms are termed'.[1] It is still possible to find such cottages lived in by elderly people, but most have degenerated into stores and chicken sheds. More and more are being demolished now, their stonework and tiles being used to improve the farm tracks. Thatch was prevalent in the seventeenth and eighteenth centuries, but the red pantiles which are still widespread came into fashion by the end of the eighteenth century. Later the Scottish blue slates were found to be less costly to maintain and they, too, are widely found today. Some buildings, even churches, still carry a flaggy sandstone 'water table' as the masons call it, a roof composed of slabs of stone that were laid on wet and gradually took the shape of the underlying timbers. Such roofs were immune to fire and are not rare in the area nearest the Allendale and Slaley quarries where horizontally-bedded stone occurs, and is being quarried even today for decorative stonework, such as fireplaces.

The classic revival continued by John Dobson, most famous for his work in Newcastle, but active, too, throughout the county in church restoration, in modernizing mansions and even in small essays in landscape as at Bolam, gave way to a new Gothic romanticism with the rediscovery of the medieval period under the influence of Sir Walter Scott. In place of the measured achievements of Dobson at Nunnykirk and Beaufront (possibly his greatest), and the Greek classicism of Sir Charles Monck at Belsay, came the extraordinary extravagancies of Abbotsford and Ayton, near Berwick, full of turrets and Gothic spires, looking far more like legendary castles than the ubiquitous ruins themselves. Scott purchased Abbotsford (when it was still called 'Clarty Hole') from the proceeds of his best-selling poetry, but his grand building schemes led to financial embarrassment. What he fondly referred to as a cottage grew into an extraordinary amalgam of castle and monastery with turrets resembling oriental minarets. The dark interior is moodily romantic and cluttered with the relics and antiquities of the owner's collecting passion. The whole structure is a fantastic shrine to the memory of the man who virtually opened the door to the appreciation of the Border landscape and tradition to the European sensibility. It was also one of the first houses to be lit with gas light, an interesting link with Cragside at Rothbury, the first house to be lit by electric light. This mansion, 'a pretentiously romantic assemblage',[2] was created by Norman Shaw in 1870 for the Tyneside industrialist, Lord Armstrong. The same wealth rebuilt Bamburgh Castle in 1894, one of the most impressive piles of stonework, by sheer size, in the whole

---

[1] H. M. Neville, *Under a Border Tower* (1896).
[2] B. Allsop, *Historical Architecture of Northumberland* (Oriel Press, 1969).

region, the medieval core being buried in a mass of rather nondescript building. At the same time, Sir Edward Lutyens was rebuilding another coastal fortress on Holy Island, now a National Trust property.

The 'improving' centuries also saw a spate of church building and rebuilding, especially north of the Border where much destruction had been wrought not only by punitive English raids but by the riots against episcopacy and by the rise of the Covenanters. Scottish armies invading across the Border in the seventeenth century also destroyed many fonts and other church furniture in Northumberland. Many fine fonts date from the restoration of the 1660s and the following decade. Presbyterianism was finally established in 1690, and many Scottish kirks were built, such as Eccles, Edrom, Polwarth, Ancrum (now ruined), Eckford, and Fogo. The last named is a good example of the plan that evolved with the nave and chancel still following the outlines of the previous church. A new extension was built on the north wall, giving the church a typical T-shape, with the communion table along the south wall and the whole church divided up with wooden box pews. This church still has three doorways on the south side, the two side ones leading to private lofts in which the lairds sat and surveyed the lower classes. The church at Morebattle not only keeps its pews, but also the allocation list of seats in the porch, showing the Duke of Roxburgh in the front pew, the schoolmaster some way back and the people from outlying hamlets and farms in descending order. Here, as with many churches, is the belfry and the outside bell-rope, now discreetly tied down. These later kirks are fairly plain inside but some retain decorative fragments, not least in a rich array of macabre tombstones. There are very fine carvings, for example, in the south wall at Polwarth (again with three doors), whilst the vestry at Fogo is in a tunnel-vaulted chamber on the site of the old chancel. Another unusual fragment is to be found above the south porch of the church at Linton, near Morebattle, a much-eroded bas-relief of a mounted horseman in conflict with two animals. This is a Norman sculpture, not uncommon in England but unique in Scotland. The same church has a good Norman font. Its setting, too, is interesting, on a hummock of glacial sand, on the edge of a silted-up lake. The old chapel buildings at Abbey St Bathans, one of the most pleasant sites in the valleys running down from the Lammermuirs, were destroyed 'on account of the obstruction they presented to the operations of agriculture'.[1]

Some of the most interesting churches, however, were built in that interim period between the medieval decline and the improvers' outburst of energy: for

[1] J. Robson, *The Churches and Churchyards of Berwickshire* (1896).

example, Cockburnspath, with its rare circular tower, and St Mary's at Ladykirk. This is a remarkable church, being constructed entirely of stone. When it was built in 1500, fire from marauding bands was a real danger. Even the pews were made of stone, much to the discomfort of the parishioners. Virtually the only alteration in this church is the addition, in 1743, of a cupola by William Adam.

Greenlaw church, dominating the splendid square in the middle of the ancient burgh, built with traditional red sandstone, has the surprise of an old prison attached to one end, part of the kirk buildings, and, again, some very fine carving.

The only comparable church on the south side of the Border is at Berwick-upon-Tweed, where Holy Trinity was rebuilt in its entirety between 1648 and 1652, one of the rare churches of the Commonwealth period, with a strong London flavour, perhaps due to its mason, John Young of Blackfriars. Its clean, classic lines are in rare contrast to all the other churches of the area.

The aftermath of Culloden and the need to get produce easily to market led to the widespread construction of new roads, based on the conception of tolls, carried out by Turnpike trusts. Roy's map still shows the ancient route of Dere Street crossing the Cheviots at over 1500 feet as 'the road to Jedburgh'. The Turnpike Act of 1751 led to the linkage of all main towns by good-surfaced roads. In this year, the Military road along the line of the Roman Wall from Newcastle to Carlisle was turnpiked, followed by Allgood's Corn Road, leading from Hexham north-east to the developing granges of Alnmouth, on the Duke of Northumberland's land on the coast. Between 1746 and 1826, nineteen Turnpike trusts controlled five hundred miles of roads in Northumberland alone. Telford worked on the new route from Wooler to Edinburgh and helped with the main road from Ponteland by way of Belsay and Otterburn to Carter Bar. These two routes are now the A696 and the A697, two of the busiest Border highways. By 1791, David Patterson was publishing his *New and Accurate Description of All the Direct and Principal Cross Roads of Scotland*, with distances between the main towns, especially the Border links by way of Berwick, Coldstream and Kelso, rather in the same way that modern mapmakers try to keep pace with new motorway developments. This entailed an equal boom in bridge construction, especially after the 1771 floods swept away all the bridges along the Tyne, excepting that at Corbridge, which still stands and tries to cope with the growing east–west traffic. At this time, only two bridges crossed the Tweed from Peebles to its mouth at Berwick. Some of the finest bridges on the Border were built at this time, most notable being that of Rennie at Kelso (later to be used as the model for Waterloo Bridge in London), that of Smeaton at Coldstream, and the fine bridge at Hexham, designed by Robert Mylne, which has recently been strengthened and widened. Not less remarkable is Captain Brown's Union Chain Bridge, a pioneer engineering achievement of 1820 spanning the Tweed at Horncliffe. The Border region is prolific in noteworthy bridges, medieval and modern.

The improving spirit led to a spate of topographical artists and writers whose interests were closely related to the pride of the landed gentry. The romantic and the picturesque occupied their talents, and most of their descriptions are concerned with the castles, the manorial residences and the more dramatic vistas such as the rocky shore in stormy conditions. There is ample visual evidence of the great coastal sites such as Bamburgh, and of the abbeys of the Tweed, but much less of the Cheviot Hills and the Lammermuirs. The man-made landscape was more to their taste than the wild. Canaletto, who painted Alnwick Castle, and Turner are among those who recorded the more famous sites. Many of the topographical guides are little more than collections and catalogues of the great houses and their occupants. Each landowner made his or her own contribution to the estate and the nineteenth century reinforced the work of the eighteenth, elaborating gardens, introducing the new conifers, rebuilding the estate cottages and adding the fashionable Gothic image to the landscape. The gentry maintained a strong attachment to the family seat; and the tradition persists. Of the English county,

> its leading families are Northumbrian families. There is none of the footlooseness which one sees everywhere in the home counties. The big and important houses do not change hands with the unscrupulous rapidity of houses in Essex and Surrey. . . . On the contrary, houses are kept up even by personal sacrifices and the sense of responsibility to estate and county is still admirably alive.[1]

This is equally true of the Scottish Border counties. Scratch a duke or earl and you find a Douglas, a Scott, a Kerr or a Hume, all the traditional families whose names filled the ballads and bitter feuds of the warring days. This was still a time when the power of the landowners was such that tenants could be turned out of home and job because they were suspected of voting for the Liberal Grey instead of the Conservative Percies in the elections of 1885.[2]

· · · · ·

[1] Pevsner and Richmond, op. cit.
[2] G. M. Trevelyan, op. cit.

The story of a lesser castle like Ford epitomizes the improving passion. One of the first courtyard castles north of the Tees, dating from 1338, following the wars of Scottish independence, it was elaborated after many vicissitudes into an Elizabethan mansion by the Carrs, to become a Strawberry Hill Gothic fantasy in the hands of the Delavals, with curtain walls and portcullis that never saw a shot fired in anger. The grand lady of the Victorian age, Lady Waterford, perhaps most famous for her pre-Raphaelite paintings in the village school, removed the pointed windows and restored the façade with square, mullioned windows and drip stones, and, incidentally, created a model village and closed the inn. Later owners in this century modernized the interior and found the ancient walls thick enough to insert bathrooms. So many of the Border mansions are amalgams of time and fashion; they present a challenge to the architectural detective. The great families remain – the Swinburnes at Swinburn, the Swintons at Swinton, for example – maintaining a special type of organized landscape and traditional social pattern which has survived even the pressures of the twentieth century, their interest still dominantly in the land, its sport and its produce. Many of the estates have become limited companies and farming on a large scale is carried out as an economic enterprise. Of the Duke of Northumberland's 98,000 acres it has been said that 'there are few larger private estates in this country and certainly none more imaginatively managed'.[1]

The pattern of present-day farming is deeply influenced by the historic evolution of the region and the survival of large estates. The landed gentry as a group are increasing rather than decreasing their land-holding, for modern farming exists in a highly competitive market and the larger units with greater capital resources tend to be the more efficient, able to adopt expensive new machinery and experiment with new breeds of sheep and cattle, such as the Charolais. In many of the large estates, a somewhat feudal social atmosphere still exists, the tied cottage and the estate village tying the labourer and estate worker to his job and his place. Tenant farmers and shepherds have little security in face of a modernizing owner who may decide that trees offer more return than sheep or that his farm units must be enlarged. But the conditions of the soil and of the climate make effective limits within which farming experiment takes place, though the increasing use of fertilizers can overcome, even if only temporarily, the soil deficiencies and make it possible to replace a traditional crop rotation with year after year of barley.

· · · · ·

[1] H. C. Pawson, *The Agricultural Survey of Northumberland.*

The total area of tillage in Northumberland's 1,276,000 acres is only just over a quarter (284,000 acres), and this reflects the hilly nature of much of the terrain, for more than half the county is under grass. The amount of ploughed land rises to nearly forty per cent in the Tweed Valley and forty-five per cent on the coastal plain inland from Blyth, but drops to only six per cent in the upper parts of Tynedale and Redesdale, where the rainfall is higher and the winter appreciably longer. On the coastal plains, coated with glacial clays and sands, the dominant crops are barley and oats, grown mainly as a feedstuff for livestock. But much of the barley is of high quality and finds its way to the seed market and to the breweries and distilleries as well as being exported in increasing quantities from the coastal ports. Oats maintain their supremacy around the perimeter of the hill region, but root crops, and especially turnips, assume greater importance; the turnip has never lost the reputation it gained during the agricultural revolution when it helped to transform the farming pattern of the eighteenth century. In most rural districts barley and oats between them occupy more than sixty per cent of the total crop acreage and, together with pasture grasses (under the inspiration of Cockle Park and other experimental establishments), form the major feedstuffs of large herds of beef cattle and sheep. Many a Northumbrian farmer will summarize his activities as producing 'everything for the butcher's shop', and both the cattle and the heavy lamb crop are aimed at this market, though the wool clip is not to be forgotten, with its outlets to the West Riding and to Scottish brokers, especially in Kilmarnock, though none is used in the high quality Tweed industry. There are more than a million sheep in Northumberland alone (more than the number of people), one sheep for every acre, a number that has remained fairly steady since 1900.

Changes have been made in the beef cattle herds, with a large increase of bullocks fattened from dairy herds, and the dual purpose cow such as the Friesian increasing at the expense of the traditional Shorthorn, Aberdeen Angus, and the Irish cattle, which, nevertheless, still arrive in great numbers at Hexham market by way of the west coast ports. Highland cattle are not unusual and stock farmers are experimenting with crossing Charolais and other beef breeds with the traditional breeds. Northumberland alone supports well over a quarter million head of cattle, and one of the most impressive sights throughout the Borders is the sleek, black Aberdeen Angus bulls, the white-faced Herefords and the big Shorthorns.

Soil and climate conditions in the Merse of Berwickshire and in north Northumberland support some of the largest mixed farms in Britain, a thousand acres being not unusual. Lobes of good farming land follow the low ground of

LEADER

the valley of the Lauder and the Tweed and, while many lowland farmers have areas of rough grazing and hill pasture within their farm economy, the hill area proper imposes a quite different livestock pattern, with cattle playing a small (but growing) part and the rearing of sheep being the dominant activity. Except for the Cheviot summits, most of the hills, such as the Lammermuirs, carry reasonable grazing vegetation to their summits. Sheep steadings at 1000 feet are not unusual, but most of the hill farms are in the valleys, often at the junction of a tributary burn with the main river.

Every year brings increasing pressure on the hill economy, with poor returns from sheep and the ardours of the seasonal round making it more difficult to get younger families to take over hill farms.

Some of the thousand-acre sheep-holdings have little more than fifty acres of 'in-bye' land on which to grow oats, hay, and other fodder crops, and the purchase of supplementary feed needed until May is a heavy drain on scarce resources. Forestry, too, is taking over much of the traditional sheep areas and reducing grazing, whilst landowners are still trying to maintain the same flocks and are introducing cattle in a mixed grazing pattern. It is possible that the cattle could hinder the proliferation of bracken, the removal of which is one of the main problems in maintaining the quality of the grazing. Higher rainfall, with annual falls of up to seventy inches in the hills, leads to the leaching of soils, and the sheep need salt licks and cobalt feed.

The comparative hardness of the farming life on top of the increased mechanization of farming activities has led to an extensive and continuing drift from the land. In a hundred years since 1851 Northumbrian Tweedside lost half its population, and the number of full-time agricultural workers in Northumberland alone has fallen from ten thousand in 1925 to seven thousand, to a point where estate owners and farmers feel that a further loss will endanger the future of farming. The advent of new industries with comparatively high wages causes further dissatisfaction with the rural life, and the closure of small schools and the decline of rural transport have reinforced the pattern. Farming is just as much an industry, producing a specific product, as any other, competing in the same market for capital and labour.

The great changes in farming have led to a decline in other aspects of the social scene that so enliven the pages of earlier topographers. Even in the nineteenth century a local parson was observing that 'our large farms are really factories for the production of cattle and corn' and bemoaning the loss of the romance of the farming year – and this before the tractor and the combine harvester had driven the horses from the stalls and brought the oil pump into the farmyard.

The Borders have a tradition of female labour, and many a labourer or hind had to bring a female or a 'bondager' to his new post after his 'flitting', usually around 12 May, from one farm to another. Flitting day was one of the great occasions on the Borders, but the carts choked with the family possessions, moving from one menial tied cottage to another, often with only two rooms, are a thing of the past, although the local newspapers are still busiest advertising farming jobs at that same time of the year.

The tradition of living on the farm still exists and the typical unit of rural settlement is not the village but the farm hamlet, composed of the farmhouse, the steadings, the cattle courts, the granaries and the cottages. Many of the 'villages' of the region are, on closer inspection, merely a cluster of two or three farms, some of them favoured with a post office, general store, a chapel and a primary school, making communities that are hardly self-sufficient in today's social patterns. The modern farming landscape is almost a landscape without people, and I shall remember last year's excellent harvest for the sight of three combines thundering greedily in line across the fifty-acre cornfield with military precision under the hot sun while I was strolling along the shady avenue of the Roman Dere Street.

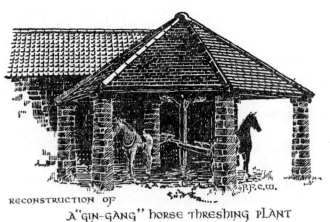

RECONSTRUCTION OF
A "GIN-GANG" HORSE THRESHING PLANT

# 7

# Burghs and market towns

And he march'd up to Newcastle,
And rode it round about;
'O wha's the lord of this castle,
Or wha's the lady o't?'

*(The Battle of Otterbourne)*

Greenlaw is one of the surprises of Border travel. It takes about two minutes to pass through on the way from Coldstream to Carfraemill, and that is all the time that most travellers devote to it. A population of about five hundred summons up the image of a 'village', yet the town is built round a large central green containing one of the most impressive town halls in the whole region, built in 1829, complete with a portico of classic proportions, facing the Castle Inn, another mirror of Georgian elegance. At the north side of the square stands the fine eighteenth-century kirk incorporating a tower built as a gaolhouse.

Here's the Gospel and the Law,
Hell's hole atween the twa'.

The old courthouse that made sense of the rhyme has now been removed from the west side of the tower. The cross which once stood in the town centre was lost after dismantling but has now been re-erected against the kirk wall. These are the ingredients of a settlement of far greater importance than the present size of Greenlaw would suggest. For this was the County town of Berwickshire from 1696 until 1853 and even then shared the status with Duns until finally losing it to its rival in 1903. The town hall was built, in fact, as the County Hall.

The fate of the two towns that originally bore the names of the counties that they administered, Roxburghshire and Berwickshire, makes a sad comment on this history of the Borders. Roxburgh moulders under the pastures west of Kelso and is forgotten except for a small, rather uninteresting hamlet and some earthworks, whilst Berwick, after many vicissitudes, was finally lost to the Scottish crown in 1483 and lies, together with its Liberty, wholly on English ground. It

139

was the loss of Berwick-upon-Tweed that necessitated the choice of another settlement as administrative centre of Berwickshire. Lauder was the only other burgh with royal status and was the site of the royal court on occasions during the sixteenth century, but the choice finally went to Greenlaw.

The original site of Greenlaw, still mapped as Old Greenlaw, lies over a mile to the south of the present town on the hump of a ridge, but already by 1598 the 'kirk-toun', grouped around the church on the lowlands by a meander of the Blackadder Water, was more populous than the old town and became a free burgh of barony with the right to a weekly market, though it is no longer a market centre. The present layout of the town has the appearance of a planned settlement around a central square. It was one of the many towns of the Merse destroyed by the punitive raids of Sir Ralph Eure in the sixteenth century, but the year after the so-called destruction 'the same towns are built and plenished

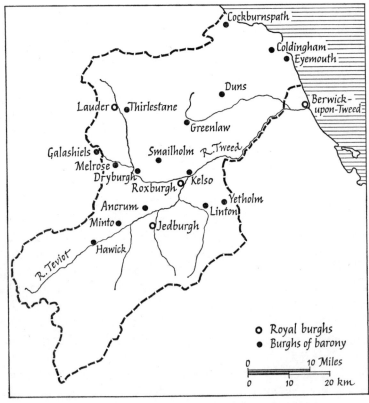

**Map 7**   *Scottish Border Burghs (12th–17th century).*

as they were before'.[1] This suggests a very simple type of house construction unlike the present strong stone buildings, which owe their appearance, as does the rural landscape discussed in the last chapter, to the widespread improvements of the eighteenth and early nineteenth centuries. Most of the market towns and burghs of the Border region were rebuilt during this period, symbolized by impressive town halls, such as that at Berwick, built by Joseph Dodds in 1754. Morpeth's had been built in 1714 to a design by Vanburgh, Alnwick followed in 1771, and Kelso in 1816. Around these central civic statements developed fine rows of burgesses' houses and coaching inns which still make many of the towns such satisfying examples of good urban architecture, worthy of preservation in our present age of further development and 'improvement' under the pressure of traffic and commerce. The Georgian architecture of Berwick's Hide Hill, Ravensdowne and the Quayside, the Woodmarket and Town Square of Kelso, Castlegate and the High Street of Jedburgh, Alnwick's Bondgate and Bailiffgate, Morpeth's Bridge Street, the gem of Warkworth, entire and intact, even the main street of some mining towns like Bedlington, once the centre of its own shire: all these reflect the increasing prosperity of the rural areas of which they were the administrative and market centres and make the region's towns so pleasant to be in. They all have minor accretions of fussy 'Victorian gothic' and jolly Edwardian façades but, on the whole, it is the very lack of more recent growth, their existence outside the main industrial developments of the nineteenth century, that has enabled the market towns to retain an identity and coherent shape. They can still be seen as towns, lacking the penumbra of indifferent townscape, neither good town nor good country, that makes the approach to so many modern towns unsatisfactory. The Scots still keep a useful word, the 'landward', to describe the land outside the towns. The limit is still clearly defined in many cases. The approach to Jedburgh is amongst the finest examples, dominated by the Abbey. Alnwick, approached from the north down the A1, still hides behind the bridge and the castle that protects it. Kelso lies, awaiting the visitor, beyond the bridge and the Abbey. So, too, does Hexham, its magnificent skyline still dominated by medieval buildings seen from the north. Greatest of all is Berwick-upon-Tweed, whether seen from the railway bridge or approached over the old seventeenth-century road bridge – 'one of the most exciting towns in England' as Pevsner calls it. This satisfaction diminishes somewhat with the woollen towns of the Upper Tweed and fades completely in the coalfield towards Newcastle. But between these extremities lies most of the

---

[1] Calendar of Border Papers.

region of pleasant rural landscapes speckled with towns richly endowed with good urban architecture, the centres of Border life.

In contrast to Greenlaw and its imposing, though somewhat fading, planned centre is Lauder, still occupying its ancient site and growing 'in the Scottish manner, out of a single street, a high and windy street on the crest of a ridge', as George Scott-Moncrieff said of Edinburgh. Lauder's present charter as a Royal Burgh of Scotland dates from 1502, though this was almost certainly the confirmation of an earlier charter. The single broad high street widens to create the market place, and in this broader section stands the old Tolbooth, and Town Hall, a simple structure with a small bell tower and flight of steps all recently renovated. Behind it has developed the Mid-Row, a group of buildings with no gardens or burgess strips attached. They probably began as temporary market booths and became permanent structures in the course of time. This often happens in old market places such as that of Alnwick, where a whole group of stone buildings and market halls disguises the pattern of the original open central space. Adjacent to the Tolbooth are the old coaching inns and the church, with its octagonal steeple and unusual plan, built as a Greek cross. Running parallel with the High Street are two back lanes giving access to the rear of the burgess strips; they were once known as the Under or North Backside and the Upper or South Backside, but are now called Castle Wynd to the north and Croft Road leading to Factors Park to the south.

The large number of grants of the status of 'burgh' to settlements such as Lauder on the Scottish side of the Border – eighteen between 1489 and 1695 – suggests that this was a period of active town development, and some of the towns may have been planned at that time.[1] But many burghs are earlier in origin. The original Royal Burghs were established partly by the deliberate efforts of the English-educated Scottish king, David I, who also stimulated the growth of the Border abbeys.[2] The burghs were 'planted' 'by the side of new royal castles to help civilize and hold in subjection'[3] the local inhabitants. The two great centres on the Borders were Berwick-upon-Tweed and Roxburgh, two of the original Court of Four Burghs of the twelfth century, together with Edinburgh and Stirling. Jedburgh achieved royal status by the thirteenth century, and Kelso and Lauder followed, though Kelso's main period of growth followed the destruction of nearby Roxburgh in the fifteenth century.

---

[1] See discussion by Whithand and Alauddin in 'Town Plans of Scotland', *Scottish Geographical Magazine*, September 1969.
[2] See Chapter 4.
[3] T. C. Smout, *History of the Scottish People, 1560–1830* (Collins, 1969).

Towns grew as centres of administration and as market centres for the exchange of goods, and achieved a monopoly of trading rights in their areas. The Scottish Royal Burghs had a monopoly of trade with foreign countries until 1672. One of the surprises of the Border region is that no major Roman centre was utilized, like London, Lincoln, or York, for later urban growth. Melrose grew near Trimontium, Corbridge near Corstopitum; but only near, not on the same site.

It is possible that Newcastle itself may stand on a camp at a strategic bend of the Roman Wall near a suitable crossing of the Tyne, the old Pons Aelius, but there is little evidence of this on the ground. Even the later centres of the Northumbrian kings, at Bamburgh, at Yeavering and Milfield, and at Corbridge have shown little growth. Bamburgh still has a village grouped beneath the castle crags; Corbridge has a good market place but no market. Yeavering and Milfield are subjects for the archaeologists only.

Town life on the Borders grew with the Norman domination, and the instability of Border life meant that commerce could only flourish under the protection of a powerful territorial lord, physically expressed by the presence of a fortification, or of the Church, symbolized by the abbeys. The close proximity of market place to castle or to abbey is striking: it is possible to group most of the border towns into two categories: the 'castle towns' and the 'abbey towns'.

The castle site and associated town is preserved in a remarkable way, almost like a fossil in the bedrock of its past, at Warkworth, where the present small town has scarcely outgrown its medieval confines in a meander of the river Coquet. At the river crossing to the north stands the narrow stone bridge and the medieval gatehouse. To the south, at the top of the hill, guarding the vulnerable neck of the peninsula, stands the magnificent castle of the Earls of Northumberland. In between, slopes the one main street of fine eighteenth- and nineteenth-century town houses down to the market place and the Norman church – a perfect urban pattern, on the minor scale. Six miles to the north-west where the Great North Road crosses the river Aln stands the other great Percy stronghold, Alnwick. It is a busy market town of more than seven thousand inhabitants, the administrative centre of a large rural district; the cobbled and paved triangular market place stands about two hundred yards to the south of the castle enclosure, outside the parkland surrounding the fortification. This town has been subject to one of the most detailed studies accorded to an urban area,[1] with its growth from early origins in the Anglo-Saxon period as a village

[1] M. R. G. Conzen, 'Alnwick, Northumberland. A Study in Town Plan Analysis', *Proceedings of the Institute of British Geographers* (1960).

round a triangular green being traced in great detail, with the aid of early maps and other documents, step by step to its present urban pattern – a classic work of detection and analysis of evidence that heightens one's appreciation of what is meant by the word 'town'.

There were three separate units in the origin of Alnwick, one of them being around Bailiffgate ('gate' in this context meaning 'street' rather than 'gateway') to the west of the Barbican of the castle where the retainers of the castle were housed. The old parish church of St Michael's is situated at the west end of this alignment. Another was Fullergate, running down towards the river, the home of the fullers, the clothworkers. The third was the junction of old roads running from Lesbury near the coast (once the more important of the two settlements but now a village) to the early Anglo-Saxon settlements of Eglingham, Whittingham, and Edlingham, all near the line of the old Devil's Causeway, the Roman Road. At this fork developed a triangular village green, marked by the present Bond-gate, Clayport Street, and Fenkle Street. The development of the political frontier meant that the early Northumbrian 'capital' at Bamburgh declined in importance and Alnwick became the bastion on the Great North Road, the first major Norman castle south of the Tweed line of fortresses. A cross once stood outside the Barbican in Castle Square, suggesting that this was once the hub of the town's life, but the village green developed as a market place and the cottages surrounding it became transformed into the town houses of the burgesses with frontages on the main commercial centre and long burgage strips running back from the houses. These frontages have maintained their importance and are now the main shopping area of the town. Alnwick was granted borough status near the end of the twelfth century, with market rights confirmed in 1297. It was important enough by 1434 to need the protection of a surrounding wall, the only walled town in the region outside Newcastle and Berwick. Only one of the old gates remains, guarding the southern approach – the Hotspur Tower or Percy Gate, with its massive stonework.

As the town grew, so pressure on space led to new buildings being erected on the burgage plots, causing the sort of overcrowding that is common in many of the Border towns, areas that in many cases are now rather run down and derelict. The great space of the four-and-a-half-acre market triangle was interrupted by new buildings, the Shambles, small shops and the Assembly Rooms, all adding to the congestion at the centre, but at least creating a busy hub of the town's life, a real living centre. New turnpikes in the mid-eighteenth century led to new growth, and the rebuilding of that period still dominates the town's appearance – a good, solid, stone prosperity. The power of the Dukes of Northumberland prevented

13. *Extract from William Roy's map of 1750 showing the surviving pattern of run-rig cultivation near Smailholm with the beginnings of eighteenth-century enclosure and the improvements of the Mellerstain estate.*

14a. *Eighteenth-century mansion and parkland at Swinburne, superimposed on medieval plough-lands. The Swinburnes still live on the estate.*

14b. *Floors Castle, reconstructed in 1839, home of the Duke of Roxburgh.*

15a. *Dipping Cheviot sheep at Cocklawfoot.*

15b. *Auction of Suffolk sheep at the Hawick Mart.*

15c. *Milne Graden, typical 'enclosure' farm group on the Berwickshire Merse, with farmhouse, byres, courts, granary and threshing chimney.*

16a. *The Royal Burgh of Jedburgh, the long high street running down the ridge from the old castle site to the River Jed; the Abbey and the textile mills (now demolished) line the main road from the south.*

16b. *Berwick-upon-Tweed guarded by the bastions of the Elizabethan walls, linked by the seventeenth-century bridge with Tweedmouth; the town hall at the centre of the street pattern; seventeenth-century church and eighteenth-century barracks in the near corner of the walls.*

later growth towards the Castle precinct and the parks, and the railway was allowed only as a branch intrusion. The spacious Victorian villas and the new public buildings, schools, fire station, gasworks, infirmary are all found on the available land to the south and west and it is to the south, especially along the main A1, that new factory development is taking place to introduce new sources of employment so vital to the continued well-being of these ancient towns.

While Alnwick's walls are remembered only as a gateway and a street pattern, to the north, those of Berwick-upon-Tweed still enclose the thriving town with Elizabethan grandeur.[1] An almost rural calm surrounds the red-tiled roofs and grey stone of the town, poised in the limbo of its own special Liberty, for so long mentioned specially in treaties signed on behalf of England, Scotland and the Liberty of Berwick-upon-Tweed. We are north of the Tweed here but still four miles from Scotland, which begins at Lamberton Toll. To the north of the Scots Gate is the mound, fragmentary bastion and watch tower of an even earlier Norman wall built during one of the periods of English possession, which enclosed an even greater area and shows the importance of this erstwhile Royal Burgh, the major port of medieval Scotland, whose harbour dues amounted to nearly a quarter of all English ports. Much of the wool from the Border abbeys and the products of the burghs found their way to the port. But it never really recovered its prominence after two hundred years of siege and counter-siege that made it an anvil between the hammer-blows of two embattled nations and led to it changing from one Crown to another no less than thirteen times. Parts of the body of Wallace, the Scottish liberator, were displayed here and Edward III hanged two sons in the sight of their Scottish father from the ramparts. The sparse remains of the once-great castle and the White Walls protecting the approach from the Tweed are reminders of bloody days. The castle was destroyed less by the furies of Border warfare than by the energy of Robert Stephenson, who chose this as the most suitable site for the new railway station, linking it in 1850 with the south side of the Tweed by the soaring stone arches of the Royal Border Bridge, one of the greatest engineering achievements of its time. A plaque on the main platform still marks the site where Edward I mediated between rival claimants to the Scottish Crown and led to the town's great time of troubles, which did not end until the Union of the Crowns in 1603. That moment, too, is symbolized by a bridge, for James VI of Scotland, crossing on to English ground, found the old bridge treacherous and caused the building of the superb fifteen-arch

[1] See Chapter 5.

bridge, which was not completed until 1624, the highest arch of the bridge marking the old boundary between the Liberty and the territories of the Bishopric of Durham, known as Norham and Islandshires. The third bridge, now the main road bridge, was opened in 1928 and was built partly as a palliative to local unemployment during the period of inter-war depression. The tragedy was that this new bridge was driven into the heart of the old town, creating a new centre at Golden Square and a terrible traffic problem for today. If only it had followed Stephenson's line and led outside the walls, much of today's debate about new by-passes and the destruction of the gates and part of the walls would have been avoided.

Berwick's return to prosperity was marked by a flowering of Georgian architecture which lines most of the principal streets and the quayside walks, and by the construction of the barracks, designed by Vanburgh (or at least with his advice) in 1719, the oldest in the country and still occupied, although the garrison is being rapidly run down. It would be nice to think that a really imaginative use will be found for these splendid buildings, quite apart from the present military museum. The military air is always present in Berwick. The old armoury still stands alone just inside the walls on the coastal side and many of the finest houses, some from the early nineteenth century such as Wellington Terrace, were occupied by officers. One still sports a fine bust of the Iron Duke above the front door. The Guard House with its Tuscan portico that once graced the entry to the town at Marygate has been re-erected on Palace Green near the Salmon Fisheries. This period found a suitable chronicler in John Fuller,[1] whose history of the town is both affectionate and accurate. At the heart of Berwick, at the foot of the High Street, where all the shopfronts have had a face-lift in recent years and the market stalls still survive, is the old trading centre, where the Woolmarket and Hide Hill meet. At the foot of the hill is the Corn Exchange, where in recent memory the hiring of farm labour still took place with a hand on the shoulder. The old butter market under the Town Hall has been cleaned up and restored and made into a fine shop and café, much more tasteful than some of the brash intrusions of new flats along Woolmarket. The livestock market is still busy but is now located near the railway station, having spent a long interval on open space, now utilized for car-parking, just outside the walls by the Scotsgate.

Most industry is now drawn together on the trading estate across the river at Tweedmouth, dominated by processing industries. During the barley harvest, the place is alive with haulage contractors and the port has an increasing export

---

[1] John Fuller, *History of Berwick* (1799).

of barley, giving a much-needed boost to coastal shipping. Here too is the Rangers' football ground, part of the Scottish League, symbol of Berwick's very special status, an English town with Scottish overtones.

Writing four hundred years ago, Leland considered Alnwick to be less pleasant than another 'castle' town, the market town of Morpeth, nineteen miles nearer to Newcastle. Morpeth was 'a long town, metely well builded with low houses, the streets paved. It is a far fairer town than Alenwicke. Morpeth castle standeth by Morpeth Town. It is set on a high hill and about the hill is much wood.' The setting of the town in a broad meander of the Wansbeck is still surprisingly well-wooded – its coat of arms granted in 1552 asserts 'We dwell amongst woods and rivers' – and its name suggests its location by a path leading over the moors. 'Peth' is still frequently found as a street name. But not many visitors would put Morpeth above Alnwick for interest or pleasure. Situated on the western limit of the coalfield, it was part of the rapid nineteenth-century growth that submerged the south-east of the county in rows of brick terraced houses and little amenity. It is a busy town, a main transport centre on the A1 and now growing rapidly with new estates and factories spreading up on the plateau that surrounds the quite impressive gorge of the Wansbeck. This type of development leaves the town centre looking a bit neglected, and behind the pleasant Georgian façades of Bridge Street is a motley jumble of yards and battered buildings. But the main street, Bridge Street, still has much of interest, including fragments of the original bridge, now used for pedestrians only. The new road bridge was built by John Dobson, the Northumbrian architect, and Thomas Telford, the engineer. By the bridge is the old Chantry, a fourteenth-century edifice, built by the Bridge Building Brethren, which has suffered all sorts of humiliations since, including use as a factory. But the broadening of Bridge Street to make the junction with Newgate is marked not only by the fine Town Hall building fronting the old market place (the market is now down by the river) but by the unusual clock tower at the entrance to Old Gate. The lower part was once a prison and the clock still chimes the eight o'clock curfew. The house of Admiral Lord Collingwood stands beyond it, in Oldgate.

What is left of the castle of the de Merleys is in private hands but, together with the parish church of St Mary's, it stands on the south side of the river, on the river cliff outside the meander. The de Merleys gained a licence for a market in their borough as early as 1199 and it is possible that the 'town' at this time was grouped near the castle. The recent opening of the by-pass up-stream, a difficult engineering feat due to the instability of the glacial sands and gravels that line the Wansbeck in this area, has taken some of the pressure off the town centre, especially on summer Sundays when Tyneside migrates to the north-east coast and to the Cheviots.

There are many other castle sites like Morpeth where the original defensive site has mouldered even farther under the grass but was possibly the *raison d'être* of the settlement that remains. Wark-on-Tweed is a fragment of masonry on the summit of an elongated mound of glacial gravels, and a small hamlet still exists in its lee. Wark-on-Tyne, once the administrative centre of Tynedale, has only the earthworks, still called the Mote, extant, but a solid-looking township built round a square still thrives by the river at its feet. At Bellingham, with a population of one thousand, still the centre of a large Rural District covering much of the traditional areas of Tynedale and Redesdale, the castle site lies to the east of the present town, one main street broadening out to an open space on two levels, dominated by the thirteenth-century St Cuthbert's church.

Here are many of the activites of the small but important town in the sense of the services it offers to the people of the dales – shops, pubs, bank, local offices, Forestry Commission offices and even cafés catering for the weekenders. A Youth Hostel contrasts with the relics of mining and iron foundries from the last century when this was an industrial town.

Harbottle, administrative centre of the medieval Middle March, is a repetition of the Wark-on-Tweed story, a small street hamlet beneath a few remnants of the once-great castle. But at nearby Elsdon, favourite picnicking place for cyclists and motorists on the afternoon run from Newcastle, are more of the intimations of past greatness as befitting the medieval centre of the Lordship of Redesdale, a place given as much prominence as the market towns of the county by Morden's map in the early eighteenth century. Here a broad spindle-shaped green nearly a quarter of a mile long flanks Elsdon burn, with the perfect outline of a Norman motte-and-bailey on the high opposite bank of the river. On the green itself is St Cuthbert's church with its fine belfry and medieval work; towards the northern apex of the green is the Parson's tower house, one of the best on the Borders. Cottages and some shops are loosely gathered round the perimeter of the green. Old drove roads led north and south from the green, and when the Turnpike came in 1751 the 'township' still found itself off the main road system then developing. Today, it remains an unusual and attractive village, much visited, not least for its good eighteenth- and nineteenth-century stone houses that were built following the Enclosure period, giving it 'its characteristic unity of building materials'.[1]

[1] M. R. G. Conzen's essay on Elsdon in *Northumberland National Park Guide* (H.M.S.O., 1968).

Wooler, with a population of two thousand, the administrative centre of the Glendale Rural District, has never benefitted from fair words from its topographers. The Reverend Hodgson called it 'a cold, uncleanly place' in 1818 and many similarly unflattering descriptions have been recorded before and since, but it still has one or two good buildings grouped round its market place, with some very sparse chunks of masonry by the church on the mound to the south marking the site of the castle of the Muschamps, early Border barons. Set on hummocks of glacial sands and gravels overlooking the Milfield Plain, it is one of the main towns on the periphery of the Cheviot Hills and one of the best centres for exploring those hills and the lovely moorland arc that approaches it from the east.

The lack of great Norman castles north of the Border makes it more difficult to pursue this relationship of town origins and castle sites, excepting Berwick-upon-Tweed and the long-gone Roxburgh. But there is a relationship still, though much more nebulous. Lauder, for example, is close to the castle of Thirlestane, a much-changed mansion, the grounds of which run with the north side of the town, where the back lane is called Castle Wynd.

Duns, the present county town of Berwickshire, is related to a fortified site, although the castle, originating in the fourteenth century, stands more than a kilometre uphill from the present town centre, just to the west of a British camp which may be the origin of the Celtic name of the town, and shows an interesting persistence of the defensive site. But Duns (known earlier as Dunse), in the manor and lands of the Earl of Moray, was burnt by Sir George Bowes and his English raiders in 1558 – the last of many raids – and rebuilt farther down the hill. The market square, recently opened up by the demolition of the Georgian town hall, is approached by North Street, South Street and Easter Street, the two-first-named streets containing some good urban architecture of the eighteenth century, but the oldest houses today are found, ironically, in the so-called Newtown, which is linked by Castle Street and Willis Wynd to the 'old town'. It is in Newtown Street that most of the county offices are grouped – the County Office, the excellent main library, police headquarters and branches of the ministries. The old High School, the most important in the county, is now housed in a new building. The town has spread south towards the railway (now closed) and a fine park is embellished with the Mercat Cross and a statue of Dune Scotius, the medieval philosopher whom Duns claims as its most distinguished forebear. The proud motto that 'Duns ding a'' was derived from a resounding defeat of the Earl of Northumberland in 1377 when the rattling or 'dinging' of dried skins threw the English camp into confusion. It was in the next century, in 1489, that the town was created a Burgh of Barony. Even with modern growth and its county status, the town still has under two thousand inhabitants, compared with Alnwick's seven thousand and Morpeth's fourteen thousand.

Jedburgh is almost a miniature Edinburgh in its basic pattern of a castle high on the hill dominating a long straight high street more than a half mile long, with the market place roughly in the middle, dividing the town into an upper and lower part, scene of a traditional ball game between the 'uppies' and the 'doonies'. The castle site, once a favourite residence of Scottish kings and one of the greatest strongholds on the Border, is now occupied by the old county prison but is still referred to locally as 'the castle'. The long street has many names – Townhead, Lawnmarket, High Street and Black Quarter according to Wood's map of 1823, although the modern town plan refers only to Castlegate and High Street. At its foot, by the river, was the old horse market. The street is still dominated by good town houses from the seventeenth century onwards, and looks very much in character. Recent new housing in Castlegate shows a bold attempt to match the interest of the older houses such as Nos 7–11, once occupied by Bonny Prince Charlie in 1745 on his way to the last invasion of English ground by a Scottish army, and now bearing his name. The burgage plots behind these town houses have been filled in by later building but are still fascinating in their pattern of narrow wynds and closes. Around the market place and along the High Street is the main shopping centre and a great congestion of traffic coming over the bridge along the A68 trunk road from Newcastle to Edinburgh, a bridge that was opened shortly before Wood drew his map of the town. Until that time the main access to the town was by the 'auld brig', a superb three-ribbed arched bridge now scheduled as an ancient monument and confined to pedestrians. This old bridging point led by Canon Gate to the market place, completing the main pattern of the town's streets.

In Queen Street, one of the medieval backlanes, stands Queen Mary's house, one of the finest examples of a fortified town house still standing, belonging to the Kerrs but made famous by the short stay of the tragic Queen in 1566 *en route* for her meeting with the Earl of Bothwell, then Keeper of Liddesdale, at Hermitage Castle. It is now a much-visited museum full of the Queen's personal possessions and mementoes.

The most important item of Jedburgh's townscape is the Abbey, standing to the south of the market place, accessible by the unique 1761 gatehouse. The lovely ruins of the Abbey are the first sight that greets travellers from the south and many of the chimneys of mills that clustered round the river at its foot have now been cleared. The Abbey site almost certainly has greater antiquity than the castle site, some of the lovely fragments in the Abbey museum showing Anglo-Saxon work from the seventh century, the heyday of the early Northumbrian kingdom, including crosses and a part of the tomb of St Boisil, possibly removed from Old Melrose Abbey. The hub of the town's activities is by the Abbey's gate. The mills by the bend of the Jed have gone, but new factories, mostly keeping links with the traditional textile industries, are developing along Bondgate beyond the two early nineteenth-century mills that still survive.

Like Jedburgh, there are many towns on the Borders that have grown up in conjunction with abbeys, settlements for their retainers and market places under the protection of their authority: Kelso (4000), Melrose (2000), Coldingham, Coldstream (1000), Tynemouth (now 70,000 in the Urban District), and Hexham (10,000).

Melrose, at the foot of the Eildon Hills, is beautifully complete. A broad triangular market place just outside the limits of the old 'mantel wall' that marked the monastic enclosure, fed by four narrow streets, gives the impression of a pattern that has survived all vicissitudes. The market cross, still in place since 1662, is surmounted by a unicorn and the Royal Arms of Scotland, emblems of a Burgh of Regality, granted in 1621. Here the shops and inns cluster around the site of the town well that stood by the cross, and there above them, so close as to seem part of the town's silhouette, is the mellow outline of the Celtic 'oppidum' on the north summit of the Eildons. A new section of road has been added to the north of the market place since John Wood's map of 1826 and the town hall is situated in Abbey Street. The Masonic headquarters in the High Street marks the oldest lodge in Scotland and the ritual procession of masons in December is one of the traditional festivals. New residential areas have developed both to the west above the town and along the Galashiels road by the Greenyards, the famous rugby ground, home of the seven-a-side game that is followed with fanatical enthusiasm in the Scottish Border towns. The town also manages to cope with demands by visitors for car parks and caravan sites and yet maintain its role as a most desirable residential area, right in the heart of the busiest part of the Tweed Valley, yet quietly withdrawn, as if to play its own special role, with no aspiration to greater urban functions.

Kelso, Jedburgh's great rival, is situated on a high bank of the Tweed, the chalk-heugh which gives its name to the town and along which the main street of the early settlement stretched, considerably shortened by the enlargement of the parkland around Floors Castle in the eighteenth century. Before the destruction of the royal burgh of Roxburgh and the great castle, its sparse ruins only a mile to the west, the town of Kelso was essentially an appurtenance of the abbey, at one time the greatest of the Border abbeys but now the least in terms of physical survival. For Kelso itself was also subject to the usual periodic destructions by fire and Englishman.

> The town is built much after the fashion of the Dutch and German cities, consisting of a spacious square or market place, with four streets and some considerable wynds, diverging from it in different directions. The market place is a square of large dimensions, chiefly composed of modern buildings, and containing the principal shops.[1]

Haig's description of his beloved town in 1825 is equally appropriate today. The great square with its planned look is still intact and the street names of Horse-market, Woodmarket and Coalmarket are still in use, running parallel east from the square on either side of the fine town hall, built in 1816, replacing the old tolbooth. Most of the buildings in the centre date from the same period. The setting gives the town a unique continental flavour. This square, still cobbled, was once the site of the famous St James' Fair, on 5 August, and much frequented by the gypsies from Yetholm with their horses and merchandise. The fair is now discontinued but Kelso is still the focus of a large area of the middle Tweed, and the ram sales, for example, held on the Border Union showground, are one of the greatest in Britain. The race-course, founded in 1822, lies on another open space to the north of the town. Hemmed in to west and south by the river (very good fishing) the town has grown towards the race-course and some interesting modern development of residential property is capped by the fine new health centre. This is most pleasing in a town that has been designated as of 'exceptional architectural value' – a reference not only applied to the buildings of the town square. Along Bridge Street is Ednam House, one of the finest Georgian town houses in the region. It is set well back from the road and is best admired from the riverside walk. Near it is an older medieval fragment, Abbey Court, the narrow street that once linked the Abbey with the old bridge. John Rennie's new bridge, that makes such a picturesque entry to the town, was started in 1800.

Farther down-stream, on another steep bank of the Tweed, is Coldstream, protected on one side by the natural moat of the Leet Burn. Nothing of the Cistercian Priory remains except the name of Nun's Walk. The market place remains but is almost a backwater, all the life of the town flowing along the one main street in which all the principal buildings are concentrated, though they do

---

[1] James Haig, *History of Kelso* (1825).

not have the architectural merit of other Border towns. The original home of the Coldstream Guards still stands in the old square.

To the north of the high street is the Hirsel, the home of Sir Alec Douglas Home, with its fine gardens open to the public. Coldstream is linked to English ground by Smeaton's 1766 bridge. At its northern end stands a small marriage house, the eastern equivalent of Gretna Green, recently restored but no longer in use for runaway couples. It is the river and the splendid panorama south to the Cheviots that gives Coldstream its charm, shared by campers and cara-vanners on the riverside haughs.

Another Berwickshire priory was Coldingham, near the rugged headland of St Abb's, but the market place and its cross are sadly neglected and have little attraction, though there are some good individual buildings, especially the inns. Although granted burgh status in 1638, it is now merely a village, very busy in summer, being only a mile from the magnificent coast.

One of the most exciting 'abbey towns' is found south of the Border, in the shelter of the Tyne valley, near the junction of the south and north branches of the river. Hexham began with St Wilfred's seventh-century abbey built of Roman stones from nearby camps such as Corbridge, known in the early medieval period as the finest building of its kind north of the Alps. It is situated on hummocky glacial moraine on the south bank of the river where two small burns, once known as the Hextol and the Halgut, cut small denes down to the main river. The streams are still there, flowing through the open space of the Seal that stands in the town centre, once the private precinct for monkish contemplation but now the possession of the town. The settlement that grew up near the burns was once known as Halgutstad, but the alternative of Hextol-desham was the origin of the present name. To the east of the abbey imme-diately outside its precinctual walls, still existing in 1862, stands the market place and the Shambles built in 1766, confronted on the west side by the massive stonework of the Moot Hall, a fourteenth-century tower-house now used as a library and exhibition centre. It was once the court house of the Archbishops of York, who controlled the Liberty and Regality of Hexham. An archway leads beneath it to Hallgates, where another fourteenth-century tower stands, even grimmer in aspect than the Moot Hall. This was once the prison. In this precinct also stand the new council offices and the old grammar school, dating from 1684. The three great medieval buildings dominate the skyline when approached over the river from the north, a unique silhouette only interrupted by the back of the cinema that fronts the market place. From the bridge the steep slope of Hall Stile leads back into the market where three other narrow streets lead out,

Gilesgate leading downhill to the junction of the two burns known as Holy Island, where a fine seventeenth-century house of almost pure Elizabethan style still stands. Many of the houses here have lintels (often over the back door, so not easily found) with seventeenth-century dates carved on them. It was once the centre of the skinner's trade and the local pub is suitably named.

The fellmongering business still survives in Gilesgate, a link with the monastic past, when fleeces and parchment were a main item of trade. On the south side of the market place two lanes lead out – Fore Street and St Mary's Chare, accessible by a narrow arch that shows fragments of St Mary's church that once stood there. They both lead to the main east–west street that is now the effective centre of the town. Here Priestpopple (the priests' people), Cattle Market (no longer) and Battle Hill combine to make the main shopping centre, together with the main inns, bus station, banks and business premises. The livestock auction marts, some of the busiest in the north of England, drawing cattle from as far afield as Ireland, are grouped at the east end of the main street, with many ancillary services, such as banking, feedstuffs, machinery, and the Farmers' Union.

The last of the 'abbey towns' is Tynemouth, now the centre of a county borough of more than seventy thousand people and, in effect, part of the great urban sprawl along the north bank of the Tyne estuary. Until the early nineteenth century, when the full effect of the coalfield activities became apparent, Tynemouth was composed of simple ingredients, which still preserve their identity remarkably well and make it a most pleasant cornerstone of the county, linking coast and estuary in the splendid views to be obtained from the cliff-lined peninsula. Here stands the coastguard station, and the still-fine ruins of the Benedictine priory with its fortified gatehouse, sometimes mapped as the 'castle', separated from the broad avenue of Front Street by a moat. At the end of Front Street, open to the keen easterlies, stands a statue of Queen Victoria erected in 1905 and beyond it terraces of solid town houses of the 1800s. Tynemouth has not lost its slightly superior atmosphere, although, as a town, it had to await the industrial age before achieving growth and status. The monks, powerful as they were, were never really able to break the monopoly of the Newcastle merchants on river traffic and failed to establish the full privileges associated with other medieval 'boroughs' in the county.

The main market centre of Coquetdale, administrative centre of a large rural district in mid-Northumberland, is Rothbury, with an air of a Scottish Victorian watering place in one of the loveliest settings in the entire region. Here the river Coquet, a notable salmon river, cuts through the Fell Sandstone ridge, giving an enclosed sense to the town, overlooked on both sides by moorland and extensive forestry, especially of the Cragside estate of Lord Armstrong. Here is neither castle nor abbey to account for the site, yet its market rights date back to a visit by King John in 1205. The notes issued by the local authority are headed 'the village of Rothbury' and it has yet to reach a population figure of two thousand. The railway came in 1870 and gave it a boost, closed in 1963 and caused a comparative slump, though the livestock market is recovering again, perhaps due to the heavy cartage rates which are leading generally to a revival of small markets.

The old town stands to the north of the medieval bridge, around a large, sloping open space, a steep grassy bank dividing two forking roads, on which most of the shops and main buildings are situated. At the south-east corner of the 'square' stands the church of All Saints, a largely Victorian restoration in which is found a very fine fragment of an early Anglo-Saxon cross-shaft (supporting the seventeenth-century font) suggesting that the settlement has early origins. The 'roth' element may come from the Celtic meaning 'cleared place'.

Isolated in Upper Teviotdale, yet thriving on its specialist woollen industries, is Hawick. It calls itself a 'comfortable town' and has an air of prosperity in the bright shopfronts along the Victorian High Street that runs parallel with the river. Between the main valley road and the river stand the mills that produce the town's prosperity and make Hawick and 'tweed' names that are known far outside the boundaries of the region and, indeed, the country. But it is not just an industrial town of more than sixteen thousand people; it is also a major market centre for the livestock region of Teviotdale, and its auction market is one of the busiest on the Borders. The historic core of the town lies to the south of the town hall, at the low-lying and flood-devastated area around Tower Knowe where the river Slitrig joins the Teviot. Here a congestion of narrow streets with names like Tower Dykeside, Howegate, Back Dam Gate and Cross Wynd shows medieval origins. The 'tower' referred to in street names was the fortified house of the Douglas family, now the Tower Hotel. The town achieved burgh status in 1511 and soon after was subjected (as were all Border towns) to the decimation of its menfolk at Flodden Field. The defence of the town by the younger men gave rise to the most famous 'riding' on the Borders.[1] However, in spite of the common riding which had its origin much earlier in the preservation of the 'bounds' of the common land, the great common lying to the south-west of the town was finally divided up, enclosed and lost to the town's people in 1777. It was at about the same time that Baillie John Hardie introduced the stocking frame

[1] See Chapter 10.

into his workshop and virtually founded the hosiery trade. By the end of the century the town had grown to nineteen thousand, far outstripping the other burghs on the Scottish side of the border. The importance is shown by the fifteen burghal representatives at the County Council meetings, with four from Jedburgh, four from Kelso and two from Melrose. Some of the early nineteenth-century mills still survive along the Weensland Road. Another unusual survival lies about two hundred yards uphill from the old town centre beyond the old 'port' at Drumlanrigg Square. This is the Mote, a Norman earthwork, now surrounded by a small park and new council flats. From its summit is a splendid view back over the town, so outstanding that it may suggest that Hawick, too, began under the shadow of a castle. The town's name is derived from two Anglo-Saxon elements, the first 'haga' indicating a hedged enclosure.

Hawick's great rival is Galashiels, another wool town of more than twelve thousand people, situated on the Gala river just up-stream from Melrose. Although in Selkirkshire, it is so closely associated with new developments taking place in the Melrose–St Boswells area of Roxburghshire that it can hardly be omitted here. The 'shieling' of the Gala originated as a small settlement for pilgrims on the way to Melrose Abbey. This may have been on the site of what is called 'the old town' on John Wood's survey of 1824, alongside Gala House. In spite of much recent rebuilding of that area, the old manor house and the cross still remain in what is now called Scott Crescent.

The Wilderhaugh Mill shown on Wood's map can make claims to be the first woollen factory in Scotland, with new methods of carding and spinning introduced in 1791. To the first mills coal was brought by pack-horse, and even in the early nineteenth century when Miss Wordsworth decried 'ugly stone houses taking the place of the broom-roofed thatched cottages' the population was only just over a thousand. By 1850 it had reached four thousand and by 1919 had grown to become one of the biggest urban centres on the Borders with more than fifteen thousand inhabitants.

The group of towns assembled at the strategic centre of the Tweed Basin, where the main east–west route following the Tweed crosses the main northern route still approximating to the alignment of the Roman Dere Street, is completed by St Boswells, which originated as Lessudden (from St Aidan) and was anciently a grange of Melrose Abbey. The older town is set on a hill overlooking the Tweed opposite Dryburgh.

Grouped round the imposing edifice of the old railway station at Newtown St Boswells is an important group of agricultural services, banking, Farmers' Union offices, forestry and advisory services. Here too are the new impressive administrative offices of the Roxburgh County Council. The old St Boswell's was important enough to have no less than sixteen tower-houses, all destroyed by the English armies in 1544, but the main street has some pleasant urban architecture and the town is still the headquarters of the Duke of Buccleuch's Hunt.

Other Scottish settlements carrying burgh status remain, or have declined to, villages with no functions outside their immediate vicinity. Such are Cockburnspath, Ancrum, Linton, Town Yetholm, Maxton, Smailholm and Minto, many of them with central greens or market places. In three of them, at least, market crosses remain.

The growth of the modern road system and, in its time, the railway, led to the decline of many local markets and the increased concentration on fewer, larger centres. The major market centres of Roxburgh are now only Hawick and Newton St Boswells, whilst Kelso and Duns survive in Berwickshire. Reston, a village on the main railway from Newcastle to Edinburgh, has an important livestock market. Berwick-upon-Tweed is the market centre for much of Berwickshire as well as north Northumberland. Northumberland now has ten livestock markets of importance, and two of them, Scots Gap near Rothley, and Acklington, are related to nineteenth-century railway developments rather than to historic towns. Scots Gap is an odd survival, now that the railway has closed; a new council estate stands by a Temperance hotel, with a scatter of buildings by the auction mart, looking something like a pioneer settlement in the American mid-west. Ponteland livestock market is situated in what was once a village on the main road north-west out of Newcastle to Carter Bar but which has now developed as a dormitory town of Tyneside. Of the twelve weekly markets recorded in Ward's Guide of 1851, only eight remain – at Berwick, Belford, Wooler, Alnwick, Rothbury, Hexham, Morpeth and Newcastle. The annual fairs at Blanchland, Harbottle, Norham, Stamfordham, Whittingham, Weetwood Bank and Stagshawbank have all ceased to function. One other useful indication of modern status, apart from population, is the presence of a secondary school. They are concentrated in a few main centres with special bus services feeding in from wide rural districts, and reflect the increasing importance of the main towns and the comparative decline of the smaller towns and villages.

Berwickshire, for example, is reorganizing its secondary education system around three main centres – Eyemouth, Duns, and Earlston, covering the west, middle, and east sections of the county respectively. Both the Royal Burgh of Lauder and the erstwhile County Town of Greenlaw are reduced to the status of supporting primary education only. Northumberland is now introducing the Middle School system so that only the four main market towns of Berwick,

Alnwick, Morpeth and Hexham, together with Haydon Bridge, will offer educational facilities up to the age of sixteen.

The market towns and burghs of the Border are amongst its greatest pleasures, still strongly rooted in the rural scene, at once their source of strength and vitality but also a potential cause of decline because of the loss of the surrounding rural population.[1] But the largest concentrations of population in the region are based on other resources than the rich fertility of the 'landward' areas and it is to these resources that we shall now turn, to landscapes of chimneys, cranes, and pit-head gear.

The Abbey Tower-house, Kelso.

[1] See Chapter 9.

# 8

# The new age of iron

I lived for some years in the small village of Ford, seven miles south of the Tweed, situated on a large private estate. Apart from the cottages of the estate workers, it contained a church, a primary school, a shop and a hall. With a population of about one hundred people, it was, and is, a very quiet place. I was surprised, when coming across a copy of Whellan's Directory of 1855, to see the occupations of the inhabitants at that time, which gave the impression of a hive of local activities. The complete list is worth quoting. There was an ironmonger, two joiners, a colliery agent, four stonemasons, two cornmillers, a manufacturer of spades, shovels and farm implements, a victualler, three grocers, two drapers, two gamekeepers, two shoemakers, a slater, a blacksmith, four tailors, two school-masters, a forester, the bailiff and the rector. Four farmers completed the list.

The remains of the old forge and the mill are still down by the river. The forge wheel was still intact and used for cutting and creosoting timber until quite recently, but the manufacture of spades and shovels, started by the Delavals in 1767, died out early in this century. Some of the implements manufactured there were not only for local farms but also for the colliery up on the Moss, where the shallow seams of the Scremerston Coal were worked. The adits and shallow pits can still be identified, although they have all been filled in to stop livestock and people from falling down them. The old 'mining village' can still be traced, mostly by the rhubarb that grows luxuriantly in what were once back gardens. Coal was last mined here before the First World War and elderly men remember going down the 'pit' with a rope tied round their thighs, 'walking' down the narrow shaft. Marsh gas, water and the competition of bigger pits farther south finally closed the workings, which had once been active in supplying small coal for the local agricultural improvements of the eighteenth and nineteenth centuries. Nearby, across a geological fault, the old quarry in the Fell Sandstone remains with much of its gear intact, though the quarry is only occasionally opened for new facing stones in the locality. A mile to the east some overgrown lime pits can still be identified. In the early nineteenth century, the traffic in coal and lime and freestone across the Border into the Tweed area was so heavy that local landowners drew up plans for a horse-drawn railway. Many local men were engaged in the extractive industries and in cartage. Throughout the rural areas is ample visual evidence of these local industrial activities. In the Milfield Plain below Ford were clay and tile works. Across the plain at Wooler were fulling mills and tenter grounds associated with the woollen industry. Any sheet of the Ordnance Survey map of the region still shows ample evidence of industrial archaeology, especially in the hill-lands of the Pennines, in the lead and silver mining areas around Hexham. Up in the North Tyne, now submerged beneath the advancing ranks of new afforestation, are the scars of stone quarries, lime pits and kilns, and coal workings. Bellingham was the site of an iron industry that supplied one-fifth of the ten thousand tons of iron used in Stephenson's High Level Bridge built across the Tyne in 1850. Even in the first decade of this century, railway lines were still being extended into the rural interior in mid-Northumberland for freight and passenger traffic.

The major inland industry to survive, outside the 'black triangle' of south-east Northumberland, is the woollen industry of the Upper Tweed, still flourishing even in the comparatively isolated parts of Teviotdale, well away from the main industrial areas and the major routeways. Culley and Bailey's *General View of Agriculture* records woollens still being made at Alnwick, Mitford, and Acklington in the 1790s, and a cotton mill at Netherwitton, and the Statistical Accounts of Berwickshire and Roxburghshire are full of references to local textile industries, although very few remain outside the main Tweed area.

The monastic establishments throughout the region, especially the Cistercians, encouraged the growth of sheep-flocks and the production of wool. Berwick-upon-Tweed was a major exporter of wool and enjoyed the privilege of shipping all that grew between the Coquet and the Tweed, in Teviotdale and in other parts of Scotland.

More important was Newcastle, which had the monopoly of all wools grown between the Tees and the Tyne, which went to Bruges and Middelburgh. It is probable that an area with such a dominance of sheep-flocks would have small local hand-loom industries from an early date, but the first mention of 'wauk

17a. *The market-place at Alnwick in the nineteenth century.*

17b. *Warkworth on the River Coquet protected by the moated castle and a gatehouse on the medieval bridge at the far end of town.*

18a. *John Dobson's own sketch of the interior of the Central Station at Newcastle upon Tyne, built 1846–50.*

18b. *The bridges of Newcastle upon Tyne; from the camera, New Tyne Bridge, the Swing Bridge, Stephenson's High Level Bridge and Redheugh Bridge.*

mills' (walker meaning fulling) occurs in Galashiels in 1587, together with
Flemish craftsmen and Scottish apprentices. The first Weavers' Corporation was
set up in the same town in 1666. By the seventeenth century there were three
mills making 'hodden grey'. The Act of Union shattered many industries as production costs in England were between ten and fifteen per cent lower than in
Scotland. Much of the wool from the southern counties of Scotland went south
by a long land passage to Yorkshire for manufacture, but in 1728 grants were
being made by the Board of Manufactures to skilled workers in wool in Galashiels, Hawick, Lauder and Jedburgh. By 1800, Galashiels mills were producing
shepherds' plaids and tartans, though Jedburgh claims the authorship of the first
cloth made from yarns of different colour. But Galashiels perfected the many-
coloured cloth, adding it to its list of famous cloths Gala 'blues', 'greys', and
'drabs'. In nearby Melrose, the traditional linen weaving died out, leaving 'the
still loom and the silent wheel', while the woollen industry concentrated on a few
growing towns. In Hawick in 1730 a spinning school was set up. Carpets were
made, trading with Newcastle and Kendal. But the great break-through in
Hawick came with the introduction in 1771 of four stocking-frames by Baillie
John Hardie, the founder of Hawick's woollen fortunes. By 1791, 362 people
were employed, and lamb's wool had ousted linen for hosiery. In the same
decade, William Watson introduced the factory system for spinning yarn with
new carding machines and spindle hand-jennies. In 1826, the first use was made
of imported high-quality wool, and within fourteen years more than eighty per
cent of wool used was imported. Today, no local wool is used in the Tweed
industry, the fine knit-wear being produced from Cashmere, Botany and other
fine wools. The fine-quality cloth, among them the 'tweels', found a ready
market in London and it was in the misreading of correspondence between
London and Hawick that the word 'tweed' originated in 1832, a name which
therefore has only an accidental connection with the Scottish river on which the
industry developed. The concentration on fine cloth enabled the industry to
survive the competition of Leicester, though during a later slump redundant
knitters from Hawick were offered twelve shillings 'tramping money' to go to
Leicester and Nottingham, which had strange echoes in the last decade when
redundant miners from the Northumberland pits have been offered inducements
to go south to the Midland Coalfields. Some of the early nineteenth-century
mills still survive, in Hawick and Galashiels and in Jedburgh. The Cumledge
Mill near Duns is still making blankets as it has done for more than 130 years, a
most impressive architectural survival of the pioneering industrial days.

Both Hawick and Galashiels are essentially Victorian towns, symbolized in the

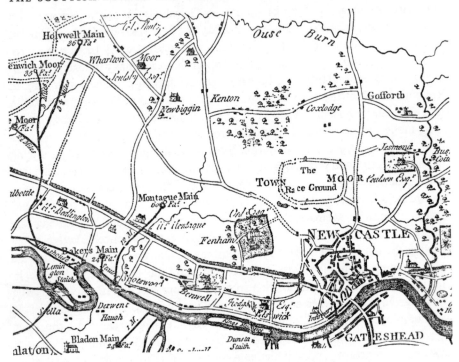

**Map 8** *John Gibson's map of the Tyne Collieries, 1787.*

latter by the Burgh Chambers erected in 1867. This was the period of the introduction of power looms, the railway from Edinburgh assisting in the transport of coal. In 1801 Hawick had a population of three thousand. By 1891 it had nineteen thousand. In the same year, Galashiels had grown to seventeen thousand with a turnover of more than £1,000,000 in contrast to its 1790 turnover of £1000. 'Cardigans' for the Crimea and the constant introduction of new processes and machinery were among the contributory factors. By 1909, Galashiels had established the Technical College to become the centre of training in Scotland, while Hawick's Henderson Technical School followed in 1929. Although essentially a machine industry, much of the finishing of the garments, now entirely aimed at the luxury and fashion trades, both heavy earners of foreign currency, is still done by hand even by the traditional 'putting out' to local villages, which are scoured for suitable labour. Nearly 3500 workers are now employed in the 'Tweed' woollen industry.

. . . . .

It was the gifts of the sub-soil, the outcropping of abundant coal seams, that brought about the final association of the north-east and heavy industry, giving rise to a common view of Northumberland as being almost synonymous with Tyneside, appearing in atlas maps with the industrial area just included in maps of England and the rest lost in the forgotten corner of the map of Scotland. The coal-extraction industry, like the woollen industry, has its roots in the monastic past with the monks, especially of Tynemouth and Newminster (near Morpeth), creating wealth from the early pits. Aeneas Sylvius, the future Pope who travelled in the Borders in the fourteenth century, reported that the Scottish monasteries put 'black stone' at the gates as alms for the poor. By 1239, Henry III had granted the freemen of Newcastle the right to dig coal, thick seams outcropping within the vicinity of the town on what is now the Town Moor. Local people speak of coal still being found there during the 1939–45 war. Geological investigations carried out with a view to opencast working showed the Moor to be honey-combed with early 'bell-pits'.[1] By the thirteenth century, the name 'carbo-maris' or sea-coal was already in use. The early seams were either worked on the surface or by levels in the steep banks of the Tyne and its tributary denes, adjacent to sea transport and available for local use and exportation in wooden craft. The coal used in the embryo industries growing up along the Tyne banks, such as salt pans, glass, pottery and copperas, was the 'land-sale', whereas the exported material was called 'sea-coal', a name to become famous over the centuries, especially during the rebuilding of the City of London following the Great Fire. The monks of Newminster operated salt pans at Blyth as early as the twelfth century and by the end of the seventeenth century there were two hundred pans on Tyneside alone: one of the long-distance route-ways across the county, head-ing over the Border hills into the Upper Tweed, is still called the Salters' Road, and a medieval bridge still survives in some neglected lanes at the back of Gosforth Park known as the Salters' Bridge.

By the Tudor period the acute shortage of timber for fuel greatly stimulated the mining of coal, and the Duke of Northumberland was using it in Alnwick Castle. A contemporary wrote that coal 'crept from the forge into the kitchen and hall', and some of the fine firebacks still to be found in Border mansions date from the need to protect stone and brick chimneys from the heat of the coal. The winning of coal was widespread throughout shallow workings as far north as Jedburgh, but the centre of the activity was within two miles of the Tyne where coal was carried by wains down to the loading places or 'staithes' (a Saxon

---

[1] See K. Hudson, *Industrial Archaeology* (J. Baker, 1966).

word meaning 'bank') on the river and drawn up again by horses. A special group of sailors developed, the keelmen, responsible for the river traffic, many recruited from the Border dales. A special suburb grew up to the east of Newcastle's walls at the mouth of Pandon Burn where the keelmen congregated. They were controlled in turn by the Society of Hostmen, merchant adventurers of the City who received their monopoly of the coal trade from Elizabeth in 1600, at which time nearly 200,000 tons of coal were being shipped out of the Tyne.

A network of wagon-ways grew up, of wooden rails with horse-drawn wagons replacing the horse and wain. The credit for their introduction is difficult to establish, though one of the first was constructed from Bebside pit to Blyth. They were in general use by 1670 and known throughout the country as 'Newcastle Roads'.

When writing of Newcastle in his series of county studies at the beginning of the eighteenth century, Thomas Coxe could enthuse that

> the coal trade is incredible, it being almost surrounded by coal-pits and having always great coal fleets, sometimes 500 sail, whose station is at Sheales nigh the river's mouth, continually attending for loading. London alone is said yearly to spend 600 thousand chauldrons.[1]

Yet Newcastle at this time still had a population of only eighteen thousand people, having nearly doubled since the Tudor period and yet being still safely harboured within its medieval walls apart from the keelmen's suburb of Sandgate and small growths along the banks of the river. The city had its origins in an encampment on the line of the Roman Wall where it ran close to the river, probably the bridging-point known as Pons Aelius. Probably a major supply point for the Roman garrisons, its early history is obscure but it emerges as the keystone of the Norman control of the northern marches, epitomized by the great stone keep of Henry II, together with its curtain wall and projecting gatehouse, the Black Gate, which still dominates the skyline on the railway approach from the south, on the edge of the steep banks of the Tyne. The Keep and Black Gate have been recently cleaned, repointed and restored under the custody of the Corporation, which is maintaining them as museums. To the north side, the early markets developed by the cathedral of St Nicholas – the streets are still narrow and bear names like the Bigg (barley) Market, Groat Market and Cloth Market – clustered round the old guildhall, rebuilt by Trollope in the seventeenth century and now an exhibition hall. The old centre is almost isolated physically

---

[1] T. Coxe, *Northumberland* (c. 1725).

by the deep trench of the Lort Burn, now followed by the cobbled lane of the Side. Radiating from this fortified core were the three main routeways of Pilgrim Street, Newgate Street and Westgate, hemmed in to the east by Pandon Burn and to the west by Skinner Burn, their steep banks making building difficult, but giving rise to a series of steep steps like the Dog Leap Steps that gives the city some of its special flavour. By the thirteenth century, it was reorganized into four parishes – those of St John's, St Andrew's, St Nicholas and All Saints, the four churches still surviving, though All Saints was rebuilt in 1786 in a remarkable elliptical form by David Stephenson. In that same century, the town walls, amongst the strongest in Europe, were built.[1] Close inside the walls in Friars Street, a fragment of the medieval town survives in the dilapidated cloister of the thirteenth-century Dominican building of Blackfriars. Much of the buildings show modification by the later Guilds. The quayside itself still holds some of the fragments of Coxe's Newcastle, some wooden structures such as Arthur's Cooperage on the Close and Bessie Surtee's House on Sandhill surviving innumerable fires. These five-storey houses seem to grow up the bank, the roof-tops being level with the castle.

Newcastle was not to burst out of its walls until the full force of prosperity based on the extension and industrialization of the coalfield boosted its populaton to twenty-eight thousand at the time of the first census in 1801.

Meanwhile, some of the wealthy coal-owners formed a group known as the Grand Allies, and energetic 'improvers', often landed gentry like the Delavals, developed their industrial sites, such as the new harbour at Seaton Sluice, a great cut through the rocks being made in 1761 by Lord Delaval to improve the 1628 harbour built by Sir Ralph Delaval. The sluice, as a loading base for coal and a glass industry, did not 'die' until the 1850s and still has a possible future as a yachting basin and marina. A wealthy Newcastle merchant took a lease of land at Blyth Dene, typical of many of the lovely denes that still survive on the industrial east coast, and used iron ore found in the banks, water power, and timber to create a new iron industry, making nails, which, by 1750, supported fifty-nine furnaces, whilst Blyth down-stream was busy developing a shiploading industry. 'Hartley Pans for sailors, Bedlington for nailers' went the jingle, but soon the nailers gave way to the 'railers' and Bedlington became one of the main centres of iron rail manufacture favoured by George Stephenson in his railway developments.

Water was the great enemy of the mining industry, and even in the 1850s it was estimated that thirty times as much water, measured by weight, was drawn

[1] See Chapter 5.

up from the pits as coal. By the middle of the eighteenth century the central basin of the coalfield was drowned out. Deeper seams needed new equipment and especially a means of pumping out water and lifting coal. Of four steam engines in use in Britain in 1714, two were in Newcastle pits – one of them a Newcomen engine – and in the next sixty years 138 steam engines were brought into use. An engine designed by Smeaton, the bridge builder, was in operation at Longbenton in 1772. Steam power was first used for surface haulage at Birtley in 1808. The conditions were ripe for a new period of mining colonization in the difficult ground north of the ninety-fathom dyke, the great fault line that cut across the coalfield from the Tyne at Blaydon, then north of Newcastle to the coast at Cullercoats Bay.

This was the world into which George Stephenson was born, son of a fireman at Wylam Colliery. After working on a farm, George drove a gin horse at Black Callerton, the principle being similar to the horse-gins used in threshing barns in the big farms. He made rapid progress first as fireman, like his father, then as brakeman, during which time he met the engineer Robert Hawthorn, whose new engine was to be installed at Ballast Hill down-river, where Stephenson soon found himself until moving to the West Moor Pit at the Grand Allies. Here he settled in the small cottage which is still preserved at the entry road to the brave new world of the 'new town' of Killingworth. The dial above the door was designed and built by George and his son, Robert, and the wagonway that ran by the back garden can still be traced in the lines of the council housing estate across the road. By 1811, he established his reputation as an engineer by over-coming the problem of draining the New High Pit at Killingworth, and was put in charge of all machinery in the pits controlled by the Grand Allies. The pro-gress of George Stephenson and son from then on symbolizes the development of industrial Tyneside, the greatness of which depended not only on a happy conjunction of natural resources, such as abundant coal and a deep estuary, but on the quality and invention of its people, a quality of self-help and endurance that may owe something to the turbulent history of the Border country. An iron railway had been used from the Walker Pit to the Tyne back in 1797 but Stephenson developed a complete network from pit-heads to coal-staithes which, by now, were large timber constructions designed to give gravity feed into waiting ships, which, incidentally, finally broke the keelman's monopoly. He developed underground haulage engines and made a new safety lamp, reaching the same conclusion as Sir Humphrey Davy by his own pragmatic methods. So the Geordie engine and the Geordie lamp passed into Tyneside lore and by 1814 he had designed the 'Blucher' for the Killingworth wagonway, the first locomotive of modern design, a development based on the locomotive that had first been used in 1805 near his old home at Wylam. Cast iron rails and flanged wheels and new forms of suspension laid the basis of the new locomotive works, first at Killingworth, then at Newcastle, that finally led to the spectacular triumph of the first passenger railway in the world when Stephenson's 'Locomotion' with three hundred passengers drew into Stockton Quay to the roar of forty thousand onlookers.

The new system of railways, direct descendant of the old 'Newcastle roads', transformed the mining scene and enabled mining to take place far from the coasts and rivers, and, incidentally, laid the foundations of a new engineering industry, producing rails, locomotives, boilers, mining machinery, and the like. By 1839, the railway to Carlisle was completed with the aid of a bridge at Scotswood, and plans were going ahead for a line to the north. Three railway stations built on that line – Corbridge, Riding Mill and Wylam – are amongst the oldest railway stations in the world still to be in use for passenger traffic, Wylam probably holding the distinction of being the oldest, having been continuously in use since 1835.

In spite of the opposition from landowners who did not want the railway through their land (such as the Duke of Northumberland) and those inland who did, favouring a North Tyne route, the main rail link to the north and Edinburgh took shape. By 1846 work had started on two great bridges of stone and iron that still survive and function today, impressive memorials to the Stephensons, father and son.

Newcastle Central Station, designed by John Dobson, was opened in 1850, and the portico, originally intended to be even more extensive, was added by 1865. One of the finest railway stations in the country, it was also the culmination of the rebuilding of the city that had started in 1825 with the construction of Eldon Square outside the walls of the old city.

One mid-Victorian visitor was quite overwhelmed by his first view of Dean Street.

> Before you opens one of the noblest and most magnificent streets you ever beheld! Here all that is old at once ceases. You are in the midst of lofty and modern mansions. You walk into what has been long termed the Coal Hole of the North, and find yourself at once in a city of palaces; a fairyland of newness, brightness and modern elegance. And who has wrought this change? It is Mr. Grainger.[1]

[1] William Howitt, *Visits to Remarkable Places* (The Silver Library, 1907).

It was not only Richard Grainger, but also the architectural talent of John Dobson and the financial help of John Clayton that transformed medieval Newcastle and created a new town centre out of the 'erst-time fields and gardens of the nuns and friars and the crooked alleys which bounded them'. The 'commodious streets' such as Grainger Street, Clayton Street and Grey Street, focusing on the monument to Earl Grey, the reformer, still give the city one of the most elegant centres in Britain, comparable in some respects with the New Town in Edinburgh. Grey Street has been cleaned up and now looks what it was once called – 'the finest curved street in Europe' – in spite of new frontages developed by banks, insurance and other commercial companies. Grainger Market, at its time, 1835, one of the most spacious covered markets in Europe, also survives as a market, though the fruit and vegetable markets have been moved recently to a new site in the Team Valley, south of the Tyne.

The new city reflected the aspirations and confidence of Tyneside, and the city boundaries, now with a population of 87,000 people, were enlarged to take in the townships of Elswick, Jesmond, Westgate, Heaton and Byker, doubling its area. It was in the fields at Elswick, where speculators were planning new villas, that W. G. Armstrong decided to set up a new factory for the manufacture of hydraulic equipment. By this time, coke was in general use for smelting iron, and Bedlington's iron industry had survived the loss of its local timber by using the coal that outcropped in the Blyth Dene's banks. The Crimean War, which had boosted the Tweed woollen industry with the production of 'cardigans', also assisted Armstrong's fortunes, and the production of his new breech-loader gun at Elswick Ordnance Company soon dominated the north bank of the Tyne.

Whereas the first half of the nineteenth century is the story of mining colonization and the development of the railways, the second half of the century belongs to the river, the shipyards and associated engineering industries. The formation of the Tyne Improvement Commission in 1850, the same year that saw the climax of the railway construction in the opening of the High Level Bridge, led to the progressive development of the river Tyne as a deep estuary, navigable by large iron ships and lined by shipyards and engineering works, as far up-stream as Newburn. The piers at the bar were started in 1854, and the estuary was dredged, giving depths of up to twenty-five feet up to Newcastle Quay, which was itself rebuilt from 1866 to 1884. New docks were developed – the Northumberland Dock near Howdon in 1857, the Tyne Dock at South Shields in 1859 (a dock which has shipped more coal than any other dock in the world), and the Albert Edward Dock in 1884 beyond Whitehall Point. The Point was still being developed in 1904, the railways feeding out like a river delta from Percy Mains and the pits inland to Backworth, Burradon and Seghill. Coal shipments from the Tyne (fourteen million tons by the end of the century) reached the peak of twenty-one million tons in 1923, and have fallen now to about four million tons. The staithes, operated by the National Coal Board, can load one thousand tons of coal per hour. The opening of the swing bridge, driven by Armstrong hydraulic equipment, on the alignment of the original bridging-point of the Tyne in 1876, improved navigation to Elswick and beyond. The Crimean War provided a market, too, for the new ironclad warships from Palmer's yard at Jarrow, which mushroomed, as had Elswick, from a village to a town of forty thousand people in 1900 with such a dependence on the one works that its closure in 1934, as a result of the depression in world trade, almost signed the death warrant of the town, 'the town that was murdered'.

By 1868, Armstrong was in the gun-boat business, and amalgamations between shipyards and between shipping and engineering interests produced the internationally famous companies of Armstrong-Whitworth which moved from Elswick to a more convenient site down-stream at Walker. Hawthorne-Leslie, a conjunction of shipbuilding and locomotives, specialized in marine engineering. In 1872 the names of Swan and Hunter were linked together with a four-thousand-foot river frontage and an interest in the Wallsend Slipway. After all the trials of depression and war and the fluctuating fortunes of the shipbuilding industry, it is Swan Hunter that remains as the controlling force behind all the shipyards of the Tyne and maintains the traditions of the river in launching the quarter-million-ton tankers of today. Tyneside lays some claim to have launched the first oil tanker, the *Vaterland*, in 1872. Until the launching of the *Esso Northumbria* and the super tankers now under construction, the great days of Tyne launchings were the *Mauretania* in 1907, and its contribution to the First World War in the form of fifty-five warships and 290,000 tons of merchant shipping. The Tyne is still second in the league of British ship-launching estuaries. The growth of the shipyards stimulated associated engineering activities and the enormous increase in the use of iron, yet, paradoxically, the period witnessed the loss of the iron industry. The famous Bedlington Works, which had started with nails and flourished with rails, closed in 1860, followed by Winlaton, Wylam, Lemington and Walker by 1891, due to the competition of the Teesside industry close to the rich ore seams of the Cleveland Hills.

The shipyards took over much of the riverside areas that had been occupied by the once-flourishing glass, soap and pottery industries. The alkali industry, which had produced half the country's output in 1867 after pioneer beginnings at Walker early in the century, formed the nucleus of the United Alkali

Company of 1890, forerunner of I.C.I., which was also to leave Tyneside except for a post-war plant at Prudhoe.

By 1884 C. A. Parsons were experimenting with steam turbines for ship propulsion and with turbo-dynamo for electric supply to ships. Their small s.s. *Turbinia* dashed through the lines of the Spithead Review in 1894 at over thirty-four knots, leading to the adoption of their engines for the new dreadnoughts. Later, amalgamation with A. C. Reyrolle produced the giant electrical engineering company at Hebburn.

The electrical engineering industry was yet another breakthrough on Tyneside. The Swan Electric Lamp Co. was founded in 1885 and new power stations at Pandon Dene and other Tyneside sites gave the new Newcastle Electric Supply Company the prototype of the National Grid. Swan's original filament lamp, together with his bust and a modern commemorative sculpture, form the centre-piece of the new office development in the Pilgrim Street roundabout complex.

The great days of iron are reflected in the cheek-by-jowl displays in the Museum of Science and Engineering on the edge of the Town Moor, where models, prints, maps and machinery jostle for space. The emphasis is on mining, marine engineering (including a special room for the s.s. *Turbinia*), transport (including the 'Billy' locomotive of 1830), electrical engineering, and armaments, with Armstrong's No. 1 gun of 1855 confronting visitors as they enter. It is a fascinating place, for adults and children, but Tyneside's industrial heritage deserves more space, especially as the visible evidence in the landscape diminishes.

The industrialization of the entire estuarine area and the enormous demand for fuel stimulated the final wave of mining, especially for steam coal, that completed the colonization of the coalfield as far north as Amble and was effective in creating some of the largest mining settlements around Ashington, known for decades as the largest 'mining village' in the world. Public buildings and major shops all show dates between 1890 and 1910 and the settlement, now with a population of 26,000, is an example of a town that grew rapidly on the basis of one resource. Its main street is dominated by the Cooperative stores and speckled with the opulent façades of working men's clubs. To the west stretch the earlier rows of terraced pit cottages, many of stone similar in style to the simple terraces of tied cottages that were transforming the rural estates at the same time. To the east lies the great grid of later brick rows with rear service roads, outdoor privies and the pile of miners' coal by the wall. The rows were often designed to face inwards on to gardens and green areas, being built after the Local Government acts of the 1870s, and often sport idyllically pastoral names in place of the more pragmatic numbered row. Local authorities and the National Coal Board, one of the largest land and house owners in the county, have effected great changes by modernizing the houses and removing some of the rows, giving a much greater sense of space.

But, though many of the pit villages were literally planted on the landscape, many were grafted on to existing rural communities, such as Cramlington, Killingworth and Earsdon, where a fine street of solid stone buildings, often with a farm cluster still surviving, stands like a fossil trapped in the later brick accumulations around it. The pithead gear, the railway sidings and the pitheap complete the scene. Bedlington is particularly fine, with its broad main street still embellished by a market cross and several fine late-Georgian frontages that keep a memory of a pre-industrial age and its ancient glory as the centre of a separate shire attached to the Bishopric of Durham. Many of these settlements stagnated during the economic depression of the inter-war years but the pace of change in recent years has been accelerating, especially with the closure of smaller inland pits and the bulldozing of the poorest property. Even the stone pit rows at Burradon, which the town-planner of Killingworth regarded, together with its pit heap, as a monument to great endeavours worthy of retention, have fallen before the demolishers and it will not be long before an authentic pit row will have as much antiquarian interest as a medieval castle. But the coalfield is a much greener place than its image has projected south of the Tyne, in spite of what are jovially referred to as the 'Ashington Pyramids'. Many of the villages are finding renewal as new residential areas linked with fast roads to Tyneside and the new light industries being brought into the region.

But the coal itself is far from exhausted and an estimate in 1945 reported a reserve of 1760 million tons, five per cent of the nation's output at a time when extraction was running at about twelve million tons a year. The National Coal Board, which took over all the major mine workings on vesting day in 1948, still has sixteen pits in operation, mostly within six miles of the coast, and one of the most modern pits in the country is now operating at Lynemouth in conjunction with the development of the giant Alcan aluminium smelter. Some of the biggest holes in the country change their pattern every day in the major opencast workings inland from Druridge Bay, with giant machines gorging themselves on the near-surface coals between Widdrington and Chevington, producing over a million tons of coal with a labour force of just over a hundred men. Blyth, which can lay some claims to have as long a pedigree as an industrial port as Tyneside itself, was shipping 200,000 tons of coal by 1854 from its own staithes, and later decline was staved off by improvements after 1882 which gave it fifteen feet of clear water and new coaling wharves which shipped out two million tons by 1891. By 1912, it could offer twenty-four feet of water, not much less than the Tyne, and in 1961 it shipped out six million tons of coal and claimed to be the largest coal-shipping port in Europe. It also exports barley and scrap metal and imports pit-props, timber, pig iron, fertilizer, oil and other cargoes for farm and factory, and is now undergoing further improvements for bulk ore imports for Alcan. Blyth, with 36,000 inhabitants, manages to keep the real smell of the sea in its nostrils with the aid of inshore seines and cobles in the South Harbour – a busy little port with coal mines, power station, great wooden staithes, fish and retail markets all cheek by jowl.

The enormous energy and engineering talent of such industrial enterprise are reflected in the continued growth of Newcastle itself. This manifested itself in the redevelopment of the town centre – though nothing as adventurous as the Grainger-Dobson rebuilding was to take place until the 1960s – in the progressive clearance of some of the most congested areas by the quayside by fire and for new commercial premises, and in the rapid spread of the suburbs until there was in effect one urban belt stretching from Newburn in the west to Tynemouth on the coast, enveloping Byker, Walker, Wallsend, Willington, North Shields and Tynemouth as well as the townships of North Durham from Blaydon, Gateshead and Felling to South Shields, producing one of the greatest conurbations in the British Isles. The character of the late-Victorian period is still indelibly stamped on Tyneside. This period saw the growth of new hotels around the Central Station and the development of the commercial district which still dominates the area between Grey Street and the Quayside. A flurry of new church and chapel building spread throughout the new suburbs, and by 1911 the population reached 696,000. By 1882 a new diocese of Newcastle was set up with St Nicholas as the cathedral church, and the town was created a city by Royal Charter with the chief citizen to be known as the Lord Mayor. Improvement in housing was heralded by the local government acts of the 1870s and new drainage, paving and lighting alleviated the high death rate. The upper-class citizens moved out to new residential suburbs of Jesmond and Heaton.

North of the city was the unique open space of the Town Moor, an area of rough grassland that brought the country right into the heart of the city, meeting by the Barras Bridge over Pandon Burn at the Haymarket, now the main bus station, still lined with pubs bearing rural names. The Town Moor, with twelve hundred acres, larger than Hyde Park in London, had been confirmed as common land controlled by the freemen of the town as early as 1357. The names of its various parts, such as Nun's Moor and Castle Leazes, still reflect its medieval origins as grazing land and hay fields associated with the secular and religious institutions. Even after the 1835 reform of local government, the freemen maintained their rights, which led to dual ownership, the Town Council owning the ground but the Freemen controlling the use of the grass. The Moor has always been the main mustering ground for large assemblies, whether of popular protest after the Peterloo Massacre, the Chartists, the Miners' Union or the crowds at the annual Race Week 'hoppings'. It was also the race-course after 1721 – remembered still by the name of Grandstand Road – until the horses moved to Gosforth Park in 1882. In its place was instituted a Temperance Festival, which has survived as one of the biggest fairs in the country, whilst losing much of its temperance.

It is no small pleasure to be able to walk out of the city centre and within five minutes be on rough grazing with a herd of good cattle, a string of horse-riders and a smattering of amateur golfers, and gaze over the landmarks of the city – the new carillon of the Civic Centre, the rising towers of the expanding University, the floodlights of St James' Park and the neo-Gothic spires of the late Victorian suburbs.

The growth of the city is reflected in the pressures on this great open space so near the centre, a paradise for speculators, if only they could get their hands on it. The nineteenth century nibbled away at the edges. The first parks laid out were Brandling Park and Leazes Park in 1873, and by 1888 a new site had been found for the College of Science (attached to the university of Durham), later to be called Armstrong College, near Barras Bridge. In 1895, the West End football team joined the East End team to form the famous United Club with its home on St James' Park, which proceeded to stir up regional enthusiasm by winning the League championship three times and reaching the Cup Final five times in the space of seven years. Yet another site on the Town Moor was allocated to the new Royal Victoria Infirmary opened in 1906 to commemorate the Queen's silver jubilee, as a result of public subscription. The new building on the southern edge of the Moor has been reinforced by extensive university development, by the new Civic Centre in its green oasis and a new educational precinct, as well as the Hancock Museum which has had the effect of pulling the focus of city life away from the river up to the Haymarket. The once elegant houses and gardens beyond the medieval walls along Pilgrim Street and Sidgate are now part of the major shopping and entertainment centre, and Haymarket itself is due for further 'improvement' as a key section of the new urban motorways that will encircle the old city centre.

The city almost turns its back on its estuarine origins, and the neglect of the riverside is in striking contrast to the bright new buildings lapping against the Town Moor, though the new tower office blocks of the Pilgrim Street roundabout do make an impressive statement of the city's renewal schemes at the entrance from the south along the Tyne road bridge (opened in 1928), and the reconstruction of the derelict area around All Saints Church is now underway. Yet surprisingly the view of the city from the Gateshead Toll has many points of similarity with the famous 'delineation' of the brothers Buck, two hundred years ago. It is a strong city of stone and iron and brick, with the skyline only now being punctuated by new tower blocks. The riverside itself is very quiet and the Tyne Quay is liveliest on a Sunday morning when the street traders hold their weekly market. Meanwhile, the livestock market down by the railway station still operates, and the shops adopt new façades, cinemas, theatres and night-clubs flourish as befits a regional capital and the major urban centre of the Border region.

The river comes into its own down-stream from the slipways of Wallsend to the bar at Tynemouth, where the cargo vessels and the regular shipping lines bound for the Baltic hoot irately at the nuisance of pleasure yachts and huddled fishermen, watched over by the enormous statue of Admiral Collingwood musing on the long maritime traditions of his home county. The Tyne is still the major ship-repair area in the country and everything from ferry-boats, deep-sea trawlers and whalers, to oil tankers and cargo vessels can be seen. A trip up the estuary from the Tyne Quay is as rewarding in its own way as a walk over the Cheviots, or a tour of the Border abbeys. The fish-quays of North Shields, speckled with Polish words, and the basin at Tynemouth are backed by elegant terraces and squares that reflect the great days of the river and, even now, maintain a slightly superior air. Beyond them, Whitley Bay gazes at its fine cliffs and wide sands and cannot decide whether to keep up the image built by big hotels and seaside mansions or to enjoy the brashness of the weekend resort for Tyneside's thousands, with bingo, fun arcades, cafés and donkeys on the sands. It is within easy reach of the city centre since the completion of the coastal road and is a growing residential area, many of the large houses finding a new lease of life as flats and apartments. To sit up on the red cliffs by Tynemouth Priory and gaze out over the bar, and follow the great sweep south past the promontory of South Shields, with its Roman fort trapped in terraced housing, as far as the yards of Jarrow and the grim mud flats of the Slake where oil storage tanks and timber yards huddle by Bede's old monastery of St Peter's, to see the great highway lined by cranes and docks, is to witness a river that has known great vicissitudes yet still receives the commerce of coast and continent with each tide.

Both the Olsen and the Bergen lines operate from Tyneside and the commerc of the estuary is still orientated towards Scandinavia and the Baltic, with North America, West Africa and the Netherlands as the next most important trading areas. Whilst the Tyne Improvement Commission operates most public port facilities and maintains responsibility for river conservancy and policing, there are several quays owned by various corporations and private companies and coal staithes operated by British Rail and the National Coal Board. A recent national report recommended a new authority to coordinate all these functions, for the Tyne is an estuary that is fighting for survival against the competition of better-placed rivals.

# 9

# The planned environment

Changes now taking place in the landscapes of the region will be as dramatic in their impact as the 'improvements' of eighteenth-century landowners and the restless advance of nineteenth-century industrialists. Planning is not new. The sixteenth-century monarchy 'planned' the defence of their borders, often in scrupulous detail. The Dukes of Northumberland and Roxburgh 'planned' changes in their vast landholdings on a not very much smaller scale than the operations of the Forestry Commission and National Coal Board today. But what makes today qualitatively different is that every corner of the region is subject, to some extent, to planning considerations.

It is inevitable that the most obvious indications of change are apparent in the urban areas. There the traditional patterns give way most readily before the bulldozer. There the traveller is most aware of new motorways, by-passes, spine roads, tower blocks and a flourishing of housing estates. Yet the rural areas, too, show that all landscapes are in a constant state of flux. We may bemoan the loss of 'traditional' aspects of the countryside, but every 'tradition' was a newcomer to the scene at some time. Here a new concrete barn breaks the pattern of a stone steading. There roadside timbers are felled, a hedgerow rooted out. Trim ranks of conifers obliterate a familiar moorland scene. Change will take place, albeit slowly, and the local authorities produce their plans and classify the land in the avowed hope of maintaining and improving the quality of the Border environment both for its inhabitants and for those who visit it. This involves two major considerations – the preservation of what is good and useful in the present landscape (but who decides what is 'good'?) and the removal of what is ugly and harmful, such as sub-standard housing, industrial wastelands and unemployment.

The Northumberland National Park was confirmed in 1956, the ninth of the
National Parks, covering an area of about three hundred and ninety-eight square
miles, including most of the Cheviot Hills, with a long extension south to include
the best-preserved stretches of the Roman Wall, especially where it accords with

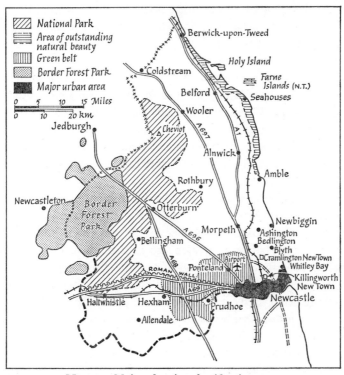

**Map 9**   *Major planning classification areas.*

the magnificent outcrop of the Whin Sill. An eastern lobe of the Park extends to
include the Rothbury Fells, the highest section of the Fell Sandstone Arc that
traverses mid-Northumberland.

Two years later, in 1958, the whole length of the coast from Warkworth to
Berwick-upon-Tweed was designated as an Area of Outstanding Natural Beauty,
some forty miles in length. The third major area afforded protection is the Green
Belt that runs in an arc to the north-west of Newcastle and its suburbs and is
intended primarily to restrict urban sprawl in that direction. Most of the landscape within the Green Belt is intensively farmed and lacks the visual quality of
much of the rural area, though the area along the Tyne Valley as far as Hexham
is very fine.

177

To these areas may be added a fourth – the extensive Forestry Commission holdings, most of which are now included in the Border Forest Park, in which tourist access and facilities are being extended. The same designation is found north of the Border, in the northward extension of the Kielder Forest into Wauchope. At the moment Scotland has no designated National Parks, though the need for controlled access to, and enjoyment of, the open spaces of the Border region is catered for by the creation of the Countryside Commission under the Countryside (Scotland) Act of 1967.

The whole of Berwickshire is effectively one countryside park, with landscapes of high visual quality throughout, culminating in the splendours of the coast and the Lammermuir Hills. That sounds attractive, but there is a danger of the county fossilizing into a beautiful relic, lacking the amenities and economic activities to keep its population. The countryside cannot stand still, for its basic economy is under pressure and the local people need more than beauty and the admiration of tourists to keep them in their native land.

The large landowners, who have considerable influence in local affairs, do not necessarily see the need for new opportunities of employment brought into the region, especially those that would offer higher wage rates than farming and estate work and cause an even greater loss of their own labour force. 'Rural depopulation is a rejection of the status of working-class countrymen' claimed a sociological survey of a Cheviot parish, and pointed out that 'the position of the shepherd is more heavily rejected than any other',[1] and already there is a shortage of skilled stockmen and shepherds in the region. At one time, mechanization forced away the men. Now, to some extent, the shortage of labour is compelling even further mechanization and changes of land-use and farming techniques.

Nine of the ten rural districts of Northumberland lost 6,700 people in the period 1951–65. The farm labour force fell by thirty per cent in ten years from 1956[2] and the loss of jobs was in no way compensated by the increase of the forested area, only about seven hundred people being wholly employed in forestry.

The Eastern Borders Development Association has initiated an idea for the increase of market gardening at the expense of the traditional barley and fodder crops. It has been estimated that seven thousand acres could be turned over to more intensive crops and form the basis for new processing and canning industries in Berwick and Eyemouth. Pilot schemes have been carried out and the results are promising. But such changes could only affect a small part of the

[1] J. Littlejohn, *Westrigg: The Sociology of a Cheviot Parish* (Routledge & Kegan Paul, 1963).
[2] Northumberland County Development Plan, 1967.

farming area. Declining rural settlements might be revived on another basis, by the increased mobility of the urban population and the acceptance of a longer daily journey to work for the pleasure of living in the 'country'. The completion of the Alnwick and Morpeth by-passes has increased the accessibility of the rural north, and the search for the summer cottage is increasing. The Forestry Commission is now building new wooden houses in the Wark Forest for sale.

The very mobility that has resulted from increased ownership of private transport has contributed, ironically, to rural depopulation because of the loss of revenue on rural bus services and their consequent decline.

A recent report, *Plan for Expansion: the Central Borders*,[1] considers that the revival of the rural areas or, as the Scots call it, 'the landward', lies in the economic health of the larger rural centres and it is there that scarce resources must be concentrated in increasing amenities and employment so as to counter-attract the most creative and energetic section of the community – the young.

> Unless the Borders can generate a sufficient pull into itself to offset these strong pulls north and south to lusher surrounds, it may well fall apart, to find its future simply as a pastoral enclave in an industrial world or as the playground and retreat for its wealthier neighbours ... a sort of huge holiday camp for Edinburgh, Glasgow, and Newcastle.

The general theme of the County Plan for Northumberland, for example, is to concentrate future development, such as council housing, industries, new amenities and services, in four market towns and in selected 'sub-centres' or 'consolidation points', smaller settlements (that often once held market status) that by nature of their location, such as Wooler and Rothbury, are important centres for large rural districts. The sub-centres are large 'villages' of more than seven hundred inhabitants though some smaller villages with populations of over two hundred and fifty are also chosen as 'consolidation points'. The rural areas, with their natural amenity, good water supply, and potential, though small, labour force, could be attractive to small industries, while the growth of the tourist industry could have a seasonal effect. It is within this general pattern that other organizations such as the Rural Community Council, an autonomous body set up as the Rural Development Commission by Lloyd George back in 1909, are expected to operate. The activities of the Council are concerned not only with such fringe activities as 'Best Kept Village' competitions but with the

[1] Scottish Development Department (H.M.S.O. (Edinburgh), 1968), 2 vols.

development of recreational facilities, village halls and, especially, the stimulation of appropriate small industries.

The general strategy for maintaining the economic health of the rural areas could be affected adversely by the Government White Paper on Local Government in England (1971) which would create a truncated and comparatively poor rural county, with a population of only 251,000 and a rateable value of just over £8,000,000, the lowest by far in England and Wales. The main population centres in the south-east of the county would be merged administratively with two enlarged 'urban counties' of Newcastle and Tynemouth. Even the 'new towns' of Killingworth and Cramlington would be lost to the county.

The emphasis on the importance of the main market towns in the revitalization of the Borders is shown in all the current plans, and the concept is supported by the recent census figures[1] of the Eastern Borders, for example, which show a further loss in the last ten years of 11·6 per cent of the 'landward' population, but a small but heartening increase of 3·5 per cent in the market towns and burghs, especially Kelso and Eyemouth. Each town has its own plan for growth and change but there are features common to all of them. They seek growth, yet each has a traffic problem on market days and Saturdays. They seek new industries but want to preserve the amenities. They want new shopping facilities and other services yet need to preserve the urban façades and spaces that make them so attractive to residents and visitors. In a region of fine towns with a growing tourist industry, this is of no little economic importance. New zones for industry are set aside, with the hope of government advanced factories, often sited by the now-disused railway yards where the livestock marts are also to be found. The 'High Street' becomes a pedestrian precinct with traffic moving on a new circulatory route utilizing the alignment of the medieval 'back lanes'. The decayed 'backs' become the site of car parks and access paths to the shopping area. Each town has its own special problem posed by its history (such as Berwick's walls) and physical setting (such as Hawick's cramping valley sides) but the plans do not differ fundamentally.

Melrose shows the plan in comparatively simple form. The Working Party for Melrose considered in 1966 that 'traffic will reach its limit of bearable congestion in five years from now'. With its function as a pleasant residential area, a traditional market centre and the site of an abbey of national importance, the first requirement for the burgh is a new distributory road taking east–west traffic away from the burgh centre. Within the burgh, the plans envisage a pedestrian

[1] Figures for 1971 supplied by A. J. Reid, Development Officer of the Eastern Borders Development Association.

precinct in the market-place fed by car parks and access routes from the obsolete properties behind Market Square and High Street. Already a new car park and caravan site have been developed to the west of the burgh. It is planned to extend the Abbey Precinct to include the ground that traditionally lay within the Mantel Wall.

Another 'abbey town', a burgh proud of its royal status, Jedburgh, shows a more complex plan due to a more difficult physical setting on the steep banks of the Jed and the need for new industries. Situated in the heart of Teviotdale, with engineering and textiles industries employing about five hundred people, it has a major traffic problem, with the main A68, especially busy in the summer season, threading through the centre of the burgh. Visitors want to stop and enjoy the Abbey, Queen Mary's House and a memory of Bonny Prince Charlie. The closure of the North British Rayon Factory was an economic blow, though a blessing in that it has enabled the northern entry to the town to become an open space, embellishing the Abbey precinct and thus reverting to its traditional role. New factories have been built on the open land to the north outside the medieval core and a new factory specializing in precision engineering opened up in 1958 on the hills to the east, now one of the major employers in the burgh. Many women still go to Hawick daily to work in the woollen mills, although some textile companies have opened branches in Jedburgh.

Quite apart from the Abbey and Queen Mary's House, many of the houses in the High Street are in category B,[1] buildings of national and local importance, and so its preservation is desirable as far as possible. A new road is suggested close to the Jed bank linking new bridges at the north and south end of the burgh. Circulation of traffic round a pedestrianized High Street would be made possible by a widening of Friars' Gate and Sickman's Path (the old 'back lanes'). The redevelopment of the 'backs' up Castle Gate above the Abbey has already started and new houses make an unusual and distinctive contribution to the urban landscape, utilizing changes of slope and enclosed spaces effectively. The burgh has overspill arrangements with Glasgow and 250 houses have been built since 1962 under this scheme.

Both Alnwick and Morpeth in Northumberland now have the advantage of through-traffic being taken on by-passes, the former to the east across the park-lands of the Duke of Northumberland's estate, the latter to the west on a new bridge over the Wansbeck, just skirting the edge of the new suburbs of private housing that have extended up on to the plateaux on either side of the Wansbeck

---

[1] Department of the Environment Designation.

gorge. Morpeth, on the edge of the coalfield, is very conscious of its potential role as administrative centre of the new county but plans to 'renew' the main shopping area of Bridge Street, the market place and Newgate with a new circulatory road round the back, roughly on the line of Damside and Dacre Street (a street of good houses this which deserves preserving as an entity), are delayed while the exact amount of desirable development is determined, with such possibilities as supermarket and shopping precinct in the obsolete area north of Bridge Street. An industrial estate of thirty acres was set aside as early as 1963, adjacent to the railway station and the Cattle Auction Mart to the east of the town, but an American pharmaceutical company has opened up a large factory on open farmland by the new by-pass to the west. Already, the headquarters of the County Constabulary, the Fire Brigade, the Library Service and the Highways Division are in the town and a new site has been chosen for the County Offices when they move from the county precinct oddly trapped in the medieval core of Newcastle.

Alnwick plans a circulatory system approximating to the roads following the alignment of the medieval walls to the west, to preserve and enhance the large market place and the fine Georgian frontages. Such features as the unusual cobbling of the old horse market, now used as a car park, will make greater visual impact when traffic is moved to car parks and access routes behind the shops. The shopping area is adequate for potential use and some new frontages have appeared. New council housing has already transformed some of the derelict areas within the medieval core and access to the centre is by such interesting alleyways and flights of steps as Dickens Lane and Correction House Lane.

The process of 'urban renewal', however, is most marked in the centre of the main city, Newcastle, where every visit reveals something new, even flower-beds and seats appearing in the middle of the main shopping street, Northumberland Street. Most traffic is being directed along the newly completed John Dobson Street and Northumberland Street is being taken over by the shoppers. The City Corporation publishes a regular news sheet to encourage a two-way exchange of ideas with the people of the city, and the great schemes which seemed confined to paper for so long are now really taking effect. The transformation of the city centre, the construction of a complex pattern of urban motorways and the renovation of the run-down riverside area are all taking shape.

The entry across the Tyne Bridge is confronted by a roundabout, of which a large tower block forms the central feature. A system of walkways, by steps and tunnels, links Swan House with the old Holy Jesus Hospital and even older fragment of the Austin Tower (part of the City Walls), a happy conjunction of new and old still overshadowed by the great bridges and archways of the Victorian railway builders. The unusual eighteenth-century round church of All Saints (possibly to find a new function as a concert hall) is now the centre-piece of another zone of office development on the recently derelict slopes above the quayside. North of the roundabout, new blocks are stepping across Pilgrim Street, and the new Bank of England, with concrete and copper, manages to echo the solidity and strength of the Norman Keep, still the dominant feature of the railway entry to the city. Ellison Square, a car-filled emptiness, is depressing, but the long-term plans indicate that these spaces will remain, and be embellished with new buildings and 'returned' to the pedestrian. New hotels are appearing along Newgate Street and more are planned for the area near the Central Station. Everything points to the deliberate creation of a real regional capital in which administration, commerce, education, culture and services will replace the traditional patterns of employment. The atmosphere of a university city is apparent in the many cultural and entertainment facilities – the new University Theatre, the Royal (at last, definitely 'saved') in Grey Street, the National Film Theatre, a new library, the Laing Art Gallery and at least two small private galleries, as well as the old City Hall and the lecture theatres of the University which are often used for public lectures.

The most dramatic change of landscape is taking place in the coalfield itself, in the creation of two new towns, Killingworth and Cramlington, only four miles apart. Killingworth, by its imaginative overall plan and the excellence of individual buildings, has excited international attention and has garnered a crop of awards and recommendations for factories, offices, and houses. The initial planning team, led by Roy Gazzard, was as interested in 'social engineering' as in architecture and town morphology, and, as the plan now grows to fruition, the future silhouette of urban Northumberland begins to emerge. The flanking neighbourhoods of two-storey houses, built around interlocking 'garths', lead to higher-rise flats and apartments linked by pedestrian bridges to the town's physical and social apex in the romantically-named 'Citadel'. The separation of vehicular traffic and the pedestrian, the zoning of industry, the shopping precinct, all these familiar images of the new urban scene are to be matched in this new town, but the pattern of routeways is designed to bring the 20,000-strong community into constant contact with the town centre, especially the sophisticated 'communicare' centre, dealing with the medical, social, and religious problems of the community.

Technically, Killingworth and Cramlington are not 'New Towns', as they are under the direction of the existing local authorities – Longbenton U.D.C. and Seaton Valley respectively. They were initiated in the 1950s at a time when pit closures were causing employment problems and when 'overspill' from Tyneside (especially Newcastle and Wallsend) needed new housing. The paramount need was for new industry, and both new towns have been successful in attracting new factories which offer employment to scientific and technical staff – very important in a region where the best-qualified have to move out of the region for suitable jobs – as well as work for re-trained miners. Fragments of old colliery locomotives stand in the foyer of the Killingworth Development Corporation Offices, while the pithead gear of Burradon is still visible to the north near the elegant, Italianate chimneys of the Gas Research Centre. One of the new open spaces in Cramlington – Alexandra Park – is laid out on reclaimed land from an old tip. The physical reality of the coalfield is all about but the future rests on new foundations. Cramlington earmarked 170 acres in the north-west quadrant of the town for industry and it is already full of the low, broad, clean silhouettes of new factories, the sort pioneered by the Team Valley trading estate in nearby Gateshead during the Depression. Killingworth has sought 'science-based' industry, and has the research centre of the Gas Council and the headquarters of the Northern Gas Board (both award-winning buildings of great visual quality), valvemakers, heating engineers and papermakers; and, recently, engineering consultants have moved in to occupy the tower block at the newly constructed centre of the town.

The need for such new industries is reflected in the present situation of the coal industry. Only 1,760 men are still employed in mining at the Seaton Valley (in two pits – Eccles and Fenwick), a decrease since 1955 of more than four thousand jobs. In the Northumberland areas of the Coal Board, which replaced the older regional organization in 1968, only sixteen pits are now active. Some of the modern pits, such as Lynemouth and Ellington, are designated 'long-life' pits and are safeguarded by their close association with the Alcan smelter which is now raising its fantastic outline above the cliffs north of Newbiggin-by-the-Sea. There is plenty of coal still in the ground and it is possible that the present world shortage of power and the difficulty of 'cheap' oil might make coal as much in demand as it was during the late 1940s. The Border has seen such 'rhythms' before.

The National Coal Board even has a direct effect on the 'new town' development. New housing can only be carried out after consultation with the N.C.B. as there is not much point in building new estates on ground that is likely to subside. Around Cramlington, especially, there has been a great deal of new housing built, partly by the local council but mostly (about seventy per cent) by a symposium of private builders, and the houses have proved popular, especially with the younger married couples. The old village centre, still complete with farm-buildings and smithy, has been swamped by the new housing and a new 'centre' has been built to 'feed' a target population of 62,000 people. Plenty of green spaces and the Radburn layout make it attractive to families with children.

Killingworth is aiming at a more conservative 20,000 population and at least half its housing is built by the council, architecturally more adventurous than the housing of Cramlington, and now private houses are being built along the lakeside. The low skyline of the first housing garths leads up to new blocks of flats that have overhead gantries to link them with the 'Citadel' at the centre and the out-of-town Woolco, latest statement of the superstore theme, fed by good roads which link both towns and their industries with the main motorway system of the country.

Killingworth and Cramlington are answers to urban problems, but the planned changes which will create a new linear city from Galashiels to St Boswells and transform this ten-mile stretch of the Upper Tweed are concerned primarily with the problem of the rural areas. Here is a deliberate attempt to encourage urban development, to effect in the words of the planners a 'blood transfusion' in an area of depopulation. The aim is to create 'a regional community with the amenities of a city' out of the present separate communities of Galashiels, Darnick, Melrose, Newton St Boswells and St Boswells. It is hoped that the increased population and economic activity of this 'new city' will have a benefi-cial effect on a broad area of the Central Borders, including the surrounding villages. The main 'growth point' will be St Boswells itself, the centre of the Tweed routeways, where the main A68 crosses the A699; its position on broad, level land is in contrast to the restricted physical setting of the two main Border towns – Hawick and Galashiels. As a symbol of this new regional significance, the new administrative offices of Roxburghshire have been built on a site north of the railway station.

Each town will have some expansion – Galashiels, for example, by 4,500 – but industrial estates will be zoned at special sites at St Boswells, Hawick, and Tweedbank (near Darnick). The high visual quality of some of these sites between Abbotsford and Melrose makes such plans the cause of much heated debate, and not just from local landowners. It is intended to maintain the present character of individual settlements – Galashiels as the natural commercial centre, Melrose as a 'cultural' centre – and a large Country Park, together with a wild-life reserve will be established in the hills between Galashiels and Peebles. Sites for 'cabins', caravans and camping are needed for visitors, and a new championship-class golf course. The whole scheme will be knitted together by an improved road system based on the A68 and A6091.

The problem of Berwickshire is different from the upper Tweed if only because it has no settlement with a population much over two thousand. The County Planning Department has made a provisional classification of its 'villages' with a view to selecting certain places for development, much in the way that Northumberland has selected 'consolidation points' to augment the major market towns. The 'A' category settlements have been chosen on a basis of existing population, services, and proximity to good roads. Apart from the burghs of Duns and Eyemouth, the new housing estates and hoped-for new industries are likely to be built in Earlston on the Lauder, Coldingham, Reston and Cockburnspath on or near the A1, and Greenlaw, Chirnside, Gordon, and Foulden.

The closure of all railway lines in the region, apart from the Newcastle–Edinburgh line and the cross-country link between Newcastle and Carlisle, has not helped the proposed revival. Under the Beeching Plan. it was even proposed to cut the coast route via Berwick, which would have isolated the north-east of the region from the national network.

The traditional isolation of Berwick-upon-Tweed has been perpetuated by the many recent government schemes for the reorganization of local government. Both the Maud and Wheatley Commissions (for England and Scotland, respectively) left Berwick out on a limb, still divorced from the county which bears its name. The current White Paper (1971) leaves it in a neglected corner of a neglected county. It is not surprising that local organizations which have a clearer view of the region's character and needs have put forward suggestions that the town should be recognized for what it is – the natural focus of a large rural region and as such the natural administrative centre of a Border region, independent of either Newcastle or Edinburgh. The future status of Berwick could be an imaginative exercise by governments that might accept that peace has really broken out on the Borders and that the 'frontier', time-hallowed as it is, has not always been and need not always be a fact. The ancient kingdom of Northumbria spanned the Tweed, and there is nothing sacrosanct about the river frontier.

The twin problems of the revitalization of a region and the redevelopment of a historic town are shown with particular intensity in Berwick. The railway did not bring the growth that other 'railway towns' experienced, and the population (12,500) is just a little lower than the figure for 1851 (13,121). This represents a stagnation that is not apparent in the streets of the town, for it is a lively, bustling meeting place for the people of a twenty-five-mile radius, and its traffic problem is made all the more acute by the conjuction of a right-angle bend in the A1, meeting a gateway through the Elizabethan Walls. All requests for a by-pass have been turned down on the grounds of economy, the by-passed traffic being insufficient to justify the cost of a new bridge over the Tweed. So schemes still concentrate on methods of breaching the Walls, though the government Inspector (1971) rejected the scheme that would have made a large roundabout with a second gap in the Walls. I have seen several ideas in the local journal over the last fifteen years or so, many with imaginative plans for a road following the alignment of the Walls, or the widening of the Scotsgate built in its present form in 1815. The Walls, undoubtedly, are a nuisance but the Walls *are* Berwick. Some local interests would cheerfully see the Walls go the way of the Norman Castle, some commercial interests would like to make Berwick look like anywhere else; but then who would want to visit it? One local councillor even suggested removing the one authentic Elizabethan gateway, Cow Port, to give visitors easier access to the seafront, perhaps forgetting that it is precisely the fact that the path to the sea leads through a medieval gateway that makes it a more interesting and memorable experience.

For the rest, the plan for the town is not dissimilar to those of other Border burghs. Marygate, the main shopping street, will become a pedestrian precinct with service roads leading from a new circulatory route using the line of Walkergate, Ravensdowne (a most pleasant, quiet street of Georgian houses), Silver Street and Bridge Street. The burgage 'backs' (which are less derelict here than in most of the burghs) become refurbished as pedestrian access ways from car parks to shopping centre.

A planned population of 20,000 by 1980, a sixty per cent growth after a hundred years of stagnation, would be impossible without an influx of new industry. Large extensions are planned in the industrial estate at Tweedsmouth and a second site at East Ord. New housing estates will spread along the A1 towards the limit of the Liberty, four miles north of the Tweed. Advanced factories are planned elsewhere in the area, at Duns, Kelso, Eyemouth and Coldstream, those in Coldstream and Kelso being in operation now. One of the factors being emphasized by the very active Eastern Border Development Association to potential industry is the availability of good water supplies, a point likely to be of increasing importance in the long term, but, as yet, most industry is linked in some way with the processing of farm produce, agricultural engineering and with textiles and construction work, though the expanding Jus-

Rol business shows what can be achieved by local initiative. There is a long-established boat-building and repair business at the Fairmile Shipyard, and the Salmon Fisheries are still building the sturdy inshore 'coble', but the main dock is limited to craft of about 500 tons, though 1500-tonners can cross the bar. The planners are sure that the port could be developed to take ships up to 5000 tons, which would interest firms concerned with paper manufacture, oil-rig servicing, and cargo links with North-West Europe.

What happens to Berwick-upon-Tweed is of national concern. Here is the delicate balance between necessary change and the preservation of what is unique to the town. That silver bow of the Tweed and the ragged frontier of the North Sea, the fortress town standing four-square against the elements and the violent past, is worth very special attention. The townscape reflects the long division of two nations and the essential qualities of the Border region, its strength, its independence and that extraordinary conjunction of historical and physical attraction that makes it ultimately so satisfying.

# 10

# Festivals, fairs and folklore

The gypsies they came to my Lord Cassilis' yet,
    And O! but they sang bonnie;
They sang sae sweet, and sae complete,
    That down came our fair Ladie.

(Johnnie Faa)

Anyone within earshot of St James' Park after a football victory can have little doubt that the 'United' is more than another football team. It is a symbol of regional pride. 'We are the greatest' sung by starry-eyed little boys in back alleys and the names of their heroes painted in giant letters across the walls of new flats is some form of compensation for a region that still feels itself isolated from the corridors of power in Whitehall and neglected as such. A rousing chorus of the 'Blaydon Races' is more than just another variant in the folklore of the terraces; it remembers the great days when the United won glories that took some of the edge off slump and industrial depression. The song is older than the formation of the team at the end of the nineteenth century. It is essentially a song of industrial Tyneside, yet achieves some of the regional significance of 'Land of My Fathers' for a Welsh crowd.

At the other end of the region an even more violent assertion of local allegiance is the sound of a Hawick rugger crowd shouting 'Terri bus and Terri Odin' (there are many variants of the spelling), which has been described as a Gaelic chant or even as an invocation to the pagan gods.

That the people of the Borders, be they miners or shepherds, should express themselves in song is only fit and proper where the tradition of significant song goes back at least seven hundred years, producing a heritage of ballads of national importance. Alongside the iron structure of Stephenson's High Level Bridge is a folk club where the renaissance of folk music is pursued as seriously and yet as naturally as anywhere in the country. There the young university student plays a riotous rant on a button accordion, an old miner fashions music from pipes he has made from frames of old bicycles, a shepherd from the Cheviots plays the

Northumbrian pipes and a Scots lass sings a lament for Flodden, all in the course of one evening.

The songs from the sea meet the coal-hewers' lively complaint and the industrial workers' humour and beneath their modern melodies lies the rich melancholy of the region fashioned in centuries of war and isolation, the balladry of the Borders. There is nothing chic or fashionable about the folk clubs north of the Tyne. The minstrels are as authentic as Jamie Strength, the gipsy fiddler who died in his 115th year, strong enough to lift a weight of 105 stone off the ground and independent enough not to wait for George IV during the famous visit to Edinburgh in 1822, saying 'he couldna be fashed waiting o' the king'; or as James Allen, also of gipsy descent, born in Rothbury in 1734, later to be installed at Alnwick Castle as official piper. His marvellous playing carried through a lifetime of roguery, theft and poaching. The line of minstrelsy goes back beyond the thirteenth century, but it is then that the first established name emerges, that of Thomas, prophet and bard, of Erceldoune (now Earlston) in Lauderdale, known as Thomas the Rhymer. The town still boasts his ruined tower, the scene of an annual pilgrimage during the Melrose 'Riding'.

The ridings are the keystone of Border festivals and I remember vividly my first experience of one on a warm June day in Jedburgh. A cavalcade of riders appeared from the south, led by a young man, finely apparelled, carrying the burghal banner. Behind him came the horses and the ponies, people of all ages, some in formal riding habit, some in tweed suits, bowlers and Wellingtons, all in the best of spirits. The leader, the Callant, led them in a leisurely circuit of the town, through the market-place, down across the ford, along the river Jed and back up the main street to the Abbey gates; with all the time the horn blowing and the crowd shouting. It was the festival week, of games and ceremonies and 'ride-outs' culminating in the Callant's Festival. One of the 'ridings' was up to the Redeswire stone near to the present Border crossing at Carter Bar. So the present people of Jedburgh pay tribute to the men of 1575 who rode out armed with Jeddart staffs to this last border affray against an English army under the warden, Sir John Foster: 'Stand firm and sure, for Jeddart's here.' Another ride-out follows part of the route taken by Mary, Queen of Scots, from Jedburgh to Hermitage Castle in Liddesdale in October 1566. On another occasion a sprig is taken from the last great oak of the Jed Forest, the Capon Tree, that still stands, supported by poles, between the river and the road near Hundalee.

The present festival was inaugurated in 1947 but the Riding itself has a much longer pedigree, being one of the traditional 'ridings' of the Border burghs. They represent a moment of historic self-consciousness, a tribute to the trials and glories of the past, in part pagan midsummer festivals, with the Callant, chosen for his honour and integrity to symbolize burghal virtue, as a little-disguised 'Summer King', though the 'kirking of the Callant' gives a Christian blessing on the proceedings. So great is the honour to be chosen as the Callant, or the Reiver in Duns, the Coldstreamer in Coldstream, the Braw Lad in Galashiels, the Laddie in Kelso, the Melrosian, or the Cornet in both Lauder and Hawick, that one of the young men dared the Tweed in flood in recent years and was swept to his death rather than forsake his symbolic role. Berwick, too, has a traditional riding of the Bounds, usually on 1 May, linked with its May Fair inaugurated by Royal Charter in 1604. Morpeth rides the Bounds at the end of April though it is not an annual occurrence.

The Common Riding of Hawick is one of the longest-established and most famous of these festivals and its dominant theme is the defence of the burgh against the English raiders after the disaster of Flodden. The Border wars throw their shadow over today's activities, and the defeat of a foray, probably by men under the command of Lord Dacre, by a muster of local youths is still recalled by a chase at full gallop led by the Cornet, a young bachelor, and his two supporters, the Right- and Left-Hand Men, both previous Cornets. The flag that they carry is a representation of the pennon captured that day in 1514. But the very name 'Common Riding' suggests a purpose older than Border wars. The ride out to the Town Moor, the muster at the Cairn Knowe, and the reading of the burgher roll was an assertion of the town's common rights against all comers, especially the rapacity of feudal lords, similar to the circuit of the common land in Lauder linked with the ancient custom of 'beating the bounds'. The eventual loss of much of the common by enclosure in 1777 meant that the ceremony 'survived as a mimic thing merely'[1] yet it still expresses burghal pride. The yachtsman, Chay Blyth, a Hawick man, celebrated two occasions during his lone circumnavigation in *British Steel* – one was Burns' Night, the other the Hawick Riding. The custom of wearing oak leaves (echoing Jedburgh's capon tree), the dawn muster of the Motte and the singing of Terri bus at sunrise may have links with the midsummer festival of a pre-Christian culture, with the 'boon fyr' or Beltane fire. The midsummer bonfire is still lit at the village of Whalton in Northumberland. The Beltane fire, a Scandinavian influence, has been linked with putting out the home fires before going up to the summer pastures and shielings, a pattern that, as we have seen in a previous chapter, was common throughout the hill country until the seventeenth century.

---

[1] Craig and Laing, *The Hawick Tradition of 1514* (1898).

The traditional ridings are those of Hawick, Jedburgh, and Lauder, but, since 1937, most of the larger Scottish burghs have instituted or revived old customs and the period from June to August is marked by festivals from the upper dales to the sea at Eyemouth, which now has its crowning of the Herring Queen. But the ridings are not the only festivals to survive. Jedburgh still plays 'handba' on Shrove Tuesday, reputedly linked with the defeat of the English at Ferniehurst Castle, English heads having supplied the 'ball'. Such handball games survive in many parts of the country, in Alnwick and Duns, Ancrum and Denholm, for example, and only died in Rothbury, Ford and other places in the last century. There was an attempt to stop the Jedburgh game but it survived a court case and the 'uppies' (the men above the market-place) still play the 'doonies', the men from the lower part of the town. Elsewhere, the contending sides are usually the single versus the married men.

Melrose, apart from its festival week, instituted in 1938, also has an unusual winter festival, the Masons' Walk, the oldest masons' lodge in Scotland parading round the burgh on 27 December. An even more remarkable survival is the great fire on New Year's Eve that takes place in Allendale Town in the south-west of Northumberland. Selected men of the dales blacken their faces, don fancy dress and, as 'guisers', parade around the town with half-barrels of burning pitch and tar on their heads, accompanied by brass bands. On the stroke of midnight, they hurl their cargo on to a central fire, a proceeding made even more hazardous in recent years by the large number of visitors.

The celebration of New Year's Eve is common throughout the region. It is possible that the ceremony of 'first-footing' was brought into Northumberland by immigrant Scottish families, for example, during the seventeenth century in the wake of James VI and again during the industrial growth of the nineteenth century; or even by mere proximity. But many Northumbrians regard it as indigenous to the county. The symbolism is connected with the desire to ensure adequate fuel, food and drink in the coming year.

Many of the festivals have the secondary value and intent of attracting visitors. The crowning of the Eyemouth Herring Queen, for example, coincides with the Glasgow holidays. Berwick crowns the Salmon Queen in mid-July. The Hexham Festival in late September and early October is now well established. It is usually devoted to medieval music and art, centred on the impressive setting of the Abbey and the medieval Moot Hall.

The traditional high spot of the Novocastrian year is still the fair on the Town Moor, perhaps the greatest of its kind in Britain. It was instituted as a Temperance Festival following the evils of the Race Week 'hoppings', but the spirit

19a. *Netherton, typical coalfield settlement with pit heaps, railway siding and terraced cottages in a rural setting.*

19b. *Cumledge, near Duns, an early nineteenth-century blanket mill still in operation.*

19c. *The wooden coal staithes at Dunston on Tyne.*

20a. *The new Civic Centre of Newcastle upon Tyne.*

20b. *Office complex of Swan House built within a traffic roundabout, with sculpture commemorating Joseph Swan's first electric lamp.*

of the 'hoppings' is still dominant. Newcastle Races, with the main event of the Pitmen's Derby (the Northumberland Plate), is still held at the same time, towards the end of June, but in the comely surroundings of Gosforth Park, while the Fair holds its traditional ground on the Town Moor.

The recently-instituted Newcastle 'fortnight' is a more catholic occasion, a feast of music, film, theatre and art with many 'fringe' activities to vie with its more illustrious northern neighbour, Edinburgh. It makes a lively start to the Autumn and amongst all the modern art-forms the old traditional music still forms an essential part to the proceedings. It would bring good cheer to Mrs Hogg, the mother of James Hogg, the Ettrick Shepherd, who complained to the young Walter Scott that 'there was ne'er ane o' my sangs prentit till ye prentit them yoursel' and ye have spoilt them airthe gither. They were made for singing an' no for reading; but ye hae broken the charm now and they'll ne'er be sung mair.'

Scott's compilation of the minstrelsy of the Scottish Border was a work of great scholarship which was to be the springboard of his imagination in later years. He dedicated the tales, as he called them, 'which in elder times have cele-brated the prowess and cheered the halls of his gallant ancesters', to the Duke of Buccleuch. The colourful history of the Borders and its medieval 'chivalry' was the very food of the boy who spent his youth within sight of the superb ruin of Smailholm Tower on a broad outcrop of volcanic rocks, with views on all sides, and to the west the three peaks of his beloved Eildon Hills.

> And still I thought that shattered tower
> the mightiest work of human power
> and marvelled as the aged hind
> with some strange tale bewitched by mind.

Scott was helped in his collecting by Dr John Leyden, described at the time as the most scholarly man on the Borders, with a reputed knowledge of twenty-seven languages. James Hogg, too, the self-educated shepherd born near Ettrick Kirk, and author of many poems and that most extraordinary novel *The Private Memoirs and Confessions of a Justified Sinner* (recently republished), was a great source of information, his mother being a storehouse of Border ballads and folk-lore. But it is the traditional ballads that have stood the test of time whilst the later interpretations in the romantic style are seldom recalled.

Scott was not the first collector, and he made acknowledgement to his pre-decessors such as Bishop Percy (*Reliques of Ancient English Poetry, 1765*), Herd's 1774 collection of Scottish ballads and James Wilson's *Collection of Scottish*

*Poems 1706–11.* But Scott also turned to the peasants of the region, listened to what they sang and recorded it. He gave his version of the Battle of Otterburn in part from Herd's collection and in part from elderly people in Ettrick Forest. In his way he felt he was rescuing the songs from them. Of the Douglas Tragedy (with its last lines appearing in many a modern ballad):

> Lord William was buried in St Mary's Kirk,
> Lady Margaret in Mary's Quire,
> Out o' the Lady's grave grew a bonny red rose
> And out o' the knight's a briar.

he wrote, 'Many copies of the ballad are current among the vulgar but chiefly in a state of great corruption'.

Witchcraft and superstition, unrequited and disastrous love infused many of the songs, but it is the ones that were 'a pure growth of local circumstance'[1] that rang through the Border towers and emphasized clan feelings by recalling the deeds of the great feudal families that are of most interest.

Most of the finest ballads are Scottish but one of the greatest is entirely English, that of *Chevy Chase*, described by a contemporary as the favourite ballad of the common people, concerning one of the many encounters between two of the leading feudal families of the Borders, the Percy and the Douglas. There are several points of similarity between *Chevy Chase* and *The Battle of Otterbourne*, relating to an encounter of 1388 in Redesdale. There were so many affrays between the two families, such as Homildon Hill in 1402, and Piperdean in 1436, that it is as if they are all fused into one epic story. This feeling is heightened by the use of generalized images such as 'the bent sae brown', describing the moorland grasses, 'the wan water', 'the bracken hills', giving at once a sense of specific location and yet of universality. But in *Chevy Chase* Percy is killed, whereas in *Otterbourne* he is taken captive. *Chevy Chase* was sparked off by unlawful hunting in the Cheviot Forest on the Scots side of the Border, whereas *Otterbourne* was the result of a punitive raid by the Scots through Tynedale as far as the walls of Newcastle.

However, it was the Otterburn encounter that fired the imagination of the minstrels, who interpreted it as a personal encounter between two chivalrous knights, with such effect that Sir Philip Sidney, the courtly poet, said 'I never heard the old song of Percy and Douglas that found not my heart more moved than by a trumpet; and yet it is sung by some blind crowther with no regular

---

[1] Prof. Veitch, *History and Poetry of the Scottish Borders* (1878), 2 vols.

voice than rude style'. And the Douglas' dying words were amongst the last words spoken by Sir Walter Scott.

The greatest battle of the Border campaigns, Flodden Field, was also celebrated in ballad, but the most famous version of *The Flowers of the Forest* was written by a 'lady of family', Jean Elliot, more than two hundred years after the event.

> I've heard them liltin', at the ewe-milking,
> Lasses a-liltin' before the dawn of day;
> But now they are moanin' on ilka green loanin';
> The Flowers of the Forest are a' wede away.

Both the first and the last lines appear in an earlier seventeenth-century version which must have been the model for later interpreters.

There is a group of ballads about clan leaders, men who might appear to us as unprincipled cut-throats but who emerge in the songs as men commanding the utmost loyalty of their followers, like Johnnie Armstong, Jamie Telfer, Hobie Noble, Kinmont Willie, Jock o' the Side and Dick a' the Cow. It is striking how many of these heroes operated in Liddesdale, the most barbarous part of the Border, so turbulent that it required a specially appointed Keeper at Hermitage Castle.

> Now Liddesdale has ridden a raid,
> But I wat they had better hae staid at hame;
> For Michael o' Winfield he is dead
> And Jock o' the Side is prisoner ta'en.

The ballad is concerned with the rescue of Jock from the English, and in the tale both Hobbie Noble and the Armstrongs appear. The Liddesdale men disguised themselves as corn carriers, and on the way to Newcastle cut timbers at Chollerford to help them scale the town walls. But Jock was bound fast in prison. In spite of walls and prison bonds, they effected the rescue, even fording the Tyne in flood (and Jock weighed down with his heavy bonds) and got safely back to the dales.

> Now, Jock, my billie, quo' a' the three,
> The day is com'd thou was to die;
> But thou's as weil at they ain ingle side,
> Now sitting, I think, 'twixt thee and me.

Many of the later minstrels, such as Jamie Strength, came from the ranks of the Faa gypsies whose traditional centre was Yetholm, near the border of Roxburghshire. They must have taken especial pleasure in the song of *Johnnie Faa*.

> The gypsies they came to my Lord Cassilis' yet
> And O! but they sang bonnie;
> They sang sae sweet, and sae complete,
> That down came our fair Ladie.

So sweet the song, indeed, that the lady went off with the gypsy laddie, giving up her luxurious life for the nomadic one and finding it finally wearisome. But the Lord Cassilis caught up with the gypsies and the story ended tragically.

> They were fifteen valiant men,
> Black, but very bonny,
> And they lost all their lives for one —
> The Earl of Cassilis' Ladie.

Not only have the ballads found a key place in the present folk renaissance but were taken by emigrants to the United States of America. With subsequent transformation, many of the ballads have returned across the Atlantic as cowboy and Negro ballads.

The poetic tradition of the Borders was maintained even before Scott's era, the most famous name being that of James Thomson, author of the poetic cycle *The Seasons*, who was born at Ednam. A monument near the village commemorates his work.

But it was in Hogg, Leyden, and Scott that the images revived in a romanticized form. As Scott wrote to Washington Irving, echoing Thomson's poem, 'I like the very nakedness of the land; it has something bold and stern and solitary about it.' His study of the ballads was 'the discipline and preparation for his life work' which began with the long poems such as *The Lay of the Last Minstrel, Marmion* (his interpretation of Flodden) and *The Lady of the Lake,* poems so successful commercially that he was able to buy the estate at Abbotsford.

> Still from the sire the son shall hear
> Of the stern strife and carnage dear,
> Of Flodden's fatal field,
> Where shivered was fair Scotland's spear
> And broken was her shield.[1]

Then came the Waverley novels, at first anonymously, culminating in the remarkable output of an average of one novel a year until 1825. He received his baronetcy in 1820 and effectively became an industry in himself, an industry

[1] Walter Scott, *Marmion* (1808).

196

which still survives in the annual pilgrimage of visitors to what is known as 'Scott Country'. Whatever present tastes in literature, that magic circle of abbeys, castles and landscapes of which Melrose is the centre is inescapably linked with his name. Many of the characters of the novels have been identified with real people, such as Megs Merrilees in *Guy Mannering*, who was based on Jean Gordon of Yetholm.[1] Scott's publisher was John Ballantyne of Kelso, whose house, Walton Hall, still stands in Roxburgh Street overlooking the Tweed.

The stories that Border shepherds have regaled me with on several occasions, however, have not been the romances of Sir Walter Scott but the mysterious tales written by John Mackay Wilson. A contemporary of Scott, he was a Tweed-mouth man who, after some disappointing years in London, returned north to become the editor of the *Berwick Advertiser* in 1834 and started to write and publish a weekly series of 'Tales of the Borders'. They had an instant success until he died, in 1835, at the age of thirty-one. One of his finest stories is *The Faa's Revenge*.

The Faa Gypsies are always cropping up in the folklore of the Borders. They were first mentioned in Galloway in the fifteenth century, and by 1540 'John Faw, Lord and Earl of Little Egypt' was in contact with James V, by which date they were adopting the surnames of the gentry on whose land they lived. They came to Yetholm in the early part of the eighteenth century with a grant of land and rights of pasture on the Common which was still, at that time, 'debateable land'. They were involved in the carrying trade, of coal, for example, from Ford and Etal to Kelso and Jedburgh, and were active in the smuggling trade that followed the Act of Union. They were great fiddlers and pipers, prominent in all the fairs and festivals. The territory of the Faas was effectively the same region that is covered in this book, with Kirk Yetholm as their 'capital', in which place the last of the Gypsy Queens, Esther Faa Blyth, died in 1883. The gypsy 'palace' is still pointed out in Yetholm and in recent years an attempt has been made to restore the 'crowning' of the Queen as a festival, but the gypsies are no longer a power in the land. They claimed that 'Faa' was a corruption of Pharaoh, but other derivations, such as 'faa' meaning 'sallow', have been suggested.

The regional song, reaching such poignant maturity in the sixteenth century, found a new form of expression in the nineteenth, stimulated by the industrial workers, especially the pitmen. The mid century was prolific in song and singers such as Joe Wilson and George Ridley, the 'poet laureate' of Tyneside. Both writers and adapters of songs, they drew their inspiration from regional themes

[1] W. S. Crichton, *The Scott Originals* (Foulis Press, 1912).

and found a ready outlet in the music halls, such as the Oxford (traditionally known as Balmbra's, restored as such in 1962 after the centenary celebrations and still going strong). 'Sang-writin had lang been me hobby,' wrote Joe Wilson, 'an' at sivinteen me forst beuk wes publish'd. Since that time it's been me aim te hev a place i' the hearts o' the Tyneside people, wi' writin' bits o' hyemly sangs aw think they'll sing.'[1] And sing them they did, and do, one of his most memorable being 'Keep Yor Feet Still'.

> Keep yor feet still Geordie hinney
> Let's be happy for the neet
> For Aa may nit be se happy thro' the day,
> So give us that bit comfort keep yor feet still Geordie lad
> And dinnet drive me bonny dreams away.

George Ridley, born in Gateshead, died young but became immortal by his songs such as 'Cushie Butterfield', but especially by his account of the annual race meeting held on an island in the Tyne near Blaydon.

> Aw went to Blaydon Races, twas on the ninth of June,
> Eiteen hundred an' sixty-two, on a summer's afternoon;
> Aw tyuk the bus frae Balmbra's, an' she wis heavy laden,
> Away we went along Collingwood Street, that's on the road to Blaydon.

The rest of the verses are often unknown, even to Tynesiders, but the chorus is known far and wide.

> O Lads, ye shud only seen us gannin',
> We pass'd the foaks upon the road just as they wor stannin';
> Thor wes lots o' lads and lasses there, all wi' smiling faces,
> Gawn alang the Scotswood Road, to see the Blaydon Races.[2]

The Blaydon Races were a revival of a much older fair or 'hopping' where the keelmen held a purse-meeting, and many of the famous Northumbrian songs have their origins in earlier times. 'The Keel Row' was popular before 1760; 'The Waters of Tyne' was sung in Hexham before 1793 and the charms of 'Elsie Marley' were noted down by Joseph Ritson in 1784. 'Lavender's Blue' has a long pedigree as has the haunting 'Blow the Wind Southerly' based on a pipe tune, 'Kinlock of Kinloch'.

Even 'Footy Again the Wa', describing the game where the players leapt to get

[1] *Joe Wilson Sings* (Frank Graham, 1971).
[2] Version from Joan Gale, *The Blaydon Races* (Oriel Press, 1970).

their clogs the highest on the wall, was in use in Longbenton before 1812. The written word does scarce justice to the speech patterns of the region; the songs should be heard. They owe much to the nineteenth-century collections such as Sir Richard Terry's *Shanty Books*, John Stokoe's *Collection of Songs of Northern England*, and W. G. Whittaker's *North Country Songs*. It is worth recalling the people for whom the industrial troubadours sang, the colliers, the men whose daily toil and danger made their limited leisure the more precious, to be enjoyed to the full. An outsider visiting the coalfield in 1867 recalls them vividly.

In their dress they often affect to be gaudy, and are fond of clothes of flaring colours. Their holiday waistcoats, called by them posey jackets, are frequently of very curious patterns, displaying flowers of various dyes; and their stockings mostly of blue, purple, pink or mixed colours. A great part of them have their hair very long, which on workdays is either tied in a queue, or rolled up in curls; but when dressed in their best attire, is commonly spread over their shoulders. Some of them wear two or three narrow ribbons round their hats, placed at equal distance, in which it is customary with them to insert one or more bunches of primroses or other flowers.[1]

Even today's male fashions can hardly compete with that display.

The culture of the pitmen deserves volumes of its own – their humour, their whippet races, the leek shows, the pigeon fanciers, the broad-framed sea fishermen standing along the shoreline on a winter's day, still enjoying their sport. The hard images of men picking over the coal waste, a dangerous and dirty occupation, and trundling it home in sacks poised precariously on bicycles are not yet entirely of the past. Coal is still widely 'culled' on the shoreline but the Working Men's Clubs and the night-life of Tyneside support a much more sophisticated (though not 'better') 'culture' than the whippet and the cloth cap.

Much has been written about Tyneside speech and the subtle dialect variations from the industrial south to the rural north. Several stories, no doubt authentic, give accounts of visitors from Scandinavia understanding the Tyneside dialect, and there is little doubt that, both in vocabulary and inflexion, Scandinavian influences are apparent. 'Gan hyem' would be as effective in Copenhagen as in Newcastle for 'going home'. Nancy Ridley, in one of her many Northumbrian studies,[2] shows the variations of 'home' from 'hyem' in the coalfield to 'heam' around Hexham and 'hame' near the Border, almost a linguistic bridge to the Scottish lowland tongue. In north Northumberland, the word 'moss' has the long

---

[1] *Howitt's Visits to Remarkable Places* (1867).
[2] Nancy Ridley, *Northumbrian Heritage* (Robert Hale, 1969).

vowel sound that makes it 'merse', reminiscent of the 'Merse' of Berwickshire and of the Danish word for the same feature. With some Northumbrians, the words 'ten bob' (now presumably obsolete) become 'teen berb' yet the 'o' can be shortened too so that 'no' becomes an abrupt 'na' and 'scad' becomes a peremptory way of saying 'it is cold'. The endearment 'hinney' still survives (although frowned on in some places) as a variant of 'honey', while 'canny' is one of those ubiquitous words that almost defies definition although it is generally used in a tone of approval, with obvious links with the Scottish 'ken'. A friend from Killingworth gave me a good example of this usage from the Battle of the Somme, where his uncle was lying in the bottom of a shell-hole underneath a large Northumbrian pitman. 'Eh, Geordie lad,' he said, 'a wish aa was cannily back in bonny Backworth.'

Many of these sounds are most pronounced in children's playground speech and the extraordinary 'Us'll get wrang' ('We will get into trouble') shows the frequent pronoun case reversal. The word 'man' thrown in at the end of an address can often result in the surprising 'woman, man' when the recipient is female, such as 'Houd yor tongue, woman, man!'

Fortunately, there is a reviving interest in dialect and a renewed pride in regional speech which has resulted not only in detailed research by university departments but in a crop of hilarious pamphlets on *Larn Yussel Geordie*.[1] The pride spills out into the humorous banter of folk singers such as Johnny Handle and Alex Glasgow, and reached a national audience in the recent production of 'Close the Coalhouse Door', the impact being only slightly lessened on its export from Newcastle to the London stage.

One particular quirk of Northumbrian speech which has excited attention at least since Daniel Defoe's travels is the pronunciation of the letter 'r'. This can be so strong in rural areas that it brings a word like 'Ford' almost to a halt before the final 'd' and 'Wooler' terminates in something like a gargle. Its origin has even been attributed to Harry Hotspur's speech impediment and a desire to emulate him.

The Northumbrian dialect is related to the 'Northern Inglis', which possibly had its original centre of dissemination in the Anglo-Saxon Kingdom of Bernicia, with its capital of Bamburgh, and spread to create a continuous dialect area from the Forth to the Humber.[2] 'This dialect, from which the literary English had severed itself and which now had a literature only in the Northern Kingdom,

---

[1] By Scott Dobson, published by Frank Graham.
[2] See also Chapter 4.

came to be considered as peculiar to that Kingdom and to be distinguished from the literary English as Scotch.'[1] 'Scotch', in this context, was the Anglo-Saxon dialect of the Scottish lowlands. Until about 1400 the 'lingua Scotica' still meant Gaelic, but the national feeling engendered by the Wars of Independence strengthened the linguistic difference so that the lowland Anglo-Saxon became accepted as 'Scottish' and the 'Northern tongue' south of the Tweed came under pressure from Midland English. There is, thus, a close historic link between the speech of Roxburghshire, Berwickshire, and Northumberland, and the dialect words and inflexions owe their origins to the earliest English settlers. The speech patterns of the region contain as many fossil remnants as the human landscape, which have been explored in previous chapters.

The comparative isolation of the Border country gave the dialect a chance to endure, albeit in a much modified form. Even more, the dalesmen trapped by the topography of the hills, poor communications, and the warring frontier developed highly localized variants of speech so that, even today, experts can identify dialect differences from valley to valley. Yet, although 'burns' and 'kirks' and 'laws' (hills) occur on both sides of the Borderline, one is still aware of a significant linguistic change when moving from Cornhill to Coldstream, only a mile apart but separated by the Tweed.

It is the ties rather than the differences that affect the farmers and shepherds as they meet periodically at marts and shows and fairs, whether they be on Scottish or English soil, and it is at these rural gatherings that the essence of the Border life is to be savoured. The business of buying and selling livestock and of 'showing' is seldom without the opportunity for entertainment and relaxation. The Border shows are still a landmark in the rhythm of the year and present rare opportunities for catching up with the news of old acquaintances and exchanging the season's tidings.

The isolation of the hill farmers led to the development of traditional crafts during the long winters, among them patchwork, for which Allendale achieved a reputation. Perhaps the most unusual is that of stick-dressing. The shafts are usually of hazel or holly and the horns are from as old a ram as possible. These are quite scarce because the horns are often damaged. The attachment of horn to shaft and the heating of the horn into the required shape are both tricky operations, but the real art starts with the dressing of the stick – decorating the horn – though some craftsmen continue the decoration down the shaft as well. Every

---

[1] J. A. H. Murray, *Dialects of the Southern Counties of Scotland* (1873).

artist fashions his own tools, such as specially-shaped nails for fine work to supplement the more common knife and sandpaper. One of the finest collections is with Norman Tulip, living on a lowland farm, who spends up to two hundred hours on one stick, fashioning marvellous images of rural and industrial life – dog, fish, fowl, farmyard animals, pit ponies, horse and cart, even the knots in the rope hanging a pheasant. His faithful portrayal of Border life is reminiscent of the engravings of Thomas Bewick, born in 1753 near Ovingham on the North Tyne.

Bewick is regarded as the father of the modern wood engraving. After travels to London and in Scotland, he settled in Newcastle, illustrating books of fables and embarking on his great works, *A History of Quadrupeds*, *A History of British Birds*, and *Aesop's Fables*. His vignettes of Northumbrian life decorate the pages of many books of rural life. Few artists had a clearer eye or could compress so much relevant detail into such small compass. He was more than an illustrator. He was an innovator, a man of spirit in the Cobbett tradition, devoted, as his memoirs reveal, to the scenes and people he depicted, moved to anger by the destruction of the traditional country ways by the Enclosure movement. His rambles were, by our standards, marathon walks, Ovingham to Newcastle, with some fishing thrown in, being nothing unusual.

One of Bewick's apprentices, Luke Clennell, became famous in his own right, doing the original drawings for Sir Walter Scott's *Border Antiquities*. The topographical artistry of the nineteenth century was represented in the region by T. M. Richardson, who illustrated *The Castles of the English and Scottish Borders* in 1833. Together with Bewick and John Dobson, he inaugurated the first Fine Art Festival in Newcastle. Many of his sketches and paintings, together with those of J. W. Carmichael and other local artists, have been republished recently.[1] Another Richardson, Henry Burden, executed a fascinating series of sketches of the Roman Wall area on behalf of the historian, John Collingwood Bruce.

Another good animal painter born in Morpeth and well represented in Berwick's small art gallery is Joseph Crawhall. But one of the most extraordinary talents that the region has produced was that of John Martin, town planner, engineer, friend of Brunel, mystic. Born at Haydon Bridge in 1789, he became an apocalyptic visionary who expressed himself in large canvases of historic and Old Testament scenes, such as Belshazzar's Feast, the Seventh Plague, and the Deluge. He became the most famous artist of his day, visited by royalty. There

[1] In *Historic Newcastle* (Frank Graham, 1970).

are enough of his canvases to be seen in the Laing Gallery in Newcastle and the Tate Gallery in London to reflect his unique vision.

As with the ballads, it is tempting to look for links between the artistic past and present, but perhaps it is enough to recall the splendour of early Northumbrian art which reached its climax in the illuminated pages of the Lindisfarne Gospels, the rich naturalistic carvings in stone such as St Boisil's tomb at Melrose (now at Jedburgh), and the delicacy of the ivory work in the Frank's Casket, now in the British Museum. The same early medieval period produced the bestiary figures and scrolls that adorned the Northumbrian crosses. They are amongst the greatest artistic achievements of the region.

The artistic tradition continues to flourish in many localities. The Border subjects of Tom Scott of Selkirk are now attracting the attention of collectors. It was a local artist, Mrs Mills of Ovingham, who first introduced me to the delicate watercolours of Victor Noble Rainbird, who depicted the quaysides and coastal landscapes of his home area, Cullercoats, earlier this century. A leading metal sculptor, Charles Sansbury, who designed the ornamental 'gates' and flambeaux of the Newcastle Civic Centre, has his workshop in Allendale Town and, amongst other subjects, finds inspiration in Border motifs. His version of a Stephenson engine now graces the Killingsworth shopping centre.

Apart from the Laing, there are other small galleries in Newcastle such as the Stone (concentrating on the Pre-Raphaelites but with a fine collection of L. S. Lowry) and the University Gallery (with a preference for modern experimental work).

It is on Tyneside that one of the most prolific of modern regional writers, Sid Chaplin, finds his 'material'. His novels are full of the atmosphere of the industrial scene. But the rural Borders have found a new, broader audience in the voracious appetite of television, not only in new versions of Sir Walter Scott's novels but in the popular series on the 'Borderers' where such names as Slitrig and Cessford have done their best to oust the imported image of that other rustling frontier, the American west.

The modern folk hero is still found in traditional activities – the winner of the sheep-dog trial, the captain of the Sevens, the Callant and the Reiver, piper and fiddler – but some of the Border names which have achieved national fame in recent years have been men in the world of sport, such as the Charlton brothers, Ashington men who migrated south to make their fame in the tradition of 'wor Jackie Milburn', greatest of Newcastle centre-forwards. Jim Alder, the marathon runner, is a Morpeth man, but the greatest legend of all is attached to the name of Jim Clark, the racing driver, whose superlative talent and character has achieved the remarkable tributes of a monument in the centre of Chirnside and a room devoted to his career in the County Offices at Duns, leaving a permanent mark on the landscape, a man in the Border tradition.

JAMES STUART Aged 115

## 11

# Exploring by track and road

And see not ye that bonny road,
  That winds about the fernie brae?
That is the road to far elfland,
  Where thou and I this night maun gae.

*(The Ballad of Thomas the Rhymer)*

## Walking the Border 'Streets'

I have made so many references to the Border hills and the green tracks that traverse them that it must be obvious that I feel they offer the best walking in the region. Indeed, they are some of the best walking country in the British Isles, with a rare combination of historic interest, varied scenery, and good walking surfaces. Access is not entirely free, even on the English side which is designated as a National Park, and the extensive army training area destroys much of the territory around Dere Street; but there are ample rights of way, long-distance walkways that follow the ancient 'streets' over hill country difficult enough to be a challenge for the experienced walker as well as a delight for the Sunday afternoon stroll in summer.

The northernmost section of the Pennine Way bounces on its roller-coaster route from summit to summit through the same region but has none of the validity of the other ways that follow routes pioneered by the earliest hill settlers, who left slender reminders of their presence in standing stones, cairns and tumuli, used by every age since. The best of the 'streets' lie to the west of the Cheviot itself and link the peripheral settlements of Coquetdale and Redesdale, such as Alwinton and Alnham, with their counterparts in the waters of the Bowmont and the Kale, such as Mow and Hownam. They start in valleys but soon leave their shelter for the hill ridges between the valleys, for the ridges offer more direct routes and less variation of gradient than the deeply-entrenched tributary valleys. The antiquity of the routes is marked not only by the archaeological evidence

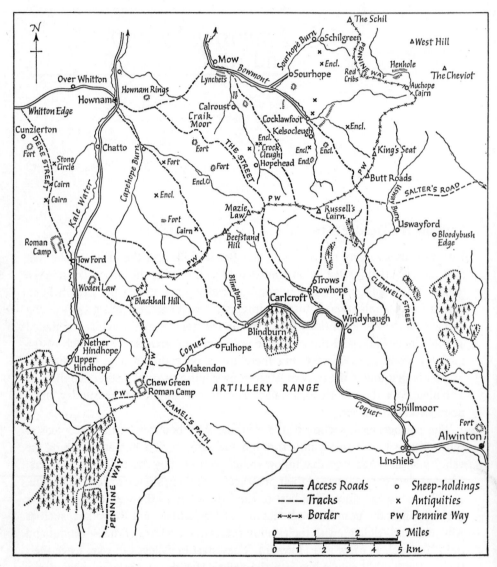

**Map 10**  *The Border 'Streets'.*

that borders them but by the long passage of man and beast that has worn them deep into the rare outcrops of volcanic rock. On marshier ground and on steep grassy slopes the tracks tend to bifurcate and a fan of deep grooves replaces the single track. These are especially prominent on the rise to the Border line, such as the approach to the Roman camp at Chew Green from the south and up to Windy Gyle from the north.

The high ground all about is littered with the hill forts, camp sites, enclosures and earthworks of the Iron Age Britons, and the streets linked tribal group with tribal group of the Ottadini as well as functioning as trade routes to the Roman south, avoiding the difficult wooded valleys. The Romans, too, used one of the routes, Dere Street, as the major axis of their military occupation from Redesdale to the Tweed, and used others of the well-beaten tracks for their reconnaissance patrols.

Used by medieval peasants taking livestock to summer pastures, the 'streets' degenerated during the Border wars into raiding paths for the clans on their hardy Galloways seeking easy pickings across the Border, rustling sheep, cattle and horses, stealing timber and goods and anything they could carry. Many of the valleys bear the name 'hope', shortened in local speech to 'up', such as Trowup, Sourup and Fleeup. The passes joining the hope-heads were called 'swires' and many of the famous swires can still be identified, such as Redeswire, the White Swire, Humble Swire, though others are remembered with such names as Butt Roads and the Red Cribs at the head of College Burn.

The Union of the Crowns saw a rebirth of the 'streets' as driving roads, bringing Scottish cattle down to English markets, though the heyday of the drovers was in the eighteenth century, when 100,000 cattle crossed the Border annually. The Union also gave a new incentive to smugglers, especially of whisky, much to the distress of the parson at Yetholm in the 1800s.

The evolution of rail and road transport, the construction of hard-surfaced roads across Carter Bar and in the fringing Wooler-to-Coldstream highway, left the Border 'streets' as a backwater, used now by local farmers for access to the outlying pastures, for some peat cutting, by the hunt and the foot-beagles, but mostly by the hill-walkers. One of the most isolated Youth Hostels was to be found at Wholehope (pronounced Woolup) on Clennell Street and for a few years it survived as a brave experiment by the Mountain Bothy Association, left open on trust to all travellers who needed its shelter.

For good walking, I prefer the early Spring or late Autumn when the bracken is low and can no longer soak you to the waist, when the sun is low enough to throw long shadows across the mellow slopes and etch out all the evidence of the varied past with startling clarity. October, too, brings the brisk nor-westers, scudding clouds and visibility of up to seventy miles, so that you just stop and stare in wonder at the supremely lovely world of which you are, at the moment, the centre.

I have often enjoyed a walk on midsummer's night, leaving Blindburn after a last beer at The Rose and Thistle at Alwinton, the best of the Border pubs, as the sun sets, mounting the track simply called 'The Street' straight up to the Border and then turning east along the ridge to reach Russell's Cairn at midnight. The sun drops to the north-west and rises in the north-east and the long twilight between is usually enough to be able to read the map without torch or match.

My favourite short walk starts from Mow in the Bowmont and follows the ridge south between Calroust Burn and Kelsocleugh up to Windy Gyle, turning east along the border, following the Pennine Way (now marked with poles bearing the ominous device of PW) to Auchope Cairn, across the tundra summit, down into the black chasm of the Hen Hole (good for lunch break even on a murderous day) and then across to Red Cribs. A track then drops gently down to the deserted farm at Schil Green, on to the research centre at Sourhope, with a final leg-stretch along the road back to Mow. But this is a gentle paradise where every hill-walker can trace out his own favourite routes.

Some stretches of Clennell Street have been churned up recently by forestry vehicles, and Salters' Road is a bit tedious in its route over the bleak moors above Alnham. Gamel's Path lies through the army training area and is not easily accessible but the Street above Windyhaugh is very fine and none of the routes on the Scottish side has any encumbrance worth worrying about.

There is good walking throughout the region, though many footpaths have been lost in the areas of high-farming – up to fifty per cent in some parishes I have surveyed. The problem is under-usage and the loss of their traditional functions in linking outlying farms and hamlets to the parish centre.

### Following the coast

There is no official long-distance walkway along the coast of the region to compare with that of the Cornish or Pembrokeshire coast, though it deserves such treatment. But there is good access for most of its length and several long stretches of superb scenery are available from, for example, Alnmouth north to Bamburgh, about seventeen miles in all, and this entirely within the area scheduled as one of outstanding natural beauty. Even within the major coalfield to the south, there are many places that combine the pleasure of sea, rock and

21a. *New pit-head gear at the Lynemouth colliery on the Northumberland coast.*

21b. *Health Centre at Kelso.*

21c. *Gas Council Research Centre at Killingworth New Township.*

22a. *Showing a prize Suffolk ram.*

22b. *Nineteenth-century photogra[ph] of bondagers working at Kirknewton.*

23a. *The Common Riding at Hawick.*

23b. *Salmon fishing on the Tweed; Kelso Abbey and flour mill in the background.*

24a. *Medieval bridge over the Till at Twizel.*

24b. *Puffins on the Inner Farnes.*

24c. *Bringing sheep down Kilham Valley.*

sand, quite apart from the less obvious delights of small resorts, harbours and mining settlements. The urban dweller on Tyneside has enough amenities of the semi-wild on his doorstep to make him the envy of most other townfolk. Tyne-mouth headland, Whitley Bay, St Mary's Island, Hartley Point, Seaton Sluice and Blyth Sands are all within a half-hour's drive from Newcastle. St Mary's Island, once a cell of Tynemouth Priory, is a lovely little spot, a rocky islet cut off at high tide, with lighthouse, café and even a coal seam near the causeway that a local miner still uses to keep his glasshouse warm. The cliffs opposite are a text-book of strata, with coal seams, fault lines and slabs of sandstone thrown around like playing cards. A cliff-top footpath leads to Hartley Point and Seaton Sluice, the seventeenth-century harbour of the Delavals and once the site of glass works and other industries. The sand dunes stretching to Blyth begin with a great heap of chalk rubble and flints which began life somewhere on the Thames Estuary and journeyed north as ballast in the colliers. Even the coaly coast at Lynemouth has its drama, especially in the fossilized forest standing upright in the cliffs near Snab Point. The church of St Bartholomew at nearby Newbiggin-by-the-Sea, battered by storms and vandals, still bearing its four-teenth-century spire (unusual in Northumberland), is a coastal landmark, and the town itself, though unattractive, at least has the smell of wet fish, crabs and lobsters landed from its inshore craft. There is enough small coal and driftwood on this stretch of the coast to keep many a family warm by 'culling' the fuel with shovel and spade and carting it off.

North lies Druridge Bay, famed for its sea birds, and now undergoing re-clamation as a Countryside Park. Large-scale opencast mining continues in the hinterland but the number of visitors (2,500 cars on Whit Sunday in 1964) led to its reclamation as a 'leisure area', complete with lake, boating, picnic sites and holiday village. Amble at the mouth of the Coquet stands at the northernmost point of the main coalfield, an industrial port full of not-very-exciting Victorian terraces, though its setting opposite Coquet Island (another erstwhile cell of the Tynemouth monks, also earmarked as a wild-life sanctuary) and its harbour might give it a new future as a yachting centre. Derelict land to the north of the harbour is now being reclaimed as a picnic site. Its enormous wooden coal staithes have a great fascination (approaching the harbour is like penetrating a meshed tunnel) although there is no coal going out, but twenty-eight registered craft bring in shellfish and wet-fish. Eider duck are commonly seen in the harbour and only ten miles up-stream is the medieval gem of Warkworth. The dunes at Warkworth have broken out into a rash of caravans but the sands north of Alnmouth are fine. The Polish trawler fleet favours this bay when the weather is adverse.

Alnmouth itself is a splendid little town, essentially one main street of stone houses, shops and pubs, with Georgian frontages, several of which remain from the great days of the eighteenth-century granges, when it was the best harbour between Berwick and Blyth. One is a Holiday Fellowship centre and others running back from the road to the shore have been converted into flats and seaside residences. The port, laid out in 1200, still has some link with the sea as a yachting centre with small boat-building yard, but the sands and the common links attract many people in the summer season. The currents of the Aln are very dangerous: a particularly strong gale in 1805 caused the river to cut through the lower part of the town, isolating the church and graveyard. They still stand bleakly on the wrong side of the estuary.

From Alnmouth to Cullernose Point is a rocky shore in which the sea and the Carboniferous Limestone combine to produce a gallery of sculptured images that can vie with any of the works of man. The different hardness of the various rock strata cause a variety of erosion forms and at Rumbling Kern the sea races in beneath the thin crust of rocks beneath your feet and roars its private messages. Long dipping rock shelves, isolated stacks, caves, blow-holes, pebbles to delight the collector and a multitude of fossils all make this a pleasure ground. Most of the sandy bays are related to geological faults.[1]

Suddenly, at Cullernose Point, the rocks change colour and direction to mark the first outcrop of the volcanic sills and dykes that enrich the scenery as far north as Lindisfarne. Craster Harbour, famed for its kippers, is hacked out of the tough quartz-dolerite, whilst the great coastal fortresses use isolated outcrops for their strategic sites, such as Dunstanburgh, that most romantic of ruins, a fourteenth-century fortress reached by a lovely footpath along the shore from Craster.

The black quartz-dolerite weathers to a rusty colour and produces distinctive patterns at inland Embleton, where cottage walls grow imperceptibly out of the solid rock. This village, sprawling over rocky knolls, has one of the best parson's pele-towers in the region. Every now and again the limestones reappear with their burden of fossils, folded and faulted by the earth's old convulsions, supporting a quarrying and lime-burning industry marked still by well-preserved kilns at Holy Island, Seahouses and Beadnell, the latter being owned by the National Trust.

The yachting centre at Beadnell is grafted on to an old settlement clustered round an ancient tower-house (now open as an inn) and some bizarre examples

[1] J. A. Steers, *The Coastline of England and Wales* (Cambridge University Press, 1964).

of seaside architecture in the 1930s. Boating at Newton-by-the-Sea, bingo, arcades and cafés at Seahouses, austere charm and memories of Grace Darling, that archetype Victorian heroine, at Bamburgh – all supplement the beauties of rock shore, sand dune and prolific wild-life that make this one of the most popular stretches of the coast, now advertised as the 'Northumbrian Riviera', though the climate is rarely favourable to bikinis. Frost is reasonably rare, snow soon disappears and winter surprisingly mild. In contrast, on occasions in summer heat inland draws in the sea-fret and blots out the sky for days, causing the thermometer to plunge several degrees.

It is not surprising that five major films have been shot on this coast in recent years, the combination of superb scenery, historic settings, clear atmosphere and comparative silence drawing the camera crews north. There are few better approaches to a town than Bamburgh seen from the Lucker road. The enormous eight-acre castle site on the whinstone cliffs is a dramatic backcloth to the trim eighteenth-century cottages and good hotels that line the Grove, the village green, tree-planted, that points to the castle. The walled garden that completes the enclosure of the green was built of Dutch bricks brought back in ballast in the seventeenth century and is a particularly fine example of the many walled gardens attached to the mansions on this windswept zone. Both the ornate tomb in the local churchyard and the museum dedicated to the memory of Grace Darling have a sense of period and, whilst it may be fashionable to debunk Victorian heroines, she does have a special place in the history of the coast and her help in rescuing eight men from the wreck of the 'Forfarshire' on the Outer Farnes became one of the most celebrated occasions of the period.

North of Bamburgh, the limestone cliffs alternate with sand dunes and broad areas of mud flats and salt-marsh such as Budle Bay and Fenham Flats, all areas of scientific importance, both for their vegetation and their wild fowl, culminating in the delights of Holy Island itself, linked to the mainland by a causeway that is covered by high tide and catches the unwary and the ambitious even now, much to the discomfort of sparking plugs and car insurance. The island is a microcosm of the region, with ancient priory, castle, lighthouse, herring houses, limestone headlands, volcanic outcrops, coal seams and sand dunes making a four-mile frame for rich farming land. This was the heartland of the once great Northumbrian civilization that declined into a smugglers' and wreckers' paradise, when the parson himself would lead his flock to pray for ships to be driven on the rocks. The causeway has brought civilization to bear but much of the insular spirit remains, not least in the private language of the residents. A handful of inshore craft still preserve the maritime tradition.

The old cottage on the Snook, now a protected area, used to belong to the Goswick fishermen, and the sand-bar stretches almost unbroken to Goswick and Cheswick, where fixed-net fishing for salmon was carried on until recently. At Scremerston the limestones re-emerge together with the first appearance of the Scremerston coal seams, a much earlier geological formation than the productive coal measures farther south. This was my first introduction to the northeast coast and still has a special place in my affections, not least for January days with the setting sun burning the crests of the pounding waves advancing unbroken from the Norwegian coast, moments when sound rather than sight dominated the senses. Berwick-upon-Tweed, a Georgian gem in a medieval mount, stands on the north bank of the Tweed but includes within its municipal boundaries the once separate townships of Spittal and Tweedmouth. Spittal, once the ship's captains' suburbs and still full of fine mansions, is a lively trippers' resort complete with funfair, bingo, new seaside flats and exposure to the sea that brought more than four feet of sand into the back gardens in the not-too-distant past. Tweedmouth preserves the barest fragments of its separate identity and has become a residential and industrial suburb of Berwick. Berwick's shoreline appears in many geographical texts as an example of synclinal basins, more easily identified as a series of rocky saucers lined up beneath the cliffs, one of which was once the Fishermen's haven and another of which protects the children's paddling pool. Northwards the cliffs become redder, horizontal beds of massive sandstones with a splendid gallery of caves, arches and stacks formed by the sea's constant attack on the jointing of the rocks. Deep bays have been cut along zones of weakness, giving a headache to railway engineers who find the main line to Edinburgh perilously close to unstable parts of the cliff. Some of these deep-cut bays, accessible to the cliff-top only by the steepest of roads, are the site of further fishing harbours – Burnmouth, Eyemouth, and St Abbs. It is possible to pass Burnmouth by rail or road and not even notice that it is there, clinging like a kittiwake to the cliff's side.

From Burnmouth right round the hunch-back of Britain to Siccar Point and the Berwickshire boundary with the Lothians extends a superlative cliff coast, as fine as anything in the entire region, hacked out of ancient Silurian rocks with occasional interruptions of volcanics, particularly at St Abbs Head. The deep bay between St Abbs and Eyemouth is carved out of an inlay of Old Red Sandstone that is seen again at Siccar Point overlying the Silurians. Easier access due to lower altitude makes this a favourite place for a day out for people from the Eastern Borders and both Coldingham, grouped round the ruins of its priory, and the clean bright fishing village of St Abbs maintain the holiday spirit late into the year when the last stragglers from the north and south take the coast road for the year's last delights. Fragments of early ecclesiastical buildings, one on the headland called the Nabbs dedicated to St Ebba, the other on Kirkhill to the south of the village, continue the pattern of early Christian coastal sites that began at Tynemouth.

Eyemouth, with over two thousand inhabitants, is the largest centre of population in Berwickshire, the most important fishing port in the region apart from North Shields, and a popular resort. A burgh of barony since 1597, it still sports the remnants of a sixteenth-century fortress on the headland protecting the harbour, often garrisoned, incidentally, by French troops cementing the 'auld alliance'. The chaos of alleyways is reproduced in the interior layout of some of the older buildings, for this was a smugglers' paradise of which it was said that there was more of Eyemouth below ground than above.[1]

A new fish market is being built, and boat-building yards are being extended up the narrow estuary of the Eye.

Angler's delight is not confined to sea-fishing, for the Ale and the Eye and Coldingham Lock have excellent sport but, as with most of the unpolluted Border burns, permits from local associations are needed.

A footpath leads from St Abbs village to the lighthouse on the headland (open to the public at certain times), but it is difficult to follow the circuit of the cliffs because of private estates. The ruins of Fast Castle, however, are accessible from the farm road to Dow Law. Cliffs of Old Red Sandstone alternating with deep bays, some with caravan sites, continue as far as the Berwickshire border which follows the Dunglass Burn beyond Cocksburnspath. An added incentive to scramble over the cliffs on the geologists' pilgrimage to Siccar Point is the ruin of St Helen's kirk by the pathway and the magnificent view along the Forth Estuary. I have known many a day of wild westerlies pouring water over the hill country when this coast has been bathed in sunshine, but its pleasures are of a sterner sort when a nor-easter blows in the winter season.

The highway crosses the Coldingham Moors, which so disturbed Daniel Defoe with its barrenness, and reaches the coast again near Cockburnspath, a small township grouped round a fine market cross displaying the emblem of the rose and thistle and its church with a unique round tower. Its earlier name was Cockbrandspath. Its ancient tower, now ruined, stands near the Pass of Pease, a route that had an evil reputation in early times (even Cromwell preferred to defend it than pass it) until the construction of the 1786 bridge gave the Post

[1] L. Scott Moncrieff, *Scotland's East Coast* (Oliver and Boyd, 1963).

Road an easier gradient. Even after it joins the A1 which follows the deep trough of Eye Water, this road still gives the feeling of approaching the Lothians and Edinburgh by the back door.

## Exploring by car

The region outside the mountain core is excellent touring country, still able to offer fairly quiet roads with good surfaces. It is traversed by trunk roads, but there are no stretches of motorway, although the A1, the Great North Road that runs parallel with the coast, linking market town to market town from Newcastle to Cockburnspath, is being improved with dual carriageways and by-passes, especially in the section from Newcastle to Alnwick. Several of the very straight roads, such as the Military Road, the B6318, that follows the alignment of the Roman Wall, and the A68 that follows part of the Roman Dere Street and links the Tyne with the Tweed by way of Carter Bar, are much more hazardous than their directness suggests, being full of changes of gradient, potentially dangerous to the motorist in a hurry. The hill country is best explored on foot, for there are no roads traversing the high ground outside the A68 which crosses the Border at 1370 feet, sixteen miles to the west of the Cheviot. There are roads that penetrate the valleys, though some of these are private, such as in the College Valley, and need access permits. The army road beyond Blindburn Farm in the Upper Coquet is open when no exercises are taking place and gives a fine sight of the inner parts of the Cheviot Range but this can be difficult in winter, even as late as March.

So the car routes I shall recommend in this chapter are designed to explore some of the quiet byways and touch many of the most interesting features of the region, including short moorland crossings as well as pleasant hours in the gentler lowlands.

One of the more usual entries to the region is the 'Roman' route from the south which reaches the Tyne at Corbridge, and it is from this point, or from Hexham three miles to the west, that a well-surfaced road takes off on a zig-zag course in a general north-easterly direction built in the mid-eighteenth century to link the farms of the mid-Tyne with the grain port of Alnmouth thirty-eight miles away. It was called the Corn road and was stimulated by Allgood, who also had a hand in the main east–west route generally attributed to General Wade. Leaving Hexham by the fine eighteenth-century bridge (recently widened) across the broad haughs of the Tyne and Hexham's industrial estate, the road follows the North Tyne past St John's Lee through the old coal-mining village of Acomb (a Saxon name meaning 'the valley of the oaks'). The poor mining terraces by the main road are in contrast to the eighteenth-century houses up the hill, where there are some good farm buildings, including an excellent gin-gang.

There is much new building at Acomb but the next village on the way is carefully protected against development. Wall has a fine square village green with sturdy yeomen's houses of the seventeenth century grouped round it. The Victorian church in the middle of the green is not unsightly and there are some medieval doorways and windows to be seen in some of the cottages grouped by it. The nearby Smithy's Arms has been translated in recent years into the Hadrian, a splendid inn. Just north of Wall by the roadside are sections of the Roman Wall, especially the Brunton Tower, with the great camp of Chesters in the parkland across the river. Move to Chollerton alongside the now-defunct North Tyne railway (some good walking along this track) to the churchyard with the stables still built into the wall, used until recently as a post office. The church is memorable for a Roman altar and Roman columns supporting the south aisle. The old railway station makes a lovely house and the view to the south-east focuses on Cocklaw Tower, the fortified heart of a small 'township'. The big farm to the north of the village sports an enormous tower, which may have been a windmill. Now the road begins its climb over open country, dominated by sweet limestone pastures, to Colwell, once busy with quarrying. Some whinstone is still quarried in the vicinity on the Swinburne estate. It is well worth making a small diversion after the reservoirs of the Newcastle and Gateshead Water Works to take the narrow road to Thockrington to see the lonely church up on the crags. Dropping gently down towards Kirkharle there are lovely views over the parkland and the estate where Capability Brown was born, against a backcloth of the Rothbury Fells with their distinctive flat plateau level. Some of the lanes here are lined by superb trees, especially that known as 'Silver Lane' that leads up to Capheaton through an avenue of ancient beeches. There are old brick kilns tucked away behind the trees. Then follows the even lovelier estate of Wallington and the National Trust village of Cambo, a planned village of the eighteenth century, with warm stone and walled gardens. Wallington Hall lies at the end of a lawn guarded on the roadside by four monstrous stone heads which came up in ballast from the City of London. Home of the Trevelyans, the house is open throughout the summer and the gardens all the year round.

Take the road on the right past Cambo church as far as a very different sort of settlement, a motley collection of cottages, garages, hotel and council estate around the pens of the livestock market at Scots Gap which grew up in conjunction with the now derelict railway. Turn left in the 'village' towards Rothbury to meet first real evidence of moorland and sandstone crags making a majestic setting for the folly of Cadgers Castle guarding the route from the north with very phoney military demean. The road to Rothbury passes a succession of geological clues, limeworkings, a small drift mine in the Scremerston Coals, before reaching the heather moorland of the Fall Sandstone Ridge. Notice the crescent sign on the Crown and Thistle Inn, the sign of the Duke of Northumberland. Much of the land ahead of you is part of his great estates. Past the flooded lime quarry of Forestburn Gate, now a most pleasant setting for a few cottages, there is a track that leads off to the left from the main road marked by the sign of the curlew, symbol of the Northumberland National Park. A well-surfaced track leads up past old deciduous woodland, out on to the moors with a splendid view in all directions. This is the real heart of Northumberland overlooking the market of Rothbury – to the north-west, the rounded humps of the Cheviots; to the west, the 1000-foot escarpment and the new phalanxes of the Harwood Forest. To the south-east, the smoky plumes of Blyth power station down on the industrial coast. A short way from the road lies an Iron Age camp and an example of sculptured rock from the Bronze Age. The track leads down through the new plantations to the road junction at Great Tosson and the ruins of a tower-house.

Along the banks of the Coquet, across the old bridge, pass into the main street of Rothbury and its unusual sloping green. There is much to detain the visitor here, not least the superb Anglian cross used as the support for the font in All Saints Church. Turn right out of the town and take the left fork towards Alnwick that leads past the impressive gardens of Lord Armstrong's Cragside Estate. The road bounces up and down across the open moors, crossing the Wooler road, then runs under the shadow of Corby's Crags. In the valley to the left lies the village of Edlingham, a remarkable sequence of buildings strung out across the pastures. First, the great hulk of the castle, still showing decorated corbels, fragments of the vaulted hall, spiral staircase in the walls and parts of the enclosing barmkin. Beyond it is the squat Norman church with vaulted porch and defensive tower. The village sprawls uphill and all around are the high-backed riggs of the medieval township ploughlands, clear as a map. Even the railway viaduct adds to the interest of the scene, though the railway has been closed since the floods of 1947, which carried many of the bridges away as far north as Wooler. The road crosses Alnwick Moor, past the inner moor parcelled up for the freemen making a distinctive farming landscape. From here, the high wall marks the parklands of the Duke of Northumberland, the most extensive in the county, leading down to the market town on the Aln clustered to the south of the great castle and its splendid barbican. Thread your way carefully through the narrow streets south through the Percy Gate and take the road beyond the Tenantry Column, proudly surmounted by the stiff-tailed lion, that leads to Lesbury and Alnmouth. Narrow lanes and narrower bridges lead past the growing village of Lesbury with its R.A.F. population, to the open skies and broad marshes of the Aln Estuary to Alnmouth and its fine eighteenth-century granges lining the one main street down the peninsula. Sand dunes, rocks, yachts and sea-scour.

## The Saxon Highway

The coast itself has been dealt with earlier in this chapter but the motorist, when sated with the delights of the 'Northumbrian Riviera', can pick up another route from the coast inland to the Tweed basin. The road begins at Lindisfarne and ends at Melrose, linking two of the most famous monastic sites. I cannot find any evidence that this was a time-honoured highway but it seems probable that a land link existed between the two centres (St Cuthbert is associated with both) as early as the seventh century, during the great days of the Northumbrian kingdom. Let us call it, then, the 'Saxon Highway', though we shall make diversions whenever something of particular interest is in the vicinity. The journey of about thirty-five miles is almost exactly the same distance as the Corn Road.

Leave Lindisfarne and the North Sea coast along the Beal road, crossing the long, fast stretch of the main London–Edinburgh railway up to the road junction with the A1 at the Plough Inn and continue across the road up the side lane to Kentstone. The road rises quickly, giving a fine view back over the mud flats and sand dunes of the Conservancy area. Just to the north on the coastal plain stands the extraordinary tower in Haggerston Castle grounds, and all around it first-class farming land for corn and stock fattening, enjoying one of the lowest rainfall figures in the British Isles; big farms with the tall chimneys associated with the steam threshers of the last century. The side road turns to join the main B6353 to Lowick, a large village stretching across the line of the Devil's Causeway, the old Roman road to the mouth of the Tweed. There is a Scottish flavour both in the coloured stonework round the cottage windows and in the general pattern of the place, basically one long street. The old green, however, is still identifiable to the south of the main crossroads. It was at nearby Barmoor, where a much-modified castle still stands, home of one of the branches of the Sitwell family, that the English army under Surrey camped before marching to victory at Flodden Field.

Take the road over the hill to Ford past old coal workings and lime quarries and suddenly be confronted with a view over the Cheviot massif. The hills look picturesque rather than formidable, an impression soon modified on closer acquaintance.

Move on down the steep slope of Ford Bank past the trim estate village on the estate of Lord Joicey, shadowed by plantations and the modernized fourteenth-century castle now used as a Field Centre. The old village school is now used as a hall and is remarkable for its murals painted by the nineteenth-century owner of the estate, Lady Waterford, whose fame was sufficient to bring Ruskin to the village. G. F. Watts, the painter, designed her gravestone in the churchyard, which has a collection of interesting stones. The church has a good example of the Northumbrian belfry, and a tomb slab in the church floor bears the earliest known picture of Northumbrian bagpipes. The overgrown stump of a parson's pele-tower stands in the pastures below the church. There are several fords over the Till, still in use during the hunting season; this was one of the most important fords, standing between the broad haughs of the Milfield Plain to the south, once a lake bed, and the gorge of the Till to the north where it cuts down to meet the Tweed. The road beyond the bridge follows a line of two-hundred-year-old beeches which are continued up to Flodden Edge to mark the line of the Scottish encampment before the disaster of Flodden. But the road turns right and left again past a series of eighteenth-century farms with expected names like En-campment and unexpected ones like Blinkbonny. A short diversion will bring you down to Branxton village and the monument on Flodden Field, which is really on Branxton Moor, where the Scots died facing their own land. Rejoin the farm road that leads west again to the valley of the Bowmont and a series of large farms which mark the site of many townships destroyed by constant border raiding. Only two miles away down-river stands the church of Kirknewton with one of the finest examples of bas-relief in the north, the Madonna and Child and the three magi, dressed appropriately in clothes remarkably like kilts. The village stands beneath Yeavering Bell, on the summit of which stood one of the 'oppi-dum' of the Iron Age Ottadini. At its foot is a stone monument to mark the site of the Anglo-Saxon capital of King Edwin. Follow the river up-stream through the broad trough cut through the lava flows of the old Cheviot volcano. At Mindrum the road leads naturally on to Kelso but a more picturesque route through the hills is followed by taking the road to Yetholm, the 'gate town' into Scotland. Both Town Yetholm and Kirk Yetholm, twin villages on either side of the Bowmont, are grouped round pleasant greens, but Kirknewton has the added fame as home of the last queen of the Faa gypsies who were a prominent feature of Border life until the first decade of this century. The Youth Hostel at Kirk Yetholm is the Eldorado of Pennine Way Walkers, a useful centre for exploring the Cheviots. Town Yetholm is the larger and more pleasant village of the two, however. Yetholm Loch nearby is a nature reserve but permits are needed to visit it. The road runs south and west over glacial moraine and old lake beds to Morebattle with many a tantalizing glimpse to the south, first up the Bowmont by Primside Mill, then up the Kale Water, into the heart of the hill country. For any visitor who has not been in the district before, it would be difficult not to give way to the temptation to explore the valley roads and enter the country of the Cheviot and Black-face sheep. I have seen them so many times yet I have never approached them without a sense of excitement.

But to return to our westerly route: Morebattle Church has a list of pew allocations in the porch which reveals more of the social life of the last century on these big estates than many books can do. Linton Church, across the 'mere', stands on a hummock of glacial gravels and has a rare medieval carving above the porch. Inside is the memorial to William Dawson, the pioneer agriculturalist who farmed at nearby Frogden. Leaving Morebattle the road follows the Kale and runs within sight of the castle of Cessford, home of the Kerrs, often Wardens of the Marches, a fine ruin up on the hill, built in the characteristic sandstone which is revealed nearby in the banks of the Kale. The road meets the main A698 at Eckford, which leads north to Kelso. But a short way along the road a narrow side road leads over a narrow bridge across the Teviot and through a little-frequented, almost forgotten, area that was once the site of the great walled town of Roxburgh. The quietness ends on joining the A699 at Roxburgh New-ton, which then follows the broad sweep of the fish-rich Tweed past Rutherford and Maxton to the great open green at St Boswells, scene of a famous medieval fair, and still one of the most important markets on the Borders. Here we join the main trunk road of the A68, following the line of the Roman Dere Street, and pass the new county administrative offices in Newton St Boswells.

Across the river lies the quiet ruin of Dryburgh Abbey in its richly wooded setting, a place for poets and for pilgrims to the tomb of Sir Walter Scott. To the west stand the three peaks of the Eildon Hills, that most famous of volcanic intrusions which has dominated the view ever since we left Morebattle. The sign-post to Melrose leads us westwards again along the A6091 between the Eildons and the Tweed's junction with the Leader Water, the most important junction of routeways, ancient and modern, in the region. Here stood the great Roman camp of Trimontium, now Newstead, marked only by a plaque by the roadside. Here now are the ruins of Melrose Abbey, partly built of materials taken from the Roman site. At the gates of the abbey stands the small town of Melrose round its triangular market-place, with the seventeenth-century market cross bearing the Royal Arms of Scotland.

Where from Melrose? There are so many fine routes to choose from: up to the lovely wooded Lauderdale to the Soutra Pass over to Edinburgh; up to Earlston and then on to the A6105 threading its way between the Lammermuirs and the rich farms of the Merse, linking many of the main towns of Berwickshire, Gordon, Greenlaw, Polwarth, Duns, Chirnside to Berwick-upon-Tweed, and passing many historic monuments and places of beauty and interest. But perhaps the logical route would be south, to link up with our starting-point at Corbridge, that other great Roman base at the other end of Dere Street.

Rejoin the A68 trunk road and head south for the Teviot crossing near Bonjedward, passing to the east the site of the Battle of Ancrum Moor in 1545, where the Scots gained something like revenge for the defeat of Flodden, and to the west the village of Ancrum, with a lovely village green and restored medieval cross well worth a short diversion. Instead of proceeding to Jedburgh, take the A698 towards Hawick but turn off down a side road signposted to Bedrule which leads through the valley of Rule Water, past the fine tower-house at Fulton, and comes out after many twists and turns at Bonchester Bridge, a crossroads hamlet surrounded by conical hills of volcanic outcrops. A mile south of Bonchester, take the right fork, the B6357, which rises into moorland country and the Commission Forests of Wauchope. This is a splendid drive in any weather, quite tricky in winter with a high pass at 1233 feet. The descent down an unfenced road leads through sheep country into Upper Liddesdale. At the small hamlet of Saughtree, a side road on the left winds back along a tributary of the Liddel Water and follows a deep glaciated channel through the Border hills, crossing into England at Deadwater, following the line of the old North Tyne railway with many of the old bridges still crossing the moorland burns, adding a touch of industrial drama to the rural scene. From Deadwater south the road lies through the impressive, man-made landscape of the Kielder Forest, one of the largest forests in Britain, past the new village of Kielder, old ruined towers and castles, ruined coal workings and sheep-holdings to the 'capital' of the dales at Bellingham. The B6320 follows the right bank of the North Tyne to the square stone village with the fortress name, Wark-on-Tyne. Here the landscape is softer, with many wooded burns running from the commons to the west and the parklands and mansions of Nunwick and Haughton. The final stretch through rich farmland brings you to Chollerford, a suitable inn and the Corn Road on which this journey began.

wayside cross.
crosshall farm. eccles.

# Select Bibliography

# Select Bibliography

The following bibliography does not profess to be comprehensive, the number of books, articles, and pamphlets being far too numerous to mention. Their numbers are increasing every year with the renewal of interest in regional history and regional culture. I have looked at so many books over the years that I can only indicate a small selection that contributed consciously and unconsciously to my knowledge and love of the Border country. The first section lists the indispensable books which are always being referred to for guidance; the second section suggests references for further reading on the topics dealt with in the respective chapters.

*Archaeologia Aeliana, Proceedings of the Society of Antiquaries of Newcastle upon Tyne.*
CROCKETT W. S., *Berwickshire and Roxburghshire* (Cambridge University Press, 1926).
*Hodgson's History of Northumberland*, 7 vols (1820–58).
*National Forest Park Guide: The Border* (H.M.S.O., 1962).
Northumberland County History Committee, *A History of Northumberland*, 15 vols (1893–1940).
PEVSNER and RICHMOND, *Northumberland* (in the *Buildings of England* series of Penguin Guides, 1957).
Royal Commission on Ancient Monuments (Scotland), *The County of Roxburgh*, 2 vols (H.M.S.O., 1956).
*Scientific Survey of North Eastern England* (British Association for the Advancement of Science, 1949).
*Scientific Survey of South Eastern Scotland* (British Association for the Advancement of Science, 1951).
SMAILES A. E., *North England* (Nelson, 1960).

CHAPTER I

BENNISON and WRIGHT, *The Geological History of the British Isles* (Arnold, 1969).
British Regional Geology: *Northern England* (H.M.S.O.).
British Regional Geology: *The South of Scotland* (H.M.S.O.).

H

CLAPPERTON C. M., 'The Evidence for a Cheviot Ice Cap', *Transactions of the Institute of British Geographers*, No. 50 (July 1970).

CLAPPERTON C. M., 'The Pattern of Deglaciation in Part of North Northumberland', *Institute of British Geographers*, No. 53 (July 1971).

GALLIERS J. A., 'The Geomorphology of Holy Island', *Department of Geography, University of Newcastle Research Series*, No. 6 (1970).

JONES J. M., 'Geology of the Coast Section from Tynemouth to Seaton Sluice', *Transactions of the Natural History Society of Northumberland and Durham* (1967).

Memoirs of the Geological Survey: *The Cheviot Hills* (H.M.S.O., 1932).

ROBSON D. A., 'A Guide to the Geology of Northumberland and the Borders', *Transactions of the Natural History Society of Northumberland and Durham* (1965).

SISSONS J. B., *The Evolution of Scotland's Scenery* (Oliver and Boyd, 1967).

TOMKIEFF S. I., 'The Cheviot Hills', *Geological Association Guides*, No. 37.

CHAPTER 2

ALDER J., 'Animals and Birds', *Northumberland National Park Guide* (H.M.S.O., 1969).

BLEZARD E., *National Forest Park Guide* (H.M.S.O., 1958).

CHAPMAN A., *Birdlife of the Borders* (1907).

CLARK W. A., 'Vegetation', *National Forest Park Guide* (H.M.S.O., 1958).

CLARK W. A., 'Vegetation', *Northumberland National Park Guide* (H.M.S.O., 1969).

'Hancock Museum', *Transactions of the Natural History Society of Northumberland, Durham and Newcastle on Tyne*.

HAYWARD and DRUCE, *The Adventive Flora of Tweedside* (1919).

HICKLING G., *Grey Seals and the Farne Islands* (Routledge and Kegan Paul, 1962).

JOHNSTON G., *A Flora of Berwick-upon-Tweed* (1829).

JOHNSTON G., *The Natural History of the Eastern Borders* (1853).

MUIRHEAD G., *The Birds of Berwickshire*, 2 vols (1895).

PERRY R., *A Naturalist on Lindisfarne* (Lindsay Drummond, 1947).

TEGNER H., *Beasts of the North Country* (H. Hill, 1961).

WALLIS REV. J., *Natural History of Northumberland*.

WHITEHEAD G. K., *The Ancient White Cattle of Britain and their Descendants* (Faber, 1953).

CHAPTER 3

ALLSOP and CLARK, *Historic Architecture of Northumberland* (Oriel Press, 1969).

BIRLEY E., *Research on Hadrian's Wall* (Titus Wilson, 1961).

COLLINGWOOD BRUCE J., *The Roman Wall* (1863).

COLLINGWOOD and MYERS, *Roman Britain and the English Settlement* (1945).

Department of the Environment,
   *Official Guide to Chesters Roman Fort.*
   *Official Guide to Corbridge Roman Station.*
   *Official Guide to Housesteads Roman Fort.*
   *Official Guide to the Roman Wall.*

DIVINE D., *The North West Frontier of Rome* (Macdonald, 1969).

*Hadrian's Wall*, Jackdaw No. 41 (Jonathan Cape).

JOBEY G., 'Enclosed Stone-Built Settlements in North Northumberland', *Archaeologia Aeliana*, 4th Series, Vol. xiii.

JOBEY G., 'Hill Forts and Settlements in Northumberland', *Archaeologia Aeliana*, 4th Series, Vol. xliii.

MARGERY I. D., *Roman Roads in Britain.*

RICHMOND I. A., *Roman Britain* (Penguin, 1954).

RIVET A. L. F. (ed.), *The Iron Age in North Britain* (Edinburgh University Press, 1966).

Royal Commission on Historic Monuments (England), *Shielings and Bastles* (H.M.S.O., 1971).

TACITUS, *On Britain and Germany* (Penguin, 1948).

WALLIS BUDGE E. A., *An Account of the Roman Antiquities Preserved in the Museum at Chesters, Northumberland* (Gilbert and Rivington, 1903).


CHAPTER 4

ADDLESHAW G., *Blanchland, a Short History* (pamphlet).

BOWEN H. C., *Ancient Fields* (British Association Pamphlet).

BUTLIN R. A., 'Northumbrian Field Systems', *Agricultural History Review*, Vol. 12, 1964.

COLLINGWOOD and MYERS, *Roman Britain and the English Settlement* (1945).

CLARK R., *Catton* (Northumberland Education Committee).

Department of the Environment, *Official Guides* to *The Border Abbeys, Dryburgh, Melrose, Tynemouth Priory and Castle.*

ECKFORD R., *Terrace Groups of Southern Scotland* (Hawick Archaeological Society, 1931).

EKWALL, *Dictionary of English Place Names* (Oxford University Press).

HANDLEY J., *Scottish Agriculture in the Eighteenth Century* (Faber, 1953).

HARDIE P. R., *The Roads of Medieval Lauderdale* (Oliver and Boyd, 1942).

HODGES and GIBSON, *Hexham and the Abbey* (1919).

HOSKINS and STAMP, *Common Lands of England and Wales* (Collins).

JOHN E., 'The Social and Political Problems of the Early English Church', *Agricultural History Review*, Vol. 18, 1970.

JOHNSON J. B., *Place Names of Berwickshire* (1940).

JOHNSON J. B., *Place Names of Scotland* (Murray, 1934).

JOHNSTON G., *The Natural History of the Eastern Border* (1853).

LAMB H. H., 'Britain Changing Climate', *Geographical Journal*, December 1967.

MAWER A., *Place Names of Northumberland.*

MURRAY J., *Dialect of the Southern Counties of Scotland* (1873).

SHIRLEY E., *Deer and Deer Parks* (1867).

*Sixth Report and Inventory of Monuments and Constructions in the County of Berwick* (1915).

SMALL J. W., *Scottish Market Crosses.*

*Statistical Accounts for Roxburghshire and Berwickshire, 1801 and 1841.*

STRANG B., *A History of English* (Methuen, 1970).

*The Venerable Bede: A History of the English Church and People* (Penguin).

WHITELOCK D., *The Beginnings of English Society* (Penguin).

CHAPTER 5

BARROW G. W. S., 'The Anglo-Scottish Border', *Northern History*, Vol. II, 1966 (Leeds University).

BORLAND R., *Border Raids and Reivers* (Fraser, 1898).

Department of the Environment, *Official Guides* to Dunstanburgh Castle, Hermitage Castle, Norham Castle, Tynemouth Castle and Priory, Fortifications of Berwick-upon-Tweed.

8th Duke of Northumberland, *Alnwick Castle* (1931).

ELDER M., *Ballad Country* (Oliver and Boyd, 1963).

GRAHAM J., *Conditions of the Border at the Union* (1905).

HUGILL R., *Borderland Castles and Peles* (new edn, Frank Graham, 1970).

JERNINGHAM H., *Norham Castle* (1883).

LONG B., *Castles of Northumberland* (Harold Hill, 1967).

MACK J. L., *The Border Line* (Oliver and Boyd, 1926).

MACKENZIE W. M., *The Medieval Castle in Scotland* (Methuen, 1927).

MCGIBBON and ROSS, *The Castellated and Domestic Architecture of Scotland*, 5 vols (1887).

RAE T. I., *The Administration of the Scottish Frontier, 1513–1603* (Edinburgh University Press, 1966).

RAMM, MCDOUGALL and MERCER, *Shielings and Bastles* (H.M.S.O., 1971).

SCOTT W., *The Minstrelsy of the Scottish Border*, 3 vols (1803).

SITWELL W., *The Border* (Reid, 1927).

*The Calendar of Border Papers*, 2 vols.

THOMSON G. H., 'Some Influences of the Geography of Northumberland upon its History', *The Historical Association*, Leaflet 28 (1912).

TOMLINSON W., *Life in Northumberland During the Sixteenth Century* (1897).

TRANTER N., *The Fortified House in Scotland*, Vol. 1, *South East Scotland* (Oliver and Boyd).


CHAPTER 6

ALLSOP B., *Historic Architecture of Northumberland* (Oriel Press, 1969).

BERESFORD M., *Lost Villages of England* (Lutterworth, 1954).

COBBETT W., *Rural Rides* (1830).

COXE T., *Northumberland* (c. 1725).

CULLEY and BAILEY, *General View of the Agriculture of the County of Northumberland* (1794).

DEFOE D., *A Tour Through Great Britain, 1724–6.*

First Statistical Account of Scotland, *Berwickshire* (c. 1801).

First Statistical Account of Scotland, *Roxburghshire* (c. 1801).

FULLER J., *History of Berwick upon Tweed* (1799).

HAIG J., *History of Kelso* (1825).

HANDLEY J., *Scottish Farming in the Eighteenth Century* (Faber, 1953).

HONEYMAN H., *Northumberland* (County Books, Robert Hale, 1949).

MACKENZIE, *History of Northumberland* (c. 1840).

Ministry of Agriculture, Food and Fisheries, *Annual Statistics.*

PAWSON H. C., *The Agricultural Survey of Northumberland.*

ROBSON J., *Churches and Churchyards of Berwickshire* (c. 1896).
ROBSON J., *Churches and Churchyards of Roxburghshire* (c. 1896).
Second Statistical Account of Scotland, *Roxburghshire* (c. 1841).

CHAPTER 7
CONZEN M. R. G., 'Alnwick, Northumberland. A Study in Town Plan Analysis', *Proceedings of the Institute of British Geographers* (1960).
CRAIG and LAING, *The Hawick Tradition of 1514* (1898).
FULLER J., *History of Berwick* (1799).
GIBSON R., *An Old Berwickshire Town: Greenlaw* (1905).
HAIG J., *History of Kelso* (1825).
HOUSE J. W., *Bellingham and Wark* (North Tyne Survey Committee, 1952).
PRYDE G. S., *The Burghs of Scotland* (Oxford University Press, 1965).
SMOUT T. C., *A History of the Scottish People, 1560–1830* (Collins, 1969).
THOMSON A., *Lauder and Lauderdale* (1880).
*Town Guides* to Alnwick, Berwick-upon-Tweed, Morpeth, Hawick, Galashiels, Duns, Hexham, Rothbury, Jedburgh, Kelso.
WHITHAND and ALAUDDIN, 'Town Plans of Scotland', *Scottish Geographical Magazine*, September 1969.

CHAPTER 8
ALLEN C. J., *The North Eastern Railway* (Ian Allan, 1964).
ATKINSON F., *The Great Northern Coalfield, 1700–1900* (U.T.P., 1970).
BERGEN C., *History of the Bedlington Ironworks, 1736–1867*.
DENDY F. W., 'Old Newcastle, Its Suburbs and Gilds', *Literary and Philosophical Society of Newcastle upon Tyne* (Northumberland Press, 1921).
GARD and HARTLEY, *Railways in the Making* (Archive Teaching Unit, Department of Education, Newcastle University).
GRAY W., *A Survey of Newcastle upon Tyne* (1649; reprinted Frank Graham, 1970).
HOUSE J. W., *Industrial Britain: The North East* (David and Charles, 1969).
MIDDLEBROOK S., 'Newcastle upon Tyne', *Newcastle Journal* (1950).
ROLT L. T. C., *George and Robert Stephenson* (Longmans, 1960).
TAYLOR T. J., *The Archaeology of the Coal Trade* (Archaeological Institute of Great Britain and Ireland, 1858).
TOMLINSON W. W., *The North Eastern Railway* (1914).
WILKES and DODDS, *Tyneside Classical* (J. Murray, 1964).
WILSON B. F. A., 'The Industrial Development of Hawick to 1872', *Transactions of Hawick Archaeological Society* (1954).

CHAPTER 9
*Alnwick Town Centre* (County Planning Department).
*Berwick-upon-Tweed Planning Objectives* (County Planning Department).
County Development Plan: *Rural Northumberland*, 2 vols (1967).
HOUSE J. W., *The Rural Problem: Northumbrian Tweedside* (Rural Community Council, 1956).

*Killingworth Township Handbook and Reports* (Northumberland County Council).
Northumberland County Development Plan: *Cramlington.*
*Reports of the City Planning Department, Newcastle upon Tyne.*
*Reports of the Eastern Border Development Association.*
*Reports of the Rural Community Council for Northumberland.*
*Reports of the Technical Working Party* on *The Royal Burgh of Jedburgh* (1964); on *Kelso* (1965); on *Melrose* (1966).
Scottish Development Department, *The Central Borders: A Plan for Expansion,* 2 vols (H.M.S.O., 1968).
'Towards a Rural Policy', *Report of the Development Committee of Berwickshire County Council* (1971).

CHAPTER 10
BEATTIE W., *Border Ballads* (Penguin, 1952).
BRODIE W., *The Gypsies of Yetholm* (1884).
BRUCE and STOKOE, *Northumbrian Minstrelsy* (1882; reprinted by the Folklore Association Inc., 1965).
Catalogues of the Laing Art Gallery, Newcastle upon Tyne.
CRICHTON W. S., *The Scott Originals* (Foulis Press, 1912).
GEESON C., *A Northumberland and Durham Word Book* (Harold Hill, 1969).
*Historic Newcastle* (Frank Graham, 1970).
LOCKHART J. G., *Life of Scott* (Everyman).
MCNEILL F. M., *The Silver Bough: Local Festivals of Scotland,* 4 vols (1968).
*Memoirs of Thomas Bewick, 1822–8* (Bodley Head, 1924).
MURRAY J. A. H., *Dialects of the Southern Counties of Scotland* (1873).
RAYNER J., *Wood Engravings by Thomas Bewick* (King Penguin, 1947).
RIDLEY N., *Northumbrian Heritage* (Robert Hale, 1969).
SCOTT W., *Minstrelsy of the Scottish Border,* 3 vols (1803).
STRANG B., *A History of English* (Methuen, 1970).
*The Monthly Chronicle* (1887–91).
VEITCH Professor, *History and Poetry of the Scottish Borders,* 2 vols (1878).
*Wilson's Tales of the Border: A Selection* (The Moray Press, 1934).

CHAPTER 11
Amongst the many books by itinerant travellers, the following few have been selected as being particularly useful and entertaining.

A Tourist (probably John Mason), *The Border Tour* (1826).
BANKS F. R., *Scottish Border Country* (Batsford, 1951).
ELDER M., *Ballad Country* (Oliver and Boyd, 1963).
GRAHAM P. A., *Highways and Byways in Northumbria* (Macmillan, 1920).
MOORHOUSE S., *Companion into Northumberland* (Methuen, 1953).
SCOTT W., *The Beauties of the Border* (1821).
WHITE W., *Northumberland and the Borders* (Chapman and Hall, 1859).

# Appendices

# Appendices

## I Buildings and structures of special interest

This list is highly selective and does not aim at comprehensive coverage of the region. It is based on the available lists of the Department of the Environment and the Royal Commission on Ancient Monuments, extracting those buildings and structures regarded as being of national and of great local importance. With all its shortcomings, it may help the visitor to find further points of interest, although the presence in this list does not indicate public access, for example, to the mansions named.

(N) – Northumberland
(B) – Berwickshire
(R) – Roxburghshire
(AM) – Ancient Monuments open to the public

| | |
|---|---|
| *Abbotsford* (R) | Scottish baronial mansion, home of Sir Walter Scott. |
| *Acomb* (N) | Several good 18thC houses in main street; fountain at top of hill. |
| *Adderstone* (N) | Hall 1819; limekiln. |
| *Allendale Town* (N) | 18thC square; old lead mines. |
| *Alnmouth* (N) | Good houses in Northumberland Street; 18thC granges; Prospect Place, 19thC; Victoria Place, 18th and 19thC. |
| *Alnwick* (N) | The Castle; Hotspur Gate, 15thC; Bailiffgate, 18thC; Bondgate mostly 18th and 19thC, Nos 71–75 late 17thC; Dispensary Lane, Fire Engine House, 1810, and Old Dispensary, 1819; Canongate Bridge, 1821; Percy Tenantry Column, 1816; Assembly Rooms, 1826; Lion Bridge (Adam), 1773; Pottergate Tower, 1768; Narrowgate No. 53, 17thC; Market Cross; Clayport Street, Old Post Office; Hulne Priory, 13thC (Carmelite). |

*Amble* (N) — Coal staithes; Hallbank Manor House (one 15thC window).

*Ancroft* (N) — St Anne's Church, Norman, with Vicar's pele.

*Ancrum* (R) — Market Cross, 16thC; triangular green; 18thC kirk (ruined); 18thC bridge; Chesters House, 1790.

*Aydon Castle* (N) — 1305, now being restored by Department of the Environment.

*Ayton* (B) — Planned village 18th–19thC; Scottish baronial castle, 1851.

*Bamburgh* (N) — Castle; triangular village green; church of St Aidan; Grace Darling monument and museum; 17thC walled garden by green.

*Beaufront* (N) — Castle, 1837–41, Dobson's most interesting work.

*Bedlington* (N) — Front Street; market cross.

*Bedrule* (R) — Norman motte; 18thC dovecote.

*Belford* (N) — Church of St Mary, some Norman work with Dobson restoration; Church Street, High Street, West Side and Market Place all good 18th and 19thC.

*Bellingham* (N) — Church of St Cuthbert, 13thC, with gatehouse pele, north side; gatehouse pele, south side; Rede Bridge, 1715; bridge, 1834 (Green); Tarset Castle, 1267.

*Belsay* (N) — Castle, 14th and 17thC; the Arcade, planned village.

*Berwick-upon-Tweed* (N) — Castle ruins, Norman (AM); White Walls, Norman (AM); Elizabethan Walls (AM); Royal Border Bridge, 1847 (Stephenson); Old Bridge, 1610–34; Town Hall, 1754–60; Barracks (Vanburgh), 1719; Trinity Church, 1648–52; Quayside houses, Georgian; Hide Hill, Georgian; Church Street, Georgian; Marygate, Georgian; Palace Green; Guard House, Palace Green, 18thC; Royal Tweed Bridge, 1925–8.

*Birtley* (N) — Church of St Giles, 11thC; limekilns.

*Blanchland* (N) — All the square, 18thC; Gatehouse, c. 1500; Lord Crewe Arms; Post Office; village restored on monastic site; lead and coal mines in area.

*Blyth* (N) — High Lighthouse, 1788; coal staithes.

*Bolam* (N) — Church of St Andrews, late Saxon.

*Bothal* (N) — St Andrew's church, 13thC; castle, 14thC.

*Bowden* (R) — Kirk, 1661; triangular green; market cross base, 16thC.

*Brainshaugh* (N) — Priory ruins; Park Mill, 18thC.

*Brandon* (N) — Ruined medieval church, on Saxon foundation.

*Brinkburn* (N) — Priory, 12thC (Augustinian).

*Buckholm* (R) — Tower-house, 16thC.

*Bunkle* (B) — Old kirk, Norman; bridge, 1770.

*Bywell* (N) — Castle, 15thC; Hall, 1760; St Andrews, Saxon; St Peters, Norman; cross.

*Cadger's Castle* (N) — Folly, 1746 (v. Jacobites).

*Cambo* (N) — All the village; pele tower (Post Office).

*Capheaton* (N) — All the village; Hall, 1668 (Trollope).

*Cartington* (N) — Castle, 14thC +.

| | |
|---|---|
| *Cavers* (R) | Westgate Hall, rare 17thC mansion; Greenview Mill; stocking weaving shop. |
| *Cessford* (R) | Castle ruin. |
| *Chatton* (N) | Westwood Bridge, 16thC, rebuilt 19thC. |
| *Chesters* (N) | Roman camp; Hall, 1771 and 1891 (Shaw); stables by Norman Shaw. |
| *Chillingham* (N) | Church of St Peters, especially Sir Ralph Grey's tomb; castle, 1344–8; planned village, early 19thC. |
| *Chipchase* (N) | Castle, 14thC +. |
| *Chirnside* (B) | Ninewalls Dovecote; paper mill; monument to Jim Clark. |
| *Chollerton* (N) | Church of St Giles (Roman columns); stable by churchyard; old windmill in farm; farmhouse; Chollerford Bridge, 1772. |
| *Cockburnspath* (B) | Kirk, 16thC (round tower); Sparrow Castle manor house; mercat cross; St Helen's kirk (Norman) on coast; Pease Bridge, 1784; Fast Castle, ruin on coast; harbour, 17thC; mill and smithy. |
| *Coldingham* (B) | Priory ruins, 7thC, rebuilt 1089 (Cistercian); mercat cross; 18thC village. |
| *Coldstream* (B) | The Hirsel (Sir A. Douglas Home); the Lees, 1770; bridge, 1763 (Smeaton); marriage house by bridge; Coldstream Guards House; grain mill by Leet Water; old brewery in Abbey Loan; Twizel Bridge, 15thC. |
| *Corbet* (R) | Restored tower-house. |
| *Corbridge* (N) | Church of St Andrew (Saxon work); all the 'village', especially Hill Street; good square; market cross, 1814; pump, 1815; Vicar's pele tower, 14thC; bridge, 1674 (only one to survive 1771 Tyne floods); old hand-made brick pottery. |
| *Coupland* (N) | Castle, 16thC. |
| *Cowdenknowes* (B) | Tower-house and mansion. |
| *Crailing* (R) | House, 1803, best Regency style in county. |
| *Craster* (N) | Tower-house; limekilns. |
| *Crawley* (N) | Tower-house, 14thC. |
| *Denholm* (R) | Planned village 18th–19thC for weaving; monument to Dr John Leyden, on fine village green. |
| *Denwick* (N) | Village pumps, 19thC; bridge, 1773 (John Adam). |
| *Dilston* (N) | Tower-house; chapel, 1616. |
| *Doddington* (N) | Church of St Michael and St Mary (altar at west end); castle house, 1584. |
| *Dryburgh* (B) | Abbey, 1250 (Premonstratensian) (AM). |
| *Drygrange* (R) | Bridge, 1779–80. |
| *Duns* (or *Dunse*) (B) | Castle; mercat cross (in park); market square, 18th–19thC; oldest house, No. 28 Newtown Street; Cumledge Mill, early 19thC blanket mill (still working). |
| *Dunstanburgh* (N) | Castle, 14thC (AM); Proctors Stead, farm with medieval work. |
| *Earlston* (B) | Rhymer's Mill (wool/blankets) Rhymer's Tower |

| | |
|---|---|
| *Eccles* (B) | Kirk, 1774; cross at Crosshall Farm. |
| *Eckford* (R) | Kirk, 1665. |
| *Edlingham* (N) | Castle ruins, 14thC; church of St John (Norman). |
| *Edrom* (B) | Kirk, 1732; old kirk (Norman) (AM). |
| *Eglingham* (N) | Church of St Maurice, Norman work; Hall, 16thC + 1704. |
| *Elsdon* (N) | Church of St Cuthbert; all the village, fine green; rectory, 14thC tower-house ('finest of all the existing rectorial tower houses of Northumberland'); motte and bailey. |
| *Embleton* (N) | Church of Holy Trinity, 13thC; rectorial tower-house, 14th and 18thC; brick dovecote, 18thC; another dovecote, 17thC; pump and fountain. |
| *Etal* (N) | Ruined courtyard castle, 1341–4; manor house, 1748–67. |
| *Eyemouth* (B) | Gunsgreen House, 1764; dovecote at Gunsgreen; watch-house in kirkyard. |
| *Farne Islands* (N) | Lighthouse, 1826; Prior Castell's tower, *c.* 1500; St Cuthbert's chapel, 14th + 19thC. |
| *Featherstone* (N) | Castle, 13th + 19thC. |
| *Felton* (N) | Mill, now grain store; riverside, good 18th–19thC houses; medieval bridge |
| *Ferniehurst* (R) | Castle, 16thC, now Y.H.; chapel, 17thC. |
| *Fogo* (B) | Kirk, 1755, with laird's lofts; bridge, 1641. |
| *Ford* (N) | Courtyard castle, 1338–41; church of St Michael, good belfry; school, 1860, with Waterford paintings; parson's pele, ruined; forge, 18thC; corn mill; old colliery workings at Ford Moss; medieval bridge, rebuilt 18thC. |
| *Foulden* (B) | Tithe barn (AM). |
| *Fulton* (R) | Tower-house. |
| *Gavinton* (B) | Planned village, 18th–19thC. |
| *Gordon* (B) | Greenknowe tower-house (AM). |
| *Gosforth* (N) | High Street, Nos 32, 34, 36, old village core; Salters' Bridge, medieval. |
| *Greenlaw* (B) | Kirk, 1675; mercat cross, 1609; new market cross, 1829; court house, 1829; County Hall. |
| *Guyzance* (N) | All the village. |
| *Halton* (N) | Castle, 14thC. |
| *Harbottle* (N) | Castle (ruined). |
| *Haughton* (N) | Castle, 13thC. |
| *Hawick* (R) | Statue to the Callant, 1914; Weensland Mills (wool), early 19thC; Wilton Mills (wool), early 19thC; Mill Path Corn Mill, *c.* 1805; the Motte. |
| *Heddon-on-the-Wall* (N) | Church of St Philip and St James, Saxon. |
| *Hefferlaw* (N) | Tower-house, 15thC. |
| *Hepburn* (N) | Castle, 14th and 16thC. |
| *Hermitage* (R) | Castle, 14thC (AM). |
| *Hexham* (N) | Abbey, 7thC, rebuilt 1093 (Augustinian); Manor Office (old |

gaol), 1330; Moot Hall, 15thC; bridge, 1785–8 (Mylne); market-place; Gilesgate and Holy Island, much 17thC; St Mary's Chare; Fore Street; Hencotes and Battle Hill; old Grammar School, 1684.

| | |
|---|---|
| *High Rochester* (N) | Roman camp; pele towers. |
| *Holystone* (N) | St Ninian's Well. |
| *Horncliffe* (B) | Union Chain Bridge, 1820 (Captain Brown). |
| *Horton* (N) | Old Grange; Belassis Bridge (medieval). |
| *Howick* (N) | Hall, 1782; the Long Row, cottages, 1841. |
| *Hume* (B) | Castle; 1794 folly. |
| *Hutton* (B) | Castle; 16thC keep. |
| *Ilderton* (N) | Roddam Mausoleum, 1795. |
| *Jedburgh* (R) | Abbey, 12thC (Augustinian) (AM); Queen Mary's House, 16thC; Canongate Bridge, 16thC; Newgate gatehouse, 1761; Prince Charlie's House, 7–11 Castlegate; Castlegate and High Street; Laidlaw Mill, early 19thC (woollens); Bongate Mill, early 19thC (woollens). |
| *Kelso* (R) | Abbey, founded 1128 (Benedictine) (AM); Ednam House, 1761, finest Georgian in the county; bridge, 1800–3 (John Rennie); Teviot Bridge; Abbey Court, houses; Walton Hall, Roxburgh Street (home of John Ballantyne); Town Hall, 1816; the Square, early 19thC; Nos 1, 2, 3, Woodmarket; Floors Castle, 18thC. |
| *Kirknewton* (N) | Church of St Gregory (fine bas-relief of the Adoration of the Magi), tunnel vaulting. |
| *Kirkwhelpington* (N) | Church of St Bartholomew, 12th–13thC; vicarage, 14th and 18thC (home of John Hodgson, local historian), 19thC; water mill and wheel intact. |
| *Kirk Yetholm* (R) | Catchpenny Old Toll; Gypsy 'Palace'; green; packhorse bridge. |
| *Ladykirk* (B) | Church of St Mary, 1500, with Adam cupola of 1743 (all stone kirk); Ladykirk House; West Lodge. |
| *Langley* (N) | Castle, 14th and 19thC. |
| *Langshaw* (R) | Tower-house, 16thC, and walled garden; Hillslap tower-house; Colmslie tower-house. |
| *Lauder* (B) | Kirk of St Mary, 1673; Town Hall/Prison; 18thC inns; gasworks, 1843. |
| *Legerwood* (B) | Dod's mill. |
| *Lemmington* (N) | Hall, 14th and 18thC; castellated farmhouse folly, 18thC. |
| *Lennel* (B) | Mansion. |
| *Lesbury* (N) | Medieval bridge. |
| *Lilburn* (N) | Norman chapel ruins, West Lilburn; tower, 15thC; Lilburn Tower, 1828–43 (John Dobson's last country house in Tudor style). |
| *Lindisfarne* (N) | Priory A.D. 635, rebuilt 1093 (Benedictine) (AM); St Mary's |

|                              | church, 13thC; castle, 16thC, restored 1902 by Lutyens; 18thC limekilns. |
| Linton (R)                   | Kirk, Norman tympanum over porch and Norman font. |
| Longhirst (N)                | All the village. |
| Littledean (R)               | Tower-house, 16thC. |
| Longhorsley (N)              | Tower-house, 16thC. |
| Marchmont (B)                | House (Adam). |
| Maxton (R)                   | Burgh cross on remnant 'green' (restored 1881). |
| Mellerstain (B)              | Mansion (W. and R. Adam). |
| Melrose (R)                  | Abbey, 7thC, rebuilt 1136 (Cistercian) (AM); Commendator's House (now museum); dovecote, 18thC; mercat cross, 16thC; Harmony Hall, regency; Darnick tower-house, 16thC. |
| Mertoun (B)                  | House, 19thC; dovecote, 1576; small meal mill, 18thC. |
| Midlem (R)                   | Planned village, 18thC. |
| Mitford (N)                  | Castle ruins, 12th–13thC; hall, 1823 (Dobson); Abbey Woollen mills, 18th–19th C; church of St Mary Magdelene, mostly 19thC. |
| Morebattle (R)               | Kirk, c. 1757; tower-house, at Corbet, possibly 16thC; tower-house, at Whitton, possibly 17thC. |
| Morpeth (N)                  | Bridge fragments, 13thC; Bridge Chantry, 13thC; Church of St Mary, 14thC; St James, Newgate, arcaded screen, 1843; new bridge, 1829–33 (Telford and Dobson); town steeple, 15thC; castle, Norman and 15thC; Collingwood House; Castle Square, Bridge Street and Market Place; Newminster Abbey, fragments, 1137 (Cistercian). |
| Nenthorn (B)                 | Hall, Newton Don (Adam, c. 1790). |
| Nether Witton (N)            | Hall, c. 1700; cross; woollen mill, c. 1800. |
| Newburn (N)                  | St Michael's Church, Norman. |
| Newcastle upon Tyne (N)      | Roman Wall fragments (west suburbs); Town Walls, 14thC; Barbican Walls, 13thC; Heber Tower; Morden Tower (with 17thC upper storey); Wall Knott Tower (with 18thC upper storey); Austin Tower; Castle Keep, 1172–8; Black Gate, 1247–50; Sallyport Tower. |
|                              | St Andrew's Church, 12thC; St Nicholas' Cathedral, 13th–14thC; St John's Church, 15thC; Blackfriars' Monastery, 13th and 19thC; All Saints, 1786–96; St Mary's R.C. Cathedral (Pugin), 1844; St Thomas' Church (Dobson), 1825–30. |
|                              | Arthur's Cooperage, the Close, 17thC timber warehouse; Bessie Surtees House, Sandhill, 17thC. |
|                              | Guildhall, 17thC interior, 18thC exterior; Trinity House, Broad Chare, 17thC; Holy Jesus Hospital, c. 1681 (now restored); Keelmans' Hospital, 1701; Custom House, Quayside, 1766; Moot Hall (Stokoe), 1812. |
|                              | Leazes Terrace, 1829; Grey Street, 19thC (Dobson); |

Grainger Market, 19thC; Royal Arcade, 1831 (now restored); Central Station, 1846–50 (Dobson); Theatre Royal, 1837.

Hancock Museum, 1878; Armstrong Building, University, 1887–1904; Laing Art Gallery, 1904; Stephenson Building, University, 1952; new Central Library; new University Buildings; new Civic Centre; new University Theatre.

High Level Bridge (R. Stephenson), 1846–9; Swing Bridge (Armstrong), 1876; Tyne Bridge, 1925–8.

| | |
|---|---|
| *Norham* (N) | Castle, 12thC (AM); St Cuthbert's Church (Norman); cross on village green; bridge, 1885–7. |
| *North Shields* (N) | Fishmarket; High Beacon; Low Beacon. |
| *North Sunderland* (N) | Presbyterian Church, 1810; Church of St Paul, 1834 (Salvin). |
| *Ogle* (N) | Tower-house, 14th and 15thC; manor house. |
| *Old Bewick* (N) | Church of Holy Trinity 'most perfect surviving small early Norman church in Northumberland'. |
| *Otterburn* (N) | Woollen mill in use; pele towers at Beanshaw and Shittleheugh. |
| *Ovingham* (N) | St Mary's Church (Saxon); vicarage, 14thC; George Stephenson's cottage. |
| *Paxton* (B) | House (Adam); Union Suspension Bridge, 1820 (Captain Brown), first of its kind in the world. |
| *Plessey* (N) | Watermill and windmill. |
| *Polwarth* (B) | Kirk, 1763. |
| *Ponteland* (N) | Tower-house, 14thC and 17thC manor house (now an inn); Church of St Mary, Norman tower and 13thC; ruined parson's pele; Bell Villas, 1841. |
| *Preston* (B) | Tower-house, now garden shed; market cross. |
| *Prudhoe* (N) | Castle, 12thC (now Department of Environment). |
| *Riding Mill* (N) | Railway Station, *c.* 1835. |
| *Risingham* (N) | Roman camp. |
| *Roberton* (R) | Harden mansion, 17thC; toll house, Greenbank, 1826; symbol stone, Borthwick Mains. |
| *Rock* (N) | Medieval tower-house (now Y.H.A.). |
| *Rothbury* (N) | Church of All Saints, mostly 19thC but Saxon cross-shaft holding font; bridge, medieval. |
| *Roxburgh* (R) | Castle fragments. |
| *St Abbs* (B) | Harbour works, 1833; lighthouse, 1862. |
| *St Boswells* (R) | Lessuden House. |
| *Seaton Delaval* (N) | Hall, 1718–25 (Vanburgh); sluice, 1761–4. |
| *Simonburn* (N) | St Mungo's Church, Saxon cross-shaft. |
| *Smailholm* (B) | Tower-house, 16thC (AM). |
| *Southdean* (R) | Pele-houses – Kilsike, Mervinslaw, Northbank, Slacks Tower. |
| *Spindlestone* (N) | Windmill. |
| *Stamfordham* (N) | Church of St Mary, 13thC with good bas-relief south aisle; |

239

|  |  |
|---|---|
|  | all the village round green; mostly 18thC with cross and lock-up. |
| *Staward* (N) | Pele house, set above forested valley. |
| *Swinburne* (N) | Castle, 17th–18thC; manor house. |
| *Swinton* (B) | Planned village, 18th–19thC; mercat cross, 1769. |
| *Thirlestane* (B) | Manor house; ruined castle to east. |
| *Thirlwall* (N) | 14thC castle. |
| *Thockrington* (N) | Church, some Norman fragments; cross base in churchyard; fine deserted village site. |
| *Tweedmouth* (N) | Most of Main Street. |
| *Tynemouth* (N) | Priory, 7thC origin, restored 11thC (Benedictine) (AM); castle (gatehouse to priory), 14thC (AM). |
| *Wall* (N) | All village, mostly 17thC; square green with fountain; Church of St Oswald on the fell, with Roman architectural fragments inside, on site of Heavenfield, 635, commemorated by wooden cross. |
| *Wallington* (N) | Hall, 17th, 18th and 19thC; 17thC walled garden; gargoyles from City of London; bridge, 1760 (Paine). |
| *Wallsend on Tyne* (N) | Holy Cross Church, 12thC fragments; Willington Viaduct, 1869; Rising Sun Colliery, 1935. |
| *Warden* (N) | St Michael's Church (Norman); cross. |
| *Wark-on-Tweed* (N) | Castle ruin, 12thC. |
| *Warkworth* (N) | Castle, 12th and 14thC (AM); Church of St Lawrence, Norman work; bridge, 1379; bridge gatehouse, 14thC; market cross; Main Street, 18th–19thC; the Hermitage, up-river. |
| *Wedderburn* (B) | Castle, 1770–5 (Adam). |
| *Weldon Bridge* (N) | Bridge, 18thC. |
| *Weststruther* (B) | Inn, 1721; Houndslow Toll. |
| *Whittingham* (N) | All the village; tower-house, restored 1845; Church of St Bartholomew, Saxon work. |
| *Whitton* (N) | Ruined tower in farm. |
| *Woodhorn* (N) | The village. |
| *Wooler* (N) | Norman motte. |
| *Wylam* (N) | George Stephenson's cottage; railway station, 1835. |

## II National Trust properties

*Allen Banks (near Haydon Bridge)* (N): 189 acres of wooded river banks.
*Alnmouth* (N): 272 acres of dunes and saltings.
*Beadnell Limekilns* (N): eighteenth-century.
*Dunstanburgh Castle* (N).
*Dunstanburgh Links* (N): 494 acres of sand dunes.
*Farne Islands* (N).

*Holystone, Lady's Well* (N): associated with St Ninian.
*Housesteads and Hotbanks on Hadrian's Wall* (N): 919 acres.
*Howick* (N): 175 acres of farmland, cliffs and dunes from Craster to Boulmer.
*Kelso Turret House* (R): not open to public.
*Lindisfarne Castle* (N): 37 acres.
*Monks House, Seahouses*: not open to public.
*Newton Links* (N): 55 acres in Beadnell Bay.
*Ros Castle (near Chillingham)* (N): Iron Age encampment.
*Shoreston Dunes (near Bamburgh)* (N): 60 acres of dunes.
*Wallington Estate* (N): 12,922 acres of farmland, parkland, Hall, gardens, and Cambo Village.
*Wylam* (N): George Stephenson's cottage (not open to public).


## III Historic houses, castles and gardens open to the public

(Situation in 1971)

*Abbotsford* (R): 24 March–31 October, daily, 1000–1700 hrs. Suns, 1400–1700 hrs.
*Alnwick Castle* (N): May–September, daily, 1300–1700 hrs. No Fridays or Sats.
*Bamburgh Castle* (N): Easter–September, daily.
*Callaly Castle* (N): 30 May–26 September, 1415–1800 hrs.
*Cragside Grounds, Rothbury* (N): Easter–30 September, daily.
*Craster Tower* (N): written appointment only.
*Darnick Tower (near Melrose)* (R): written appointment only.
*Harnham Hall (near Belsay)* (N): written appointment only.
*Howick Gardens* (N): April–September, daily, 1400–1900 hrs.
*Langley Castle (near Hexham)* (N): May–September, Weds, 1400–1900 hrs.
*Lindisfarne Castle* (N): 1 April–5 June; 28 June–30 September, daily, 1400–1800 hrs except Tues; 6 June–27 June, Weds, 1400–1800 hrs.
*Mellerstain* (B): May–September, daily (no Sats), 1400–1730 hrs.
*Seaton Delaval Hall* (N): May–September, Weds, Suns and Bank Holidays, 1400–1900 hrs.
*The Manor House, Whalton* (N): Gardens only, 15 May–26 September, Sats, Suns and Bank Holidays, 1400–1900 hrs.
*Wallington Hall, Cambo* (N): April–September, 1400–1800 hrs, no Tues, Fris; October, Sats and Suns, 1400–1700 hrs.
*Wedderlie House (near Gordon)* (B): written appointment only.


## IV Museums and galleries

| | |
|---|---|
| *Alnwick* | Bondgate Gallery: occasional exhibitions. |
| *Bamburgh* | Grace Darling Museum. |
| *Berwick-upon-Tweed* | Art Gallery and Museum. |
| *Chollerford* | Chesters Museum: Roman antiquities. |

| | |
|---|---|
| *Corbridge* | Corstopitum Museum: Roman antiquities. |
| *Duns* | Jim Clark Memorial Room. |
| *Hawick* | Wilton Lodge Museum: local Border history and crafts. |
| *Hexham* | Moot Hall: occasional art exhibitions. |
| *Jedburgh* | *Abbey Museum.* |
| | Queen Mary's House: materials relating to Mary, Queen of Scots. |
| *Kielder* | Forest Park Museum: summer weekends and August. |
| *Melrose* | Commendator's House: the Abbey and associated antiquities. |
| *Newcastle upon Tyne* | The Keep Museum; The Black Gate Museum; Museum of Antiquities (University); Laing Art Gallery and Museum; Plummer Tower (annexe to Laing); Museum of Science and Engineering; Hancock Museum (Natural History); Hatton Gallery (University); Stone Gallery (Private); Westgate Gallery (young artists). |

# V Conservation areas and sites

*Border Forest and National Forest Park:* 126,000 acres designated in 1955.

*Chillingham Castle Grounds:* herd of wild white cattle.

*Comb Rig Moss:* National Nature Reserve, 1960. Eighty acres near Kirkwhelpington available by permit only. Forestry Commission and Nature Conservancy.

*Duns Castle Grounds:* Nature Reserve of the Scottish Wildfowl Trust. One hundred and ninety acres designated in 1966.

*Farne Islands:* 80 acres. Nature Reserve of the National Trust and Farne Islands Association.

*Gordon Moss:* Nature Reserve of the Scottish Wildfowl Trust. One hundred and two acres designated in 1966. Permit needed.

*Hancock Museum, Newcastle upon Tyne:* HQ of the Natural History Society of Northumberland, Durham and Newcastle upon Tyne: publishers of many booklets on geology, flora and fauna.

*Harbottle Crags Reserve:* nearly half a square mile of Fell Sandstone moorland leased to the Northumberland and Durham Naturalists' Trust by the Forestry Commission in 1970.

*Lindisfarne:* National Nature Reserve, 1964, and National Wildfowl Refuge, 1966, covering 7,378 acres of sand dunes, salt marsh and foreshore.

*National Park Information Centres* at Lewisburn (North Tyne), Twice Brewed (Roman Wall), Ingram (Beamish Valley) and Byrness (Redesdale).

*Northumberland Coast:* 58 square miles designated in 1958 as an Area of Outstanding Natural Beauty.

*Northumberland National Park:* 398 square miles designated in 1956.

*St Abb's Head, Berwickshire:* fulmar colony.

*Yetholm Loch:* Nature Reserve of the Scottish Wildfowl Trust. Permit needed.

# Index

# Index

Abbey St Bathans, 85, 132
Abbotsford, 124, 131, 185, 228, 236
Acklington, 98, 157
Acklington Dyke, 29
Acomb, 215, 228
Adam, Robert and James, 124
Adam, William, 124, 133
Adderstone, 228
Afforestation, 50
Agricola, 71
Akeld, 78, 114
Ale Water, 39
Alexander III, 85
Allan Water, 116
Allen, James, 190
Allen Banks, 235
Allendale, 44, 97, 123, 128, 129, 131, 201, 203
Allendale Town, 192, 228
Alnham, 116
Alnmouth, 133, 210, 228, 235
Alnwick, 101, 109, 110, 118, 124, 143–5, 157, 163, 181, 182, 216, 228, 236, Pl. 17a
Alwinton, 205, 208
Amble, 39, 85, 209, 229
Ancroft, 90, 116, 229
Ancrum, 81, 96, 98, 132, 157, 229, Pl. 10a
Andesite, 25

Anglo-Saxon colonization, 45, 77ff.
Armstrong, Johnny, 105, 195
Armstrong, Lord, 112, 131, 168, 169
Ashington, 82, 170, 171
Auchope Cairn, 100, 208
Aydon Castle, 229
Ayton, 131, 229

Bailey, John, 92, 125, 126, 160
Ballads, 193ff.
Bamburgh, 29, 81, 112, 143, 211, 229, 236
Barmkins, 115
Barmoor, 217
Bastle houses, 118, 121
Battle stone, 67
Beadnell, 27, 37, 210, 235
Beaker folk, 67
Beaufront, 229
Bede, the Venerable, 79, 81, 174
Bedlington, 141, 165, 169, 171, 229
Bedrule, 127, 229
Belassis Bridge, 232
Belford, 157, 229
Bellingham, 51, 82, 148, 160, 220, 229
Belsay, 23, 119, 123, 127, 133, 229
Bemersyde Loch, 56
Bernicia, 17, 78

Berwick-upon-Tweed, 40, 54, 110, 118, 120, 133, 140, 141, 145, 157, 160, 186, 188, 191, 229, 236, Pl. 12a, Pl. 16b
Bewick, Thomas, 57, 127, 129, 202
Biddlestone, 25, 67, 120
Birds, of the forest, 53; game, 46; of the moorland, 47; of prey, 47; of the sea, 36; Pl. 6b, Pl. 24c
Birling, 81
Birtley, 80, 229
Bizzle, the, 20, 48
Black Dyke, 65
Black Law, 26
Blackbrough Hill, Pl. 7a
Blanchland, 85, 87, 114, 157, 229
Blaydon Races, 198
Blyth, 163, 165, 168, 171–2, 229
Board of Agriculture, 126
Bolam, 89, 229
Bonchester, 26, 62
Bondagers, 138, Pl. 22b
Bonny Prince Charlie, 122, 150
Border Laws, 108
Border Service, 119
Bothal, 90, 98, 229
Bowden, 96, 229
Bowes and Elleker Report, 104
Bowmont Water, 30, 33, 64, 82, 92, 218, 219
Bradford Kaim, 33
Brainshaugh, 228
Brandon, 229
Branxton, 15
Branxton Moor, 15
Breamish Valley, 22, 54, 63
Brethren Stones, 68
Bridges, 120, 133, Pl. 24b
Brinkburn, 85, 87, 229
Brocolitia, 75
Bronze Age, 66–68
Brotherston's Hole, 34
Brown, Launcelot, 125
Brownsman, 35, 37
Brunton Bank, 69, 72
Buccleugh, Duke of, 50, 114, 128

Buckholm, 229
Bunkle, 91, 229
Burghs, 142ff.
Burnmouth, 212
Burradon, 169, 171, 184
Byker, 83, 168
Byrness, 51, 237
Bywell, 89, 229

Cadger's Castle, 229
Callaly, 53, 123, 236
Calroustburn, 44, 63, 208
Cambo, 124, 215, 229
Capheaton, 123, 229
Carboniferous rocks, 26
Carfrae, 83
Carham, 101
Carter Bar, 104, 130, 133, 190, Pl. 1
Cartington, 229
Castle Heaton, 114
Catcleugh, 51, 56
Catrail, the, 65
Cattle breeds, 126
Cattle, wild white, 45
Cavers, 126, 230
Cessford, 115, 204, 230
Chapman, Abel, 47
Chatton, 92, 230
Chesterholme, 71
Chesters, 70, 72, 74, 230, 236
Cheswick, 41
Chevington, 171
Cheviot Hills, 21ff., 25, 30, 32, 43ff., 92, 137, 177, 205
Cheviot 'lake', 24
Cheviot 'moat', 22, 26
Chevy Chase, 36, 43, 122, 194
Chew Green, 59, 73, Pl. 8a
Chillingham, 45, 52, 53, 98, 113, 120, 230, 237
Chipchase, 123, 230
Chirdon, 52
Chirnside, 230
Chollerford, 236
Chollerton, 75, 215, 230

Chopwell, 52
Christianity, 78ff.
Churches, 88ff., 132–3
Churn Gut, 36
Clans, 105
Clayton, John, 70, 168
Clennell, 117, 120, 127
Clennell, Luke, 202
Clennell Street, 206, 207, 208
Clifton, 92
Coal Measures, 28
Coal Mining, 159, 163ff., 184, Pl. 19a, Pl. 21a
Cobles, 54
Cockburnspath, 133, 157, 213, 230
Cocklawfoot, Pl. 15a
Cockle Park, 136
Coldingham, 79, 82, 87, 98, 151, 153, 213, 230
Coldingham Moor, 39
Coldsmouth Hill, 19
Coldstream, 98, 106, 121, 133, 151, 152, 187, 191, 230
Coldstream Guards, 121
College Valley, 30, 44, 95
Collingwood, Admiral, 147, 174
Colmslie, 116
Comb Rigg Moss, 55, 237
Common Land, 96
Common Ridings, 190–2, Pl. 23a
Coquet, river, 22, 26, 28, 55, 87, 110, 205
Coquet Head, 59
Coquet Island, 209
Corbet, 230
Corbridge, 75, 80, 116, 133, 143, 167, 230, 237
Corn Road, 133, 214
Cornhill, 33
Corries, 30
Corsbie, 115, Pl. 12b
Corstopitum, 71, 74, Pl. 8a
Countryside Commission, 178
Coupland, 78, 230
Cowdenknowes, 105, 230

Cragside, 53, 131, 236
Craik Forest, 52
Crailing, 230
Cramlington, 171, 183–5
Craster, 114, 210, 230, 236
Crawley, 230
Crock Cleugh, 64
Crookham, 33, 78
Crosses, 80, 81, 221
Crosshall, 80
Cullercoats, 28
Cullernose Point, 210
Culley, George, 92, 125, 126, 129, 161
Cumledge Mill, 162, Pl. 19b
Curlew, 47, 56, 216

Dacre, Lord, 107
Danes, 83
Darling, Grace, 54, 211, 236
Darnick, 116, 185, 236
David I, 85, 96, 101, 142
Dawson, William, 126
Deadwater, 27, 31, 101, 221
Deer, 46, 52
Deer Parks, 98
Defoe, Daniel, 23, 200, 213
Deira, 17, 78
Delaval, family, 128, 135, 165
Denholm, 83, 96, 230
Denwick, 230
Depopulation, 119, 137, 178
Dere Street, 58, 69, 73, 97, 104, 205, 207
Derwent Reservoir, 57
Deserted villages, 96, 119
Devil's Causeway, 71, 144, 217
Devonian rocks, 24ff.
Dialect, 199–201
Dirrington Great Law, 21
Disputed Ground, 100, 101
Dobson, John, 88, 131, 147, 167, 168, 202
Dod Law, 61, 66
Doddington, 27, 77, 78, 115, 230
Douglas, family, 105, 134, 155
Drove-roads, 129, 207

Drumlins, 32
Druridge Bay, 171, 209
Dryburgh, 45, 85, 86, 97, 230
Drygrange, 98, 99, 230
Duddo, 67, 76
Dunes, 34, 42, 209, 211
Dunion, 21, 26, 62
Duns, 52, 56, 83, 139, 149, 157, 187, 191, 204, 230, 237
Duns Castle grounds, 237
Duns Law, 25
Dunstanburgh, 29, 43, 113, 230, 235, Pl. 11b
Dunston Staithes, Pl. 19c
Durham, Bishops of, 85, 111
Dykes, 29

Earlston, 157, 230
Earsdon, 171
East March, 104, 111
Eastern Borders Development Association, 178, 181, 187
Eccles, 85, 98, 132, 231
Eckford, 132, 231
Edgarhope Forest, 45, 51, 52
Edin's Hall broch, 64, Pl. 7b
Edlingham, 90, 215, 231
Edrom, 91, 132, 231
Edward I, 101, 145
Edward III, 145
Edwin's Palace, 77, 218
Edwin, King, 78
Eglingham, 231
Eildon Hills, 21, 25, 62, 73
Elsdon, 90, 96, 109, 116, 148, 231
Elswick, 168
Embleton, 116, 210, 231
Emparkment, 120
Enclosures, 97, 122ff., Pl. 13, Pl. 15c
Erratics, glacial, 30
Escomb, 79
Etal, 78, 113, 231, Pl. 10b
Ettrick Forest, 21, 45, 194
Eye Water, 32
Eyemouth, 24, 157, 178, 180, 192, 213, 231

Faa gypsies, 100, 124, 195, 196
Falstone, 44, 52, 57
Farming, medieval, 91ff.
Farming, modern, 135ff.
Farne Islands, 29, 31, 36ff., 177, 231, 235, 237, Pl. 6a, Pl. 6b, Pl. 24
Fast Castle, 113, 213
Featherstone, 113, 231
Fell Sandstone, 26, 29, 53, 63, 66
Felton, 231
Fenton, 53, 78, 119
Ferniehurst, 231
Field systems, 63, 93
First-footing, 192
Fishing, 53, 54, 209, 213
Flitting, 138
Flodden Field, 15, 103, 106, 155, 190, 195, 217, 218
Floors Castle, 124, 151, Pl. 14b
Fogo, 132, 231
Ford, 78, 90, 113, 116, 128, 135, 159, 218, 231
Ford Moss, 31
Forestry Commission, 50, 55, 178, 179
Forests, original, 44, 45, 83, 95, 98
Foulden, 231
Freestone, 23
Fulton, 231

Gaisty Law, 25
Galashiels, 156, 161-2, 185, 191
Gavinton, 127, 231
Gentry, landed, 134, 135
Geordie, 166, 200
Gin-gangs, 130, 138
Girthgate, 73
Glaciation, 29ff.
Glendale, 44, 149
Goats, wild, 48
Gordon, 115, 231
Gordon Moss, 56, 237
Gosforth, 173, 231
Goswick, 41, 42, 212
Grainger, Richard, 167, 168
Granges, 83

Greaves Ash, 63
Greens, village, 95
Green Belt, 177
Greenknowes, 115, 231
Greenlaw, 33, 133, 139, 157, 231
Grey, Sir Edward, 43, 168
Grey, John, 127
Grey's Forest, 43
Guyzance, 231

Hadrian, 71
Haig, Earl, 86
Halterburn, 67, 82, 100
Halton, 117, 231
Hancock Museum, 45, 55, 173, 237
Hand-ba', 192
Harbottle, 109, 148, 157, 231
Harbottle Crags, 55, 237
Harden stone, 25
Hardie, Baillie John, 161
Hareshaw Lynn, 55
Harnham Hall, 236
Hartford, 55
Harthope Burn, 30
Hartley, 165, 209
Harwood Forest, 52, 216
Haughs, 34
Haughton, 113, 231
Hawick, 116, 155, 161–2, 189, 191, 231,
    237, Pl. 15b, Pl. 23a
Heddon-on-the-Wall, 69, 89, 231
Hedgehope, 25
Hedgeley, 33
Hefferlaw, 231
Hen Hole, the, 30, 48, 208
Henry II, 85, 101, 111
Hepburn, 231
Heriot's Dyke, 65
Hermitage, 113, 231, Pl. 11a
Herons, family, 105
Hethpool, 92, 107
Hetton, 27
Hexham, 75, 80, 85, 88, 97, 116, 123, 151,
    153–4, 192, 231, 232, 237
High Rochester, 71, 232

Hill forts, 61ff.
Hill grazing, 48, 50
Hillslap, 116
Hogg, James, 193
Hole, 115
Holy Island, see Lindisfarne
Holystone, 232, 236
Horncliffe, 232
Horton Grange, 97, 232
Housesteads, 29, 72, 74, 236, Pl. 8b
Howden, 31
Howick, 232, 236
Hownam Law, 61, 62
Howtel, 114
Hule Moss, 56
Hulne, 85, 98
Humbleton, 31
Hume, 232
Humes, family, 105, 106, 134, 153
Husbandlands, 92
Hutton, 232
Hutton, James, 24, 126

Ilderton, 232
Ingram, 237
Iron, 161, 170
Iron Age, 44, 58ff., Pl. 7a, Pl. 7c, Pl. 8c

Jacobites, 122
James IV, 15, 106
James V, 45
James VI, 120, 145, 192
Jarrow, 79, 169, 174
Jedburgh, 85, 86, 109, 116, 142, 150, 151,
    161, 163, 181, 190, 192, 232, 237,
    Pl. 9b, Pl. 12c, Pl. 16a
Jed Water, 24, 34
Jesmond, 55, 168, 172

Kale Water, 30, 33, 58, 64, 72, 219
Kames, Lord, 126
Keelman, 164
Kelso, 85, 86, 122, 126, 133, 142, 151, 180,
    187, 191, 197, 232, 236, Pl. 21b
Kelso Trap rocks, 25

Kerr, family, 105, 115, 134
Kershopefoot, 101, 104
Kettle moraine, 33
Kidland, 52
Kidlandlee, 94
Kielder, 237
Kielder Forest, 48, 50–2, Pl. 5c
Kielder Moor, 101
Kilham, 21, Pl. 24a
Killingworth, 166, 171, 183–5, 203
Kimmerston, 78
King's Stone, 67
Kirkharle, 96, 125
Kirkhaugh, 80
Kirkheaton, 95, 96
Kirknewton, 78, 90, 96, 232, Pl. 22b
Kirkwhelpington, 95, 232
Kirk Yetholm, 96, 232

Ladykirk, 90, 133, 232
Laird's loft, 132
Lammermuirs, 45, 50, 65, 84, 105, 137, 178
Langleeford, 44
Langley, 113, 232, 236
Langshaw, 116, 232
Lanton, 78, 116
Lauder, 53, 141, 142, 149, 161, 191, 232
Lauderdale, 24, 45, 51, 97, 137
Legerwood, 232
Leland, John, 44, 45, 147
Lemington, 169
Lemmington, 117, 232
Lennel, 232
Lesbury, 232
Lewisburn, 53, 237
Leyden, Dr John, 193
Liddesdale, 50, 65, 101, 104, 195
Lilburn, 232
Limekilns, 27, 130
Limestone, 27, 210, 212
Lindisfarne, 41, 42, 78, 79, 85, 86, 87, 112, 211, 232, 233, 236, 237, Pl. 9d
Lingua Scotia, 201
Linton, 90, 132, 157, 233
Littledean, 233

Longformacus, 83
Longhirst, 233
Longhorsley, 233
Longstone, 36
Lutyens, Sir E., 132
Lynchets, 64, 92
Lynemouth, 28, 171, Pl. 21a

Macalpin, Kenneth, 101
Mack, James Logan, 101
Malcolm's Road, 73
Marchmont, 233
Marchmont, Earl of, 125
Martin, John, 202
Mary, Queen of Scots, 114, 116, 150, Pl. 12c
Matfen, 95
Maxton, 91, 96, 157, 233
Mellerstain, 124, 233, 236
Melrose, 26, 45, 84, 85, 86, 97, 151, 161, 180, 185, 192, 233, 237, Pl. 9a
Meltwater channels, 31, 32
Merse, the, 20, 21, 22, 45, 107, 110, 136, 199
Mertoun, 233
Micro-flints, 66
Middle March, 101, 104, 148
Midlem, 96, 233
Midsummer Fire, 191
Midwinter Fire, 192
Milfield, 77, 78
Milfield Plain, 31, 49, 77, 126, 160
Millstone Grit, 28
Minto, 62, 157
Mitford, 98, 109, 110, 233
Monastic farming, 96, 97
Monastic industries, 160, 163
Monastic sites, 85
Monday Cleugh, 31
Monks House, 236
Monkwearmouth, 79
Morebattle, 132, 233
Morpeth, 109, 110, 147, 157, 181, 182, 191, 233
Mosstroopers, 100, 107

Motte and bailey, 109
Mow, 84, 93, 205
Mud flats, 41
Mutiny Stones, 65

National Coal Board, 169, 171, 175, 184
National Forest Park, 50, 177, 178, 237
National Nature Reserve, 41
National Park, 177, 237
National Trust, 37, 235
Natural History Society of Northumberland, Durham and Newcastle upon Tyne, 37
Nature Conservancy, 56
Nature Trails, 55
Nenthorn, 233
Nesbit, 78
Nether Witton, 233
Netherton, Pl. 19a
Newbiggin-by-the-Sea, 209
Newburn, 233
Newcastle upon Tyne, 111, 160–9, 182–3, 233, 234, 237, Pl. 18a, Pl. 18b, Pl. 20a, Pl. 20b
Newcastle 'Roads', 164
Newcastleton, 50, 52, 128
Newminster, 85, 88, 163
Newstead, 73
Newton Links, 236
Newtown St Boswells, 156, 157, 185
Norham, 82, 90, 96, 101, 110, 157, 234
Norham and Islandshires, 85, 146
Norman Conquest, 45, 85, 101
North Shields, 174, 213, 234
North Sunderland, 234
North Tyne Railway, 31
Northumberland, Dukes of, 50, 51, 98, 110, 123, 135, 144, 149, 163, 167, 176, 181, 216
Northumbrian kingdom, 77ff.
Nunnykirk, 80

Ogle, 119, 234
Old Bewick, 90, 234
Old Melrose, 79

Old Red Sandstone, 24, 212, 213
Oppida, 62
Ottadini, 17, 62, 71
Otterburn, 51, 129, 133, 234; Battle of, 105, 139, 194
Ovingham, 80, 89, 234

Paine, James, 124
Palaeozoic rocks, 23
Parish boundaries, 84
Pawston Loch, 31
Paxton, 234
Pennine Way, 59, 205, 206, 208, 219
Pennymuir, 73
Percy, family, 106, 110, 194
Permian rocks, 28
Perry, Richard, 42
Place names, 77ff., 83ff.
Planned villages, 127
Plessey, 234
Polwarth, 125, 132, 234
Pons Aelius, 72, 143
Ponteland, 114, 116, 133, 234
Powburn, 31
Preston, 234
Prudhoe, 11, 170, 234

Quarry Hill, 26

Railways, 166, 167, 186
Raven's Cleugh, 25
Redesdale, 34, 46, 52, 94, 129, 136, 148, 194, 205
Rennie, John, 152
Reston, 157
Riding Mill, 167, 234
Ridley, George, 197
Rigg and furrow, 91
Risingham, 234
Roberton, 234
Rock, 234
Roddam Dene, 25
Roman Wall, 56, 69ff., 95, 177
Ros Castle, 43, 46, 63, 236
Ross Links, 41

Rothbury, 52, 154–5, 157, 234
Rothley, 28
Roughtinglinn, 63, 66
Roxburgh, 118, 142
Roxburgh, Duke of, 124, 132, 176
Roy, William, 125, 127, 133, Pl. 13
Royal Burghs, 142
Rubers Law, 21, 26, 127
Run-rig, 93, 127
Rural Community Council, 179
Russell's Cairn, 108

St Abbs, 212, 213, 234
St Abb's Head, 24, 39, 213, 237, Pl. 3
St Boswells, 90, 156, 185, 234
St Cuthbert, 37, 41, 64, 79, 82, 148
St James' Park, 173, 189
St Mary's Island, 209
St Oswald's, Heavenfield, 75
Salmon, 54, 188, Pl. 23b
Salters' Road, 163, 208
Scotch pebbles, 25
Scots Gap, 157
Scott, Sir Walter, 86, 114, 131, 193
Scottish Wildfowl Trust, 56
Scotts of Buccleugh, 105, 134
Scremerston Coal, 27, 159, 212, 216
Sculptured rocks, 18, 66, 216
Sea-coal, 163
Seahouses, 37, 211, 236
Seals, 40, Pl. 6a
Seaton Delaval, 124, 234, 236
Seaton Sluice, 28, 165
Selby's Forest, 43
Selgovae, 62
Shafto Crags, 28
Sheep breeds, 128, 129
Sheep farming, 136–7, Pl. 15a, Pl. 24
Shiels, 83, 94
Shipyards, 168–9
Shires, 85
Shorestone dunes, 236
Shows and fairs, 201, Pl. 22a
Siccar Point, 23, 39
Silurian rocks, 23, 24

Simonburn, 80, 234
Simonsides, 27, 66, 115
Slaley, 52, 131
Slitrig, 64, 65, 98, 155, 203
Smailholm, 26, 35, 83, 90, 114, 127, 157, 234
Smeaton, John, 133, 230
Snook, the, 41
Southdean, 62, 116, 234
South Shields, 72, 172
Soutra Pass, 21, 105
Spindlestone, 234
Spottiswoode, 45
Stagshaw, 69, 157
Staithes, 163, 166, 175, 209, 229, Pl. 19c
Stamfordham, 95, 157, 234, Pl. 10c
Standing Stones, 67, 75
Staple Island, 39
Staward Pele, 235
Stenton Forest, 52
Stephenson, George, 165, 166
Stephenson, Robert, 145, 166
Stick-dressing, 201–2
Stob stones, 67
Stone Age, 66
Stone Circles, 67, 68, 76
'Streets', 205–8
Strength, Jamie, (alias James Stuart), 190, 195, 204
Summerings, 94
Surrey, Earl of, 15, 106
Swinburne, 135, 235, Pl. 14a
Swinton, 127, 135, 235
'Swires' and 'gates', 104, 108, 207
Sylvius Aeneas, 116

Tarset, 52, 117
Telford, Thomas, 133, 147
Terraces, river, 34
Teviotdale, 64, 85, 107, 160
Thirlestane, 149, 235
Thirlwall, 235
Thockrington, 80, 90, 235
Thomas the Rhymer, 190
Thomson, James, 196

Threepwood, 45
Threestone Burn, 50, 67
Thrunton, 55
Till, river, 63, 82, 106, 218, Pl. 24b
Tosson, 114
Tower-houses, 114ff.
Town Moor, Newcastle upon Tyne, 55, 163, 172, 173, 192
Traquiar Forest, 52
Trimontium, 26, 73, 74
Trollope, Robert, 123
Turnpikes, 133
Tweed, river, 21, 26, 32, 54, 82, 83, 101, 103, 151, 186, Pl. 23b
Tweeddale, 24, 45, 136, Pl. 2
Tweedmouth, 71, 187, 212, 235
Tweed cloth, 161
Twizel Bridge, 106, Pl. 24b
Tyne, river, 22, 26, 32, 82, 168ff.
Tyne bridges, 168, 169
Tyne Improvement Commission, 168, 175
Tynedale, 94, 101, 136, 148
Tynemouth, 28, 85, 88, 151, 154, 180, 235

Union, Act of, 129, 161, 197
Union of the Crowns, 145

Vallum, 69
Vanburgh, Sir John, 124, 141, 146
Vindolanda, 71
Volcanic rocks, 25, 26, 29

Wade, General, 69
Walker, 83, 169, 172
Wall, village of, 95, 96, 123, 215, 235
Walled towns, 111, 118, 119, 187
Wallington, 55, 114, 124, 235, 236
Wallsend on Tyne, 72, 169, 172, 174, 235
Wansbeck, river, 34, 147, 181
Warden, 80, 235

Wardens of the Marches, 105
Wark-on-Tweed, 101, 109
Wark-on-Tyne, 47, 52, 109
Wark Common, 101
Wark Forest, 48
Warkworth, 80, 85, 89, 100, 109, 143, 209, 235, Pl. 17b
Waterford, Lady, 135
Wauchope Forest, 52
Wedderburn, 105, 235
Wedderlie, 236
Weetwood, 29, 157
Weldon Bridge, 235
Welton Hall, 115
Weststruther, 33, 235
Whalton, 191, 236
Whin Sill, 29, 31, 36, 71, 177, Pl. 4, Pl. 24c
Whiteadder Water, 50
Whitley Bay, 174
Whittingham, 68, 80, 89, 157, 235
Whitton, 117, 235
Whitton Edge, 58
Widehaugh, 51
William II of Scotland, 101
Wilson, Joe, 197
Wilson, John Mackay, 197
Woden Law, 58, 59, Pl. 7c
Wood, John, 150, 156
Woodhorn, 80, 235
Woodland, 44, 45, 49, 50, Pl. 5a, Pl. 5b
Wooler, 43, 149, 157, 160, 235
Woollen industry, 160ff.
Wylam, 82, 166, 167, 169, 235, 236

Yeavering, 77, 79, 143
Yeavering Bell, 62
Yetholm, 68, 83, 96, 100, 157, 197, 218, 219
Yetholm Loch, 56, 237
Young, Arthur, 126